AF290526

Leif Lorentzon

Africa – and I was 19

A travel narrative

FSC
www.fsc.org
MIX
Papper från
ansvarsfulla källor
Paper from
responsible sources
FSC® C105338

To Kajsa, Axel & Naima: you are the best!

The road is the source, it is the treasure, it is richness.
Ryszard Kapuscinski

Cultural particularities are accidental. What defines the human species are the universals of culture.
Kwasi Wiredu

Africa offers the rest of the world humanity.
Richard Dowden

CONTENTS

Högdalen

I was 19 years old when I hitchhiked around Africa and today I am 69.

Sometimes I have wondered why I journeyed out into the world, and why alone. During a few summers in high school, I had hitchhiked around Europe with some of my friends, but why was I the only one to continue? My family had never moved around much, only from Jönköping (where I was born), via Södertälje to the Stockholm suburb of Högdalen. Nor did we travel abroad; there was never any money for that. My sister, seven years older than I, had however moved to Switzerland when she was 18, but had that influenced me? No, there was something else: a rather mysterious restlessness, I guess. I had possibly acquired a taste for something during those summers thumbing around Europe.

In my early teens I had often borrowed issues of *National Geographic* from the school library at Bäckahagen, where I spent my elementary school years. Perhaps a seed was planted there when I gazed wide-eyed at the fantastic pictures.

Or maybe I was just nuts!

First I spent a year in Africa, then two in America and then another in Asia. In just over five years I hitchhiked around the world, with two ten-months intervals in Stockholm to earn money; I worked as a cleaner at Stockholm's subway stations: a great job! That Africa would end up meaning so much to me; to dominate large parts of my life, I had no idea of at the time, or when I came home. But I am sure I felt I had done something quite remarkable.

During much of the spring and summer of 1971, I had been on the floor of my room in Högdalen with Michelin's three maps of the African continent, numbers 153, 154 and 155. They would become my constant companions through 'dark' Africa. I had bought them in the cartographical shop on Vasagatan, opposite the central station in Stockholm, for SEK 8.20 each (about $1 at the time). Together they covered the entire floor and also filled me with excitement. With them I had already in my imagination travelled several times across the continent, visiting the pyramids of Giza, riverboating on the Nile and the

Congo, swimming in the Indian Ocean, crossing the Sahara and seen lions and elephants on the savannah. The two-dimensional maps could not promise that I would experience them in three-dimensional reality, but they gave me hopes and dreams. Of course, there were no blank spaces on the maps, and most African countries had been freed from colonial powers for at least a decade, so no colours separated them either.

The Michelin maps were, however, beautiful and intoxicated my nights and days with dreams of Alexandria, Wadi Halfa, Serengeti, Congo, Agadez, Marrakech... Abstract words, for me exotic place names, which I would concretize into fairly familiar places. The maps are still beautiful now that I have retrieved them from a box in the basement. They are rather worn out but hold together remarkably well with the help of some sticky tape. Of all the maps I have travelled with, these are my favourites; they are the most appealing! The colour combination is beautiful: mainly white with main roads in red, the smaller ones in yellow and white, the desert is yellow and the forest green. They also inform you which roads were passable during rainy seasons, which were dangerous or difficult, where there were unfurnished "rest-houses" or isolated hotels and good water. Information that on the floor in my room triggered my imagination.

Now my route is clearly visible on all three maps. With a pencil I marked my progress across the continent as I travelled, even marking each night with a dot, and a cross if I stayed longer than one night. This should, together with the diaries I kept, make it possible to remember now, 50 years later. The diaries were my dearest travel companion, someone to converse with, to share my experiences with. Most days I ended by putting down what had happened during the day and they now fill a drawer in my home. It is fortunate that I have them because memory is deceptive, full of holes and reconstructions. I have discovered this now as I read through them and am surprised at what I have forgotten or distorted. "The past is a foreign country; they do things differently there," as L. P. Hartley once wrote. I also have some fading photographs and my old passport with all its peculiar stamps, as well as the yellow vaccination booklet. In the basement I also found a plastic bag with all the letters I wrote home and all the letters I received from home, both from family and friends. So, no madeleine cake is needed. Where to begin and end is also beyond question; my African trip lasted exactly one year to the day. And now I will try to recount that journey to the best of my poor ability.

But is it the same Erik? The same me, who now, 50 years later, is sitting in front of a computer writing this, the same person who hitchhiked around Africa in 1971-72? Hardly. But, then again of course it is. I remember events, places and even people, but I cannot remember myself; I never see myself in those places, with those people. However, if I now am to use diaries and maps to tell where, how and why I travelled, perhaps I may even remember myself.

Skillingaryd

My parents were hugging each other on the balcony. Crying, they waved goodbye as I walked down the courtyard towards Harpsundsvägen and the tube station at Högdalen. They wondered when, and even if, they would ever see me again. I probably didn't understand their anxiety at the time. Today I do! Unbelievable that they managed to sleep, found any peace during that year when only a postcard or an aerogram would arrive rather sporadically. I had promised to write once a week, which I did, but the mail was often very slow. Still, from what I found in the cellar; it seems that all my mail arrived to Högdalen.

It was the 12th of July, 1971. The sun occasionally showed itself behind pretty cumulus clouds, neither hot nor cold: a typical Swedish summer day in the early 70s. I had been cleaning subway stations since August, saving as much as I could. Now I took the subway to Skärholmen and walked through its commercial centre to E4, Europe motorway 4 and the Esso petrol station next to it. I wore a denim jacket over a plaid flannel shirt and a pair of jeans. On my feet I had a pair of brown leather proletarian shoes (as we called them) from the workers' shop on Gamla Brogatan in Stockholm - like most of my friends – obligatory footwear for anyone in the anti-Vietnam-war marches. Over one shoulder hung an American gas mask bag, also from Gamla Brogatan, its army vintage shop. In it I had a notebook, pencils, a paperback edition of Cervantes' *Don Quixote*, a Swiss Army knife, a C-harmonica, an Instamatic camera and, of course, passport and traveller's checks.

I had opted for thick books that would last long, so in my red backpack, among an extra pair of jeans, a pair of shorts, five pairs of underwear, a thick sweater, three t-shirts, a toothbrush and a recorder, there was a thick paperback of *The Glass Bead Game*, *The Lord of the Rings* in one volume and a thin collection of the Swedish poet Dan Andersson. The latter was included to tame homesickness should it overwhelm me. On top of my backpack I had lashed a rain poncho and a sleeping bag.

At the Esso station there was already a guy hitchhiking. We exchanged a few words. He was also from Stockholm, heading to Copenhagen and had been hitching here for about fifteen minutes. I went and stood below him. I had learned that in Europe, where there could sometimes be up to 25 hitchhikers out of a big city. The last to arrive goes to the end of the line. In this case it was actually an advantage; I got just far enough out on the exit so that cars whizzing by on the highway could also see me. Maybe one of them would slow down and stop. It had happened before. I took off my backpack and rested it against a post beside the road, hung my shoulder bag on the backpack and put my thumb in the air.

Now it began!

After another fifteen minutes, the fellow in front of me got a ride. Shortly after that a Volvo Amazon came to an abrupt stop on the highway and pulled to the side. I grabbed my bags and ran to the car. The young driver said he was only going to Södertälje (35 km) but "if you want to come along, jump in!" Which I did.

Unfortunately, I was dropped off in the middle of downtown Södertälje after a hazardous drive on the highway, where he zigzagged between slower cars. I was happy to leave him, but unhappy with where. Now I had to walk through Södertälje towards the E4. However, it didn't take long; it was a smaller city then and I knew it relatively well after having lived on Erik Dahlberg's Street in the late 50s.

After a few longer lifts I ended up in Skillingaryd around five o'clock. In a small grocery store I bought a light yogurt and a sandwich. Then I headed out on Södra Vägen to continue towards Africa. But after a couple of hours without anyone stopping, I went back to a hot dog stand and bought a boiled frankfurter with bread and a chocolate drink. Some moped kids hanging around examined me curiously and wondered where I came from and where I was going.

"I come from Stockholm and am going to Africa," I said. They didn't believe me, just laughed at the fool. So I did the same, and left them.

Nothing happened. I stood on the long main road in Skillingaryd, where the residential buildings ended and the deep forest of Småland began. The few cars that passed by all ignored me and as it was getting close to nine pm, I began to plan for the night. Not that it was dark; this was in the middle of summer when the sun in this part of the country sets around eleven pm, and the nights never get dark. But the cars were fewer and it could be good to get an early start tomorrow. I began walking further out of the little town to find a tree to spread my rain poncho and sleeping bag under, without being seen.

But suddenly a woman comes running after me. She stops me and asks if I want some coffee and sandwich.

"I can't say no to that," I reply, surprised.

"My mother and I've seen you hitchhiking here for several hours now. She lives in a house close by. I've had dinner with her and we've been watching you all the time and felt sorry for you. We've put on coffee and made some cheese sandwiches if you are hungry."

So, after I tell her that my name is Erik and she tells me hers is Gun, we go up to her mother's apartment in a typical three-story apartment house from the 1950s, just like the one I had left in Högdalen. A lovely smell of coffee meets us in the apartment and soon I am sitting in the kitchen with a couple of cheese sandwiches and a cup of coffee.

"Yes, we saw you hitchhiking over there," Gun points. "And we couldn't help but feel sorry for you." They also ask me where I am heading.

"I'm going to Africa," I say, realizing how cocky it sounds; but it was true.

"But it's so far," says Gun in surprise. "And isn't it dangerous?"

"I don't think so. I've hitchhiked a lot in Europe before, so I'm sure I'll be fine."

"But why are you alone?"

"No one else wanted to join me."

"But how are you going to get to Africa? Are you going to hitchhike all the way? And doesn't it cost a lot?"

"I'm going to hitchhike to Athens and I know there are passenger boats from Piraeus to Alexandria and it's not that expensive. Then I'll see. There will be both trains and riverboats up the Nile, but then I'll probably hitchhike, or go by bus. There are people living everywhere and they travel, at least locally, and I am sure I'll be able to join them. I have no idea which route I'll take; I'll have to ask around for the best one. But I am going to Tanzania. Friends of my parents live there and I hope to visit them. And I have saved up 10,000 kronor (about US$1200 at the time), which I hope will last a year. I have some in traveller's checks with me and the rest at home, which my parents will send to me when mine run out. I don't want to carry all of it."

"But why are you traveling?" asks the older woman, who had been silent up until now.

"I don't think I really know," I answer after a while. "But it's probably because I hope something out of the ordinary will happen, otherwise I could stay at home. I want to experience new places and people. And not knowing what the next day will look like or even where I will sleep."

"And what do you think you will find?"

I think for a while before answering, and then I say: "I'll see when I get there." All three of us laugh at that.

"But where are you planning to sleep tonight?"

"I was actually on my way out of town to find a tree to sleep under when you caught up with me."

"But you can't do that!"

"Oh yes, I've done it before and I understand it's not going to rain tonight."

"No, you cannot do that. You have to come home with me," Gun says. "You can't stay in the house since my husband is away, but we have a hammock in the garden where you can sleep tonight if you like."

"Yes, thanks, that sounds fantastic."

So, we go back into the village after Gun has made sure her mother is comfortable for the night. In a beautiful garden with a yellow brick house there is a hammock. Gun asks me to wait a while and disappears into the villa. Soon she comes out with a pillow and a couple of blankets.

"I hope you can sleep here."

"No problem! And this is really kind of you."

"Don't mention it. Just hope you don't get cold."

"I don't think so. I have my sleeping bag and now you've given me a couple of blankets too."

"I'm working early tomorrow, so I'll probably be off to work by the time you wake up. Just leave the blankets and pillow in the hammock before you leave."

I promise to do so.

"Well, good night then!"

"Night, and many thanks again!"

I crawl into my sleeping bag and roll a blanket on top and lie for a while thinking about how kind people sometimes are. This is a fantastic beginning!

Around seven I woke and lay there for a while, enjoying the morning. I was in no hurry to go anywhere. The sun had been up for a long time

14

and was shining through the apple trees. On a table next to the hammock there was a thermos of coffee and a couple of sandwiches were wrapped in a foil package. I crawled out of my sleeping bag and saw that there was also an envelope under the thermos. In it was a ten-krona note and a letter: "Erik, I hope you slept well. Here's some breakfast. Just leave everything here on the table when you are done. If you remember, it would be nice to get some postcards from Africa. Good luck, Gun." And then her address.

Gun received a postcard from Cairo and one from Nairobi.

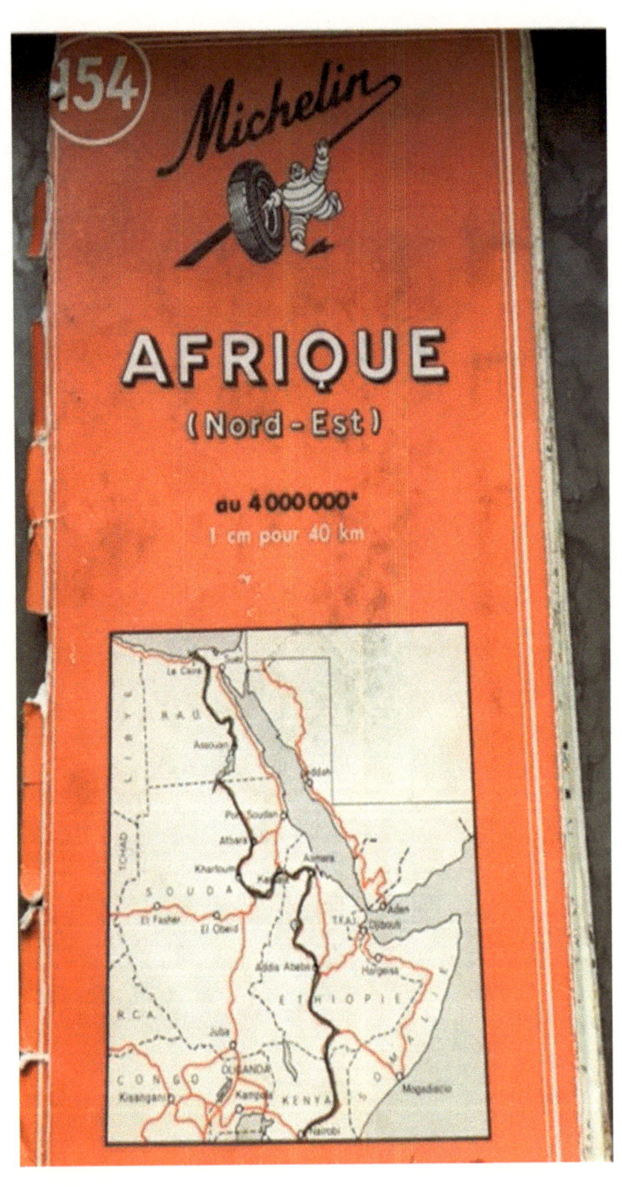

Alexandria - Nairobi

Alexandria

After an obligatory sojourn in Amsterdam, a visit to my sister in Zûrich, and a few eventful weeks in dictatorial Greece, where Brenda from Princeton, N.J. seduced me in Corfu, and I accidentally stayed in a brothel in Athens and almost got arrested, and resolved to spare myself for the rest of my life from all anise alcohol after an ouzo festival in Filopappou Park, and from Hydra hitched a ride to Athens on a yacht with a bunch of kind gay American soldiers on vacation, and in Paros stayed on the beach for a week where I finished reading *Don Quixote*, I took a boat to Alexandria on August 20. HML Cynthia left at 16.00. I caught it just in time after the ferry from Paros was delayed for more than a day due to high seas.

HML Cynthia had seen better days but still offered a small pool and a couple of nice lounges where I mostly hung out for the two days the journey across the Mediterranean Sea took. One could sense that the boat had a more glorious past: a thick carpet of unidentifiable colour was soiled with, among other things, trampled chewing gum, the leather chairs were worn and stained, as were the various tablecloths on the tables. Now the walls of the boat were mainly adorned with portraits of Gamal Abdel Nasser, even though he had been dead for a year and really botched it during the 6-day war. But he was obviously still celebrated for his pan-Arab ambitions. A sporadic portrait of current President Anwar Sadat was also visible. This was my first encounter with this phenomenon - so foreign to Scandinavia: decorating walls with current political leaders - and they were all men, of course. In every country I travelled to in Africa, almost every public space and shop was decorated with portraits of the current despot. A tasteless dictatorial innovation.

My ticket had cost 32 US$, including tax, and for that I also got a couple of meals. I had not booked a sleeping compartment but planned to sleep on deck.

Soon I befriended one of the crew members. Ali, who was from Port Said in Egypt, was pleasantly surprised when I told him I was from Sweden. He had worked for a while in Gothenburg and knew a few Swedish phrases. I could borrow his cabin if I wanted to shower. He could see that I was dirty and sticky from the salty waters of the Aegean Sea. I had not been able to shower after Paros beach so I gratefully accepted his offer. Afterwards, he also offered me and a Dutchman we met to sleep in his cabin if we wanted to, which we accepted. Ali also managed to arrange for us to eat in the 1st class lounge, which meant better food than we were entitled to with our 2nd class tickets.

I wondered a bit about his kindness and generosity. He was my first contact with the Arab world, and I certainly did not want to let my ignorance of its people turn into suspicion. But had I been alone, I might not have gone to his cabin for the night, even if he had worked in Gothenburg.

The cabin was far down and in the middle of the boat and was a bit claustrophobic without windows, but it had two beds. It looked like most boat cabins I have seen with two wall-mounted beds, one above the other and the Dutchman, Heinz, who I came to really dislike, got the upper berth and I would share with Ali in the lower one. Heinz was older than me, a trained doctor, or so he claimed, and painfully conceited. Due to the age difference, he felt he had the right to keep telling me how things were and, above all, to cast suspicion on Ali; he was after all an Arab! as he said. But he didn't mind accepting Ali's goodwill. A tiresome individual, I hoped to be rid of soon.

We all crawl into bed however and although it's a bit cramped, it would probably be possible to share the narrow bed with Ali, sleeping head to foot. Besides, he would rise at three o'clock to work, after which I would have the bed to myself, so I am fine with the arrangement. After sleeping well for a while, I wake up to find Ali's hand on my thigh. I remove it. Then he places my hand on his erect cock and moves it up and down. It takes a while for me to realize what is happening. When I do, I throw myself out of the bed and onto the floor: "What the fuck!"

"What the hell are you doing?"

"I'm not getting back up into the bed; I'm sleeping on the floor!"

"But it's ok, please, I promise not to do anything more," whines Ali, who is genuinely sad that I no longer want to share the bed with him. As if someone has taken a cake from a child, he begs and pleads. Heinz has of course woken up and is laughing his head off at the whole thing. "Bloody idiot," I think to myself and seriously dislike him even more.

18

Instead, I even feel a bit sorry for Ali, although I am disgusted at the same time. He is obviously sorry to have hurt me. But no way am I getting into bed with him again, even if I can't find any sleep on the floor. I lay there wating for it to be three o'clock. When he finally goes on his shift and disappears, I climb back into his bed and fall asleep immediately. But there were no more nights in Ali's cabin.

The next day I spent about an hour watching *Dr. Dolittle* in the ship's cinema. But I could not suffer all of it. It was more pleasant to stay in the 2nd class lounge and socialize. Heinz and I were not the only travellers going down to Africa. Together we sat in a group of almost ten and exchanged experiences and information over lots of tea. I didn't have much to offer of course, but I listened with big ears. This was before all *Lonely Planet* and *Rough Guide* books. Instead, you asked everyone you met: best way to travel, where to stay, where to change money, the best cheap food, etc. I got lots of tips, including that I ought to stay in the youth hostels in Alexandria and Cairo. A Sudanese told me that it is easy to travel by bus through Ethiopia to Kenya, which he said is better than through southern Sudan to Uganda. "But soon it's rainy season in southern Ethiopia and then the roads are almost impassable." We'll see, I thought to myself.

The second night I slept alone and well on a bench on the aft deck in the fresh Mediterranean air, and without both Ali and Heinz. Where the latter had gone to I did not know and did not care one bit about. Unsympathetic type.

The next day, HML Cynthia docked at the port of Alexandria, which was no longer the "magnificent harbour," Ibn Battúta wrote about in the mid-14th century when he said that he had hardly seen a more beautiful harbour anywhere during his extensive travels. Now it was a rather rundown and partly barricaded waterfront. Before entering the city I needed to get a visa. They had set up a small immigration office in one of the lounges on the boat. The visa cost 23 Egyptian pounds - I think; it is difficult to read the stamp in my old passport. I had no Egyptian pounds, so together with a customs officer I had to go ashore to a bank to change some money. That was the only money, US$10, that I changed at a bank for many months.

Back on the boat, it was soon my turn in the visa queue.

"Swedish?"

"Yes."

"Half price!"

I didn't understand why but of course thanked them for the discount. In customs, much the same happened. While they questioned other Westerners about how much money they had and brusquely went through their backpacks and suitcases, they just waved me on without asking questions or caring about my backpack when they saw my Swedish passport. I would experience the same benevolent treatment several times in Africa. Something that of course had nothing to do with my excellent personality or handsome physique, but only because I happened to be Swedish. This came to pass at a time when Sweden still had a good reputation among what we then called the Third World.

Once in Egypt, I was assaulted by hordes of shouting young men who all wanted to help me in every possible way. A phenomenon I here met for the first time but would get used to. Completely surrounded I managed, together with Heinz and a German couple, to find a bus that took us into town and the hostel on Port Said Street.

I only stayed a few days in Alexandria. A city the French writer Gustave Flaubert in 1849 experienced as almost European, seeing lots of Europeans everywhere. I read in my diary that I did not, instead I disliked the city. Probably because it was my first encounter with what was so radically different from Högdalen. Although that was the intention of the trip, to expose myself to "the dissimilar", "the other," the encounter was nevertheless overwhelming: the poverty, the dirt, the stench: the first city I visited outside Europe. And I was also a bit afraid by all that was so different. I was not a self-confident young man, but a cautious, slightly scared teenager encountering for the first time an environment that was completely unfamiliar: frightening. I almost had to force myself out into the streets. But it was necessary because the hostel closed for five hours in the middle of the day. This journey would teach me humility in the face of the unknown, and thus make me less insecure, but it would take time; here in Alexandria I had to struggle. At the same time, I realized that I was seriously ignorant of the world I had suddenly, but of course intentionally, entered. With some shame I realized that perhaps I should have read something other than Lawrence Durrell before arriving in North Africa.

In the spring of that year, I had read his *Alexandria Quartet* and really loved the four books. I had therefore been looking forward to Alexandria. I walked around searching for a cosmopolitan Mediterranean metropolis, but without success. Maybe it had something to do with me: a 19-year-old teenager who, of course, didn't know what to look for. But I found some famous water holes and hotels to read and feel the atmosphere in. As a European, I was able to sneak in everywhere, as long as I did not wear shorts; I quickly understood that. But even at the Spitfire pub, which had been serving alcoholic beverages since 1883, I found nothing but thirsty local men drinking beer in the darker parts of the bar, and a few lost tourists who certainly didn't exude the romantic mystique of Justine or Balthazar.

Yet I sent a postcard to Skebokvarnsvägen 209 in Högdalen and Stoffe's mother, who was the one who had recommended Durrell's quartet.

It was also much warmer than I had imagined and I was envious of the men wearing galabeya, a loose-fitting, traditional garment that reached the feet. Selma Lagerlöf, famous Swedish author and first female Nobel laureate, called them "wide pants" when she visited Alexandria on Christmas Eve in 1899 with her travelling companion Sophie Elkan, and thought "the people were incredibly funny." But even though it looked both comfortable and cool, I realized that I would look ridiculous if I put on a galabeya. A German in the hostel had done so and did look rather silly. So I took the train to Cairo after two days.

In March 2003, being 51 years old this time, I returned to Alexandria for a literary conference at the new Alexandria Library, which had been inaugurated in the fall of the previous year. The African Literature Association had brought its annual conference to the library and was the first international academic organization to convene at this hitherto rather empty library, with a stated ambition to gather all human knowledge on its shelves - like its ancient namesake. To start somewhere, they had asked all the participants of the conference to bring a copy of the books we had published and donate them to the library's shelves. Now there is a copy of my doctoral thesis in its collections! I am rather pleased about that!

I liked the city much better in 2003. As far as I could see it was not more cosmopolitan, smelled the same and was probably even more run-down. But now I liked the food, especially 'koshari,' a cheap, nutritious and tasty rice and lentil stew sold everywhere in Egypt. By 2003 I was more mature, definitely better educated and, after several trips to Muslim milieus, had come to enjoy its culture, its food and the almost limitless generosity of its people - although I still avoided wearing galabeya.

Hitchhiking was forbidden in Egypt because of the current war with Israel, so I took a train to Cairo. I travelled with Bruce from Scotland. We had of course bought the cheapest tickets: 3rd class. Bruce had travelled by train in Egypt before and knew that it was important to be early at the station to get a seat. Something we were and got. Two window seats opposite each other on simple wooden benches, which was what was offered. The windows were open so it was at least windy in the almost suffocating heat. And once we started, dust and sand soon covered us. Now there were, at least in 3rd class, no "well-sealed compartments" for women as when Selma Lagerlöf travelled by train on the same route. In our compartment all genders, ages and existences were mixed.

Next to us sat a couple of young Egyptian men with whom we soon conversed. Otherwise, the carriage was overcrowded and the aisles packed with people, animals and luggage. We were the only Europeans in the carriage so attracted some attention. Or rather too much attention. All the vendors that crowded the train inevitably wanted to sell us various food, drinks and gadgets.

At one point, a woman in rags comes and stands in the aisle next to us. She takes out a couple of light bulbs and first crushes them with her bare feet, then starts eating the glass she has broken. At first I cannot take my eyes off her, but when she swallows and stares at me, I turn disgusted to look out the window. Bruce is equally horrified but can't help but laughing. When she has swallowed it all, she wants to be paid. Naive as I am, I have not understood this, while Bruce of course has and categorically refuses. Which I also do, even though I realize that in her apparent infinite poverty she could certainly use a few of my pounds. Our Egyptian bench friends remain insightfully neutral. But when the woman starts screaming and shouting so that the whole carriage becomes involved in the racket, they explain to her that we want to be left alone, and after a while she reluctantly leaves us.

Maybe we should have paid for the light bulbs?

The journey took three and a half hours. It was unbearably hot, in spite of fresh blasts of dust and sand through the windows, and a dreadful noise all the time. Nor was the view interesting, though the beautiful sails of the felucca boats were remarkable to see. The water of the Nile was hidden from us, so it looked as if they were sailing on land. Otherwise, the debris along the railroad line dominated: mostly plastic, but really all kinds of human rubbish. We asked our Egyptian friends why it was so miserably dirty.

"Nobody picks it up."

No, that we could see. "But if no one ever does, it will look like this forever, because most of it is plastic."

"People are too poor to care. They other things to think about."

"I've been to countries in Asia that are just as poor," Bruce said. "But it sure as hell doesn't look like this – except for India of course!"

"But where will they put all the rubbish?"

"In other countries you collect it and put it in a place where you can take care of it, maybe burn it."

"Since the authorities don't give a damn, it would just remain there. That's how it works in Egypt."

And it still did in 2003; it looked just as bad then when I made the same train journey twice.

Cairo

Cairo was even hotter. Or Al-Qahira, as it is called in Arabic, was even hotter than Alexandria. I ended up staying in Cairo for just over a week as I had a few things to do here. Above all, I was waiting for money my parents would send here, which was delayed. Until it arrived, I could go no go further up the Nile. It didn't matter much as the city is truly wonderful. While I enjoyed it more than Alexandria, I didn't appreciate it as much as I did when I returned later in life. I should have done so. And it has history. Archaeologists have shown that there were settlements here at the end of the last ice age, around 10,000 years ago. On, as the city is called in the Bible, was the first city to be located here, and Max Rodebeck, in his magnificent monograph on *Cairo*, tells us that On was founded "on July 19, 4241 BC. To be precise at 4.58 in the morning." Astronomers know this because Sirius was just above the horizon at On at that time; the earliest exact date in world history, apparently. So it is possible to claim that Cairo is the oldest city in the world, even though only one obelisk remains of On, or Heliopolis, as we usually call it. The red granite obelisk stands in the suburb of El-Matariya.

But the hostel was on a small street in the Bab-Al-Louq district, fairly central. It was a bland, white, three-story building with a reception of a sort on the street level and dormitories, toilets and showers on the second floor. Three dormitories, two for men and one for women. As in Alexandria, it was also closed between 11am and 4pm every day, which later would put me in a bit of a predicament, as it turned out.

Egyptian cuisine became relatively incompatible with my young constitution, and when my stomach started to grumble, the smell of the street kitchens was enough to make me sick. But we found a Chinese restaurant near the hostel where the food was almost free; for 25 piasters, about 25 cent, you got a big plate of rice, meat and vegetables under the watchful eyes of Mao Tse Tung from the posters on the walls. I had dinner there several nights.

I always woke up every morning at five to the Adhan, the "Allahu Akbar" of the prayer callers. If I managed to fall asleep after that first call to prayer, I would soon be awakened by the incredibly piercing cries of the roaming street vendors as they rolled their carts through the city streets, loudly trumpeting their goods and services.

The hostel soon became truly like a small home, even though they closed in the middle of the day. I slept in an upper bunk in a room with five bunk beds. There was a small shelf on the wall next to the bedside lamp where I placed my books, making the bed's nook my sanctuary. It is important to find a quiet space of your own when traveling, where you can retreat, escape all the experiences and the often-incomprehensible tumult of voices - particularly in a city like Cairo. I tried to do this as often as I could.

Below me, however, was Heinz. Just as unbearable as on the boat. I avoided him as best I could. This was fortunately not difficult as there were several people staying at the hostel who were going to East Africa and Heinz was not going further than Egypt - which pleased me. That more people were going down to East Africa also pleased me, and surprised me. When I decided to travel to Africa, I had no idea, or rather did not reflect on the fact that others could have similar plans. Which was a bit naïve, of course. I was still 19 years old and happy not to be the only hitchhiker in this "mother of cities," as Ibn Battúta called it in the 14th century.

Bruce had been to Cairo before and knew of some interesting establishments, including Café Riche. An old classic restaurant where intellectuals apparently ate French. It served substandard Western food in a pleasant setting. The walls were covered with photographs of local celebrities, including two Egyptian greats at the time unknown to me, Umm Kalthoum and Naguib Mahfouz. I came back in 2003 to eat here a couple of nights, even though the food had not improved, but the environment was just as pleasant.

Bruce told us about Umm Kalthoum, about how almost incomprehensibly big she was, and is, in the Arab world. For 37 years she gave a live concert every first Thursday of the month of up to 6 hours on Radio Cairo. The entire Arab world would stop and listen. Even the Six-Day War paused, he claimed. One evening Bruce took us to Café Umm Kalthoum on Obani Street in the central entertainment district. It was named after a visit by the diva in 1948. If you were lucky, she could still slip in.

We weren't that lucky but I got to hear her amazing voice for the first time. They played her marathon long songs over the radio all the time. I may not have been so excited at the time, but I certainly am today. And I am not alone. At her funeral in 1975, over two million people took to the streets of Cairo, far more than at Nasser's funeral. They even seized her coffin and went to the al-Husssein Mosque, and if the Imam there had not stopped them, they would probably have buried her next to the Prophet's grandson. Now her tomb in al-Khalifa is still well visited and she has her own radio station that broadcasts her music every day and around the clock. At least they did when I was here in 2003 for the literature conference and listened to it in my hotel room.

Bruce also took us to the Windsor Hotel, a quaint little colonial hotel in the Haleem Basha area. It had obviously seen better days but was as cozy as British colonial establishments can be. We couldn't afford to eat but had a beer each at the bar. When I was back in 2003 I stayed here. Just as pleasant then, while I probably appreciated more the café opposite, where I sat and chatted with the local male populace, smoking hookah in the evenings.

However, the aforementioned Chinese restaurant was now in 1971, where I, to avoid the local cuisine, usually ate. There was also a café in a small square nearby where we would sit and drink tea in the evenings, Café Musa. Here I learned that I should get an international ID card certifying that I was studying Egyptology, which would give me free entry to the Egyptian Museum and archaeological sites in the country.

For this ID and the visa to Sudan, I needed to photograph myself. There was a photographer near the hostel, recommended by others. I found him in a small room upstairs around the corner and I asked if I could be photographed. "Inshallah," he smiled and sat me on a stool in front of a dark curtain. The photographer, a nice older gentleman, knew enough English to photograph hostel travellers. He took a picture of me with a beautiful old, almost antique camera, which resulted in a negative. This he put on a stand in front of the camera lens and took ten pictures of it. I had ordered ten. He wanted 30 piasters for the job, but I managed to bargain down to 20. Saved a penny! And I got to the Sudanese embassy before they closed for lunch; there I left my passport which I could pick up in a couple of days enriched with a visa.

Later that day I went to a student organization. An interesting place. Everyone seemed to be a Maoist, judging by how they were all dressed

26

in Mao-suits, and the wall decorations that were completely dominated by colourful posters from the People's Republic. I still got a student ID absurdly simple. They stapled my photo to a certificate, stamped it twice, and then it was up to me to write the details of my Egyptological studies, without having to provide any proof thereof.

I also visited the Swedish Embassy to read some Swedish newspapers. It was, and apparently still is, located on Gezira Island and the fashionable Zamalak district. Despite the nice environment, the staff was snotty, which surprised me. It couldn't be that often that some long-haired Swedish hitchhiker came by, or maybe that was the problem: my appearance. However, I did not let myself be discouraged and returned several times to read my favourite daily paper, *Dagens Nyheter*, particularly to see how Hammarby football club was doing. An obsession I cannot help. I grew up in a southern suburb of Stockholm where Hammarby has its home and fans, and with a father who was a work colleague of Gösta Lundell - who played in Hammarby until 1965, and even some nationals, so we got free tickets to all home games for several years. And I was hooked.

Looking like a hippie with my long blond hair caused some attention on the streets. If also I was wearing shorts, which in the merciless heat I usually wore during the day, there was no stopping the excitement; there was shouting and laughter and "hello mister hippie" most of the time. A bit tiring, but at the same time harmless and completely without the sometimes threatening atmosphere I experienced during my visit in 2003, when people would shout Yankee go home and throw stuff at me, due to the recent US bombings of Iraq. Now, in 1971 it, was Vietnam they were bombing. One day I walked past the North Vietnamese embassy in Cairo and they had a big wall outside the embassy covered with photographs of Vietnamese demonstrations all over the world. Probably to show the support they had in the struggle against US imperialism. There were a few photos from demonstrations in Stockholm, but I couldn't find myself.

Later one the afternoon, I was sitting in Café Musa talking to an Egyptian student my age. He was studying economics but first wanted to know if I loved Nasser and then was mostly interested in whether I had any girlfriends or not. I had to admit that I didn't love the former, but that I did have the latter. He himself did not know any girls outside his family, but had a boyfriend. I realised why there were almost no girls on the streets in the evenings, and why I often saw men walking hand in hand or arm-in-arm. When I expressed my wonder at this public and physical male bonding, he didn't really understand what I meant, and he was of course right; why shouldn't men be allowed to walk arm-in-arm or hold hands in public? This I realized even then. Graham Greene commented on this in *Journey Without Maps*, his travel book from Africa: "They [the men] seemed to like to touch each other, as if it made them feel good to know the other man was there. It wasn't love; it didn't mean anything we could understand."

In Greece, I had written to my parents and asked them to send me 1000 Swedish kronor via American Express in Cairo. I also hoped to receive letters from home. So the second day in town I navigated to Am Ex. Nothing. I was awfully disappointed. However, two days later there were some letters waiting for me: one from my sister, one from Stoffe and a long letter from my mother. The latter I read in tears on a staircase outside Am Ex. My one-year younger brother's newly purchased motorcycle had been stolen and he had also had a small accident with our father's car. It made me terribly sad and homesickness flooded me. I became exhausted, drained and wondered what on earth I was doing: why was I in Cairo? Suddenly I just wanted to go home. Hug my brother and leave all the dirty streets and smelly food stalls. Luckily, the hostel soon opened and I was able to crawl up into my bed, sleep some siesta and then read Gerald Durrell's *My Family and Other Animals*, which I had found in Greece. A well-written and entertaining book that made me feel a bit better.

The next morning we woke up to find our beds full of sand. At first I didn't understand what was happening, but soon realised that there was a sandstorm and the sand was blowing in all over Cairo. Apparently not so unusual. If it was really bad, they even closed the airport. This time it was probably not so bad and I decided to take a long walk. You just had to squint a little extra with your eyes and cover your mouth with scarf or bandana. I wanted to go to the old town next to the al-Hussein mosque and the big Khan el-Khalili bazaar. On the way there, I walked through more Western-dominated architecture. All the banks and government buildings had walled barricades, sandbags in front of the entrances and armed guards. Photographing this was strictly forbidden; in fact, it seemed that photography was forbidden in all of Cairo. I certainly didn't dare. Nor did I dare cross the streets by myself. From what I could see, motorists didn't care one bit about pedestrians. They just drove on as fast as they could. If there were traffic lights, that didn't seem to really alter the situation any. To get across without risking life and limb, I waited for more pedestrians, local ones, who knew how to execute the crossing. Together we became bold and dared the crossing with the authority of the group. But I was scared every time.

Before entering the bazaar and the old town, I visited the al-Hussein Mosque. As a man, in long pants on this day, it was okay to enter the large hall barefoot. I sat far back against a wall on the giant carpet that covered the entire floor. It was half full of men praying; no imam leading the prayer but a murmur that rose silently to the high ceiling. Soon I was joined by an older man who drew me into a small room full of books. He was determined to give me guidance literature. And I came away with a small booklet that told me in faltering English why Islam is the only true path. I saved many books during the trip, but this was not one of them.

But I leafed through it while sitting at one of the cafés in al-Hussein Square, in front of the mosque. I ordered tea. A young boy served me a tray with a pot of mint tea and a glass filled with sugar. I had already learned to like this sweet tea and seen how it was poured back and forth from pot and glass: I felt almost like a Caironian. Now it was also important to make sure not to get sand in the glass. I was sitting there appreciating the tea and the bustling life of the square when a man came up and asked if he could join me. Of course he could.

He spoke good English and said his name was George. A handsome fellow with the obligatory moustache; he looked not unlike Omar Sharif. He was quite elegantly dressed in a double-breasted suit, and surprisingly well polished shoes given the general dust, dirt and sand of the city. His hair was glossy black and well combed over his head. He had lived and studied in Bristol, England, he said. When he realized I was going into the bazaar, he wanted to join me. "It's easy to get lost in there." Since I had heard about an American couple who had had stuff thrown at them when they didn't want to buy anything, I welcomed George as my cicerone.

I wanted to be trusting, despite Ali's clumsy abuse on HML Cynthia. Otherwise, I realized, this trip would be meaningless. When I later read the Polish author Ryszard Kapuscinski, I was happy to recognise this when he writes in *Travels with Herodotus* that he considers suspicion a character flaw rather than a sign of reason when travelling.

After we had finished our tea, George and I entered the bazaar together. We left it rather soon, however, as it turned out I wasn't going to buy anything, despite all the shopkeepers' persistent offers. George helped me escape them all with my dignity intact. Instead, we continued into the old town, el-Gamaliya. Here I might not have dared to walk alone. At one point, some little boys shouted "Yankee go home!" at me and threw pebbles. George shouted angrily at them and apologized for their rude behaviour. But of course I attracted attention, even though I was wearing long pants.

el-Gamaliya was full of stalls and shops selling literally everything under the sun. It was also full of small eateries. We stopped at a small restaurant that George said "serves an excellent pigeon." It was actually more of a hole in the wall with three tables on the street and two inside. The table we sat at was covered with a sticky plastic cloth which a woman soon came out and quite successfully cleaned. George knew the owner, apparently the woman's husband who was delighted and promised to do his utmost, I gathered. Yet I had some misgivings about the lunch choice, but let myself be persuaded. And it was a pleasant surprise. Not that there was much food on the bird, but the extras made it a pleasant meal. "First good Egyptian meal I've had," I declared.

George told me that he owns a small import business which does reasonably well. Enough to support a wife and three children who are all in school now. He can often take some time off in the afternoons to go for a walk, like today. The evenings he always spends out on the town, socializing with his male friends in the city's cafés, playing dominoes and board games and drinking tea - sometimes even beer.

"Your wife never joins you?"

"No, she spends most of her time at home, with her female friends. Sometimes we can have mutual friends, usually family, over for dinner, especially on weekends. But otherwise we spend time apart. It's better that way."

"It's different in Sweden. Of course, sometimes you only meet your male friends, but I'd rather hang out with girls."

"Yes, I know it's different in Europe. But we have our traditions, which have to do with our religion, and it will probably stay that way."

"Sad, I think," and told him about the young man I met who was studying economics and his desire for girlfriends.

"I recognize that but he will meet someone to marry eventually. His family will take care of that. I remember I found it a bit difficult in the beginning in Bristol. I had a hard time getting used to the obvious equal presence of the girls at the university. I probably never learned to accept it, even though I had a couple of British girlfriends. So I think I prefer our system. Safer. Now I know where my wife is."

We didn't get much further in that discussion. And it would soon get dark so it was time to leave. I had a good walk ahead of me. George promised to accompany me to Hussein Square and from there I found my own way. Many years later, when I read about al-Sayyid Ahmad Abd al-Jawad's night walks in Cairo in Naguib Mahfouz's fantastic *Cairo Trilogy*, I remembered George.

Every day I visited Am Ex, hopeful for money. But they were delayed. Sometimes letters from home were waiting, which was always a pleasure. I answered them all by aerogram or postcard and also sent a postcard to Skillingaryd. If I did nothing else when the hostel was closed, I would go to the British Library, which was within walking distance and where I could sit and read in peace. Or I would find my way to the riverside Hilton hotel and sit in its air-conditioned foyer and write and read. Admittedly, I was an odd figure in that milieu, but I was left alone and grateful for its peace and coolness.

After a few days, my stomach started to upset me. Whether it was the pigeon's fault or not, I don't know. And it didn't matter. I come down with an intense diarrhoea; difficult as I couldn't stay in the hostel during its closing hours. When it was at its worst, I mostly sat and passed the time at Café Musa nearby; they also had a decent toilet!

One morning when I was brushing my teeth in my underwear in the shared bathroom at the hostel, I hear: "What the hell, Erik. There's shit running down your legs!" I didn't realize I was shitting myself! At least here I had access to clean underwear, toilet paper and a shower. It became worse a few days later.

I was feeling better and we decided to go out to Giza and visit the pyramids. We, me and an American couple, Mike and Debbie, took an early morning bus to be there as early as possible. The bus was only half full and maybe that's why the driver suddenly stopped and decided to spray it clean with a water hose. We all had to get off while he showered the exterior as well as the interior of the bus relatively clean. Then the journey continued.

Once there, the air was still fresh in the early morning and the sun was not yet tormentingly hot. Most of the tourist vendors had not yet opened their businesses and we could almost unmolestedly enjoy the pyramids, the environment and the desert that begins right after the wonders. With our student cards everything was also free. We could climb Cheops pyramid but the size of the stone blocks surprised and made a climb almost impossible. "No stone is less than thirty feet," Herodotus tells us in the second book of his *Histories*. There he also complains about how cruel and ruthless Cheops was, how he tormented the slaves in the construction of his pyramid. The road to Giza took ten years to build and then another ten years for the underground chambers beneath the pyramid, which took another twenty years to build. The cost was astronomical, as Herodotus illustrates with the amount of money spent on "radishes and red onions and garlic" for the workers. He also mentions that when the money ran out, Cheops ordered his daughter to prostitute herself in order to raise money: nice father!

In *Arabia Felix*, Torkild Hansen relates the Danish research trip of 1761-67 to Egypt. The participants spend a whole year in Cairo and, of course, studied the pyramids. Carsten Nierbuhr (the only one to survive the expedition) and Peter Forsskål discovered with their rather primitive measuring instruments that the "four sides of the pyramids were exactly east, west, south and north, a finding unaffected by later measurements." And, of course, they also climbed the pyramids and measured their height with so-called triangulations and the result is almost still valid. Only a difference of 71 cm, less than half a percent off compared to later, more precise measuring: the Pyramid of Cheops is 137.38 meters high. Impressive Scandinavians. And this was 36 years before Napoleon marched in and turned the pyramids into an exotic tourist magnet.

If we couldn't climb Cheops, we could at least enter one of its burial chambers. We had to crawl through a narrow claustrophobic passage to get to a room of about 5 square meters. There was nothing to look at because archaeologists and grave plunderers had preceded us for centuries. Still, it was a magic experience to stand inside a burial chamber that was 5000 years old. And I still remember it as one of the most amazing things I have ever experienced.

We took the same bus back to town. This time it was full of passengers. We barely got on, unaccustomed as we were to elbowing and pushing our way onto a bus. But we managed. And had to stand: tightly packed and unable to move. And as I stand there, I can feel it running down one of my legs. The diarrhea has returned. Fortunately, I am wearing long trousers. All I can do is squeeze as best I can and hope no one notices my misery. It's so crowded that at least no one can see what is going on, but maybe smell it?

When we arrive and I carefully step off the bus, the hostel is of course closed. Mike and Debbie, also unaware of my plight, are off to the American Embassy while I carefully make my way to the Hilton. It is a bit of a walk but it has stopped running down my leg and as far as I could see, nothing is visible on my pants, but there is some splashing in my shoes! At a gentle pace, I slide my feet over the narrow sidewalks to the Hilton, all the time terrified that it will start running again. Once there, I enter their large, shiny and clean toilet. There I can take off my pants, shoes and socks and clean them as best I am able to with paper and water, all the time terrified that someone else will enter the bathroom. But no one does. I also sneak into one of the toilet stalls where I take off my underwear and with toilet paper clean also them as best as I can - and my butt. But, of course, I have to put everything back on, which is not pleasant! Afterwards, I would have preferred to remain in the hotel foyer until the hostel reopened, but given that my pants are not very clean or dry, I did not have the nerve to sit down and soil one of their armchairs. Instead, I slowly make my way back to a café with wooden stools in Bab-Al-Louq. When the hostel finally opens, I can hand-wash my socks, pants and underwear and spend the rest of the day in my bed. I read Dan Andersson poetry to quell the homesickness that lurks heavily in my stomach.

The next day I felt well enough to visit the Ethiopian embassy in Cairo. I had already obtained a visa in Stockholm, but wanted to hear how I could enter the country, as there were rumours that one could not from Sudan. Sure enough, the border between Sudan and Ethiopia was closed due to the conflict in northern Ethiopia, now Eritrea. One had to fly from Kassala in Sudan. Again, I was also warned that the roads in southern Ethiopia are largely impassable during the autumn rainy season. No buses run but there may be jeeps and trucks taking passengers. We'll see, I thought worriedly again. It would turn out that their warning and my concerns were highly justified.

I had now decided on this route. Southern Sudan was in turmoil; war had raged on and off between the Muslim northern Sudan and the Christian and animist southern Sudan since 1962. Meanwhile, we had read about Idi Amin, who had been in power in Uganda since January. I was also curious about Ethiopia. A not so small part of my decision had to do with to the fact that most of the other travellers I had met were going that way.

There were seven of us at the hostel going down to East Africa, including a couple of Indian guys from Kenya who were going home. They had a lot to say and claimed that it was always possible to get around in southern Ethiopia, even if it was difficult. I spent most of my time now with Mike and Debbie. They were both from New York, older than me but we nevertheless had a good time together. It felt fine that we were a group that could travel together, safe for the 19-year-old Erik, who was the youngest. Now my money only had to arrive. I was looking forward to leaving Cairo, and not least the hostel, even though I had managed to enjoy my berth and corner. But the hostel was far from clean and full of cockroaches. An insect I became acquainted with here for the first time, but was to become very familiar with during the trip.

Finally, the money arrived. The fifth time I visited American Express, on September 2, after eight days in Cairo, there was a letter from a bank in the city telling me that they had 1000 SKR waiting for me. Once at the bank, they wanted to give me the full amount in Egyptian pounds, but after persistent pleading and explaining, I managed to get it in British pounds, in traveller's checks from Thomas Cook.

After that bank visit, I sat in the Hilton again and wrote a long letter home to my parents. I thanked them for the money and that I missed them, but that everything was fine. Every time I read letters from them, or wrote to them, I got homesick and for a few moments was almost ready to turn back. But I never did. Instead I wrote a few aerograms to friends in Högdalen.

I had not yet visited the Egyptian Museum. Now I did. With my student card it was free. Here too, the current war situation with Israel was evident: armed soldiers everywhere and the glass cases were taped and fronted with walls of sandbags. The museum was also too big for me. But the famous tombs were impressive. Especially the tomb of Tutankhamun which they had rebuilt as it looked when Howard Carter discovered it in 1922 in the Valley of the Kings outside Luxor. And the next day I would take the train to Luxor, as hitchhiking was still forbidden in Egypt.

It was a surprisingly pleasant, yet slightly awkward train ride. I was traveling with Don and Jim from California, both of whom were a bit crazy. The trip would take a full day and I feared the worst remembering the train ride between Alexandria and Cairo. We bought the cheapest tickets they offered: 2nd class for 1:50 Egyptian pounds. However, we ended up sitting in 1st class. When we boarded and found our seats, which looked like those on the train from Alexandria, Jim dragged us to a 1st class compartment that was empty, except for an older man in a suit.

"This is where we sit," says Jim.

"We can't do that," I say. "What do we do when the conductor comes, or someone who has these seats?"

"Pretending we don't understand. And just show our tickets. If we're lucky, they won't care and won't bother with any long-haired Europeans." Don just laughs and has probably experienced Jim's madness before.

"This is crazy. You're nuts," but I go along with it. I'd rather sit unfairly with them than alone in second class.

Soon, of course, an Egyptian couple arrives who obviously have tickets for the seats we are occupying. We look out the windows and pretend not to understand them. Then they leave and soon return with the conductor who of course wants to see our tickets. Which we show him. He and the couple of course see that we don't have 1st class tickets. But after examining us one more time, he tells the couple that they can sit somewhere else. They look very surprised and irritated, but wander off with the conductor. "I told you so," Jim laughs. I can't believe it. Just because we are Europeans and they are Egyptians, we got their seats! I was ashamed, but I stayed put. As a result, it was a very comfortable trip where we could even stretch out and get some sleep.

But it was certainly not one of my prouder moments.

It was dark when the train rolled into Luxur but we quickly found the hostel which was beautifully situated with a view of the Nile. The next morning we discovered that we could rent bikes next door. And so we did. First we cycled to the Karnak temples. Karnak means, I now know, besieged village, and it was built around 2000 BC. And is still partly standing. We walked around the ruins and let ourselves be impressed without really knowing much about what we were locking at, at least not I. It was again a bit disconcerting to see things and not understand them, without being able to name what I saw: experiencing without language. So when a local joined us and said he was a guide and could tell us about the history of the temple, we agreed. To think that the hieroglyphics, which were clearly legible, and the statues of gods and humans, whose faces bore clear features, were thousands of years old was truly 'mind-blowing,' as the Californians said. Sad to see that idiot tourists had carved their names into the thousands-year-old stones: what silly people there are!

We also visited the Luxor Temple and admired the remaining obelisk. We had all been to Paris and seen the other one in the Place de la Concorde. Its foundation was still here, next to the one that was now alone, longing for its brother - or if it is a sister - who is just as alone, longing for the Nile in the midst of all the traffic in Paris.

It was relentlessly hot; the sun was blazing from a naked sky and I realized I had to get a hat of some kind. I found a soft safari hat in a stall in town and a water bottle. Don had given me some water purification tablets, so I could now fill the bottle with tap water and drop a ¼ tablet into the bottle. However, it was so hot, 40 degrees in the shade, that for the first and only time in my life I had a nosebleed.

We spent the evening at the hostel and made a good salad with vegetables and yogurt. Then we sat on the hostel's veranda, enjoying the date palms rustling in the wind and the little boat traffic the Nile offered in

36

the evening darkness. When I went to bed, a lizard sat on the ceiling above my bed. I stared at it, unable to fall asleep, terrified that it would fall on me. But eventually I must have dosed off because when I woke up with the sun, the lizard was gone. I told Jim about it the next morning and he laughed at me.

"But Erik, it was just a gecko. They are everywhere and are the best thing you can have in a house. They eat insects, which you don't want in your house. You will get used to them and even like them."

And so I did. I got used to them as quickly as the cockroaches, althhough I never came to terms with the latter.

Next day was Monday and my malaria pill day; every Monday throughout the trip I was to take a prophylaxis tablet. Something I also did. After breakfast at a café nearby, it was time for a new bike ride, now to the Valleys of the Kings and the Queens. They are on the other side of the river so a slightly longer bike ride. But it was as always wonderful to cycle, although in the sun and wind it felt like biking into a 200-degree blast furnace. We were the only ones cycling; if you did not walk, you used a donkey. We met several men on donkeys, never women, they seemed to prefer to walk alongside - or they were not allowed to ride. And the strange thing was that men all sat with both legs on the same side of the animal; why didn't they ride astride?

The valleys themselves were not much to see. Sand and mountains. But we got to go down into several of the tombs and it was fascinating. Of course, we visited Deir el-Bahri and Queen Hatshepsut's tomb temple from the 15th century BC. Again, I did not know much about what I saw other than that it was old, very old. The colours on the walls were intense, as if they had been painted yesterday, unbelievable. In one of the tombs we saw a mummy, as intact as the ones I had seen in the museum in Cairo.

A young man in a turban and galabeya wanted to show us something special. He took the three of us to a remote part of the Valley of the Queens. There he opened a tomb, gave us a flashlight and invited us down. We only saw a steep passage deep down into the earth, but we went down the sandy stairs. He himself stayed behind. It was scary. I remember now when I read my diary that it was deep and although spectacular when we got down, we couldn't see much with just a flashlight.

When we peered up, the light at the end of the stairway was barely visible. The air was thick and short on oxygen. What if the light goes out and he closes the door and disappears? Thus my thoughts went. Don and Jim probably thought the same, although neither of us expressed our feelings. But we got up rather quickly.

Of course, the fellow was waiting for us and we showed our gratitude with a few pounds. We were the only ones in that part of the valley, so maybe it was special.

On the way home we took it easy. Cycled detours through the green palm groves of the Nile. I liked this much better than the mega cities down the Nile. Here people did not yell and scream at us. We were left alone. Nor did they seem as poor. Few, if any beggars. The only ones who were really not well off here were the horses. Not much more than skeletons that they whipped or stuck sticks in open wounds to get them to pull small carts. Depressing to see.

We bought dates to munch on and found a small café where we drank refreshing lemonade and each had a divine omelette. A dish I ate as often as I could for the rest of my time in Egypt. It was good and I imagined it was kind to my stomach, which was still behaving rebelliously. Either I couldn't poop at all, or I didn't do anything else. As Flaubert wrote from Egypt in a letter home to his mother on January 5, 1850: "Shitting must work! That is the most important thing."

When we got back to the hostel, Mike and Debbie had turned up. In the evening, after an omelette dinner at the café next door, we sat on the hotel's terrace and played charades. The others had done this much more than I, as it turned out; I was lousy at it. So I quickly eliminated myself and then enjoyed the cool evening and the company and the view. I read that I expressed happiness that night in the diary; I was happy with the 'sense of the moment' and felt elated and carefree, privileged to be sitting by the Nile with other globetrotters on a September evening in 1971.

The next day I took the train to Aswan together with Jim and Don. We performed the same maneuver also on this train. But this time we took no other passenger's seats as the 1st class car was almost empty; also here the conductor let us stay. However, Jim and Don sat in the dining car the whole trip, so I had my own compartment. Enjoyed the solitude, the beautiful Nile Valley, the train ride. Reflected on the fact that when I take the boat from Aswan up the Nile to the south in a couple of days, it all becomes more irreversible. Turning around in Aswan, as Herodotus did in the 460s BC, and travel back home would be quite easy, but once I am on the boat to Wadi Halfa, it will be more difficult. Crossing Lake Nasser would be my Rubicon River. Not that I was longing for home, at least not at that moment, rather the opposite. I could also see that I was getting used to the environment, even the flies, which I now only lamely waved away when they wanted to get into my eyes and nose.

The hostel in Aswan soon became full. Everyone was leaving on the boat south in two days. And we were really from all over the world, almost. Besides us Westerners, who were 12 now, there were the two Indian Kenyans and several Sudanese going the same way. Together we had a great time and exchanged stories and books. But I got to keep my Swedish books. No one wanted them. I was not only the youngest but also the only Swede in the group: "The Swede."

Unfortunately, my stomach started acting up again. And I had a fever. I felt terrible. I stayed in the hostel most of my stay in Aswan even if I ate some yogurt and omelette in a café next door. At least I managed to send a birthday postcard to my father, who would turn 48 in a week. I also did some shopping. For the boat trip we all bought some food, even though it was said that there would be some on the boat. I got biscuits, a cucumber, a couple of tins of sardines and four boiled eggs, nuts and dates. I did not intend to starve on the boat, if only I could get something down.

We had to wait for three hours the next day to buy tickets at a small table on the dock next to the boat. There was no shade, so we queued in the blazing sun. Excruciating but unavoidable if we wanted to get on the boat. Then there was a fight to board and find somewhere in the shade on the aft deck. However, most passengers wanted to sit indoors so we had quite a lot of space on deck. But it was several hours before we left the quay just next to the Assuan Dam.

The dam created Lake Nasser and, south of Wadi Halfa in Sudan, Lake Nubia. It dammed a 480 km long and in places 16 km wide large lake, covering 5,250 km2 and capable of holding 132 km3 of water. The first and second cataracts of the Nile were flooded and some 60,000 people were forced to move, whether they wanted to or not. But what perhaps attracted even more international attention was the relocation of several ancient monuments, notably the temples at Abu Simbel. The dam had been inaugurated by Anwar Sadat the previous year.

Traveling on the lake was, at least then, hardly a beautiful trip. All the fertile soil along the Nile had been drowned, and now all we saw along the shores of the lake was dry desert. So we did other things. Games and reading. I had traded a book by James Clavell, *King Rat*. (You read strange literature when you travel, books you would never dream of reading at home.) I had got it for *Zorba* by Nikos Kazantzakis, which I had finished in Cairo: a really good book. It was important to have some English books to swap with when traveling this way, I had now realized. And almost everyone was a big reader, except perhaps the Australian Leroy, who was just crazy.

In the evening, at sundown when the boat was moving smoothly up the Nile, Leroy dived into the lake and went for a swim. This caused an uproar among the crew. Forbidden and dangerous! Poisonous snakes swim the lake among crocodiles and the large Nile perch. Leroy was unaffected by this information and got up without haste and dried himself. The rest of us were a little jealous; he now looked cleaner and fresher than we did. But none of us had any thoughts of following his plunge. Although a swim would have done me good; I was terribly dirty. In the diary I see that I had never felt so filthy. And it wasn't helped by the fact that I felt sick, had a feverish chill in the heat. Mike and Debbie gave me some dysentery tablets hoping that would help. At least I managed to sleep some that night.

Mike and Debbie on Lake Nasser.

40

As daylight came, we passed Abu Simbel at a leisurely pace. I slept but was woken up to see the world heritage site in the morning light. I don't think it was possible to go ashore then and visit the temple. At least not for us on our boat.

Instead, we docked in Wadi Halfa at 10 a.m. and the train to Khartoum would leave at 4 pm When Flaubert visited Wadi Halfa in 1850, it consisted only of a "row of palm trees with a few houses: that is the whole village." Now it was somewhat larger: Lake Nasser and its boat traffic together with the railway to Khartoum generated activity. But it was hardly a metropolis.

The border crossing went relatively smoothly in a small hut by the quay and soon we were officially in Sudan. We had time to buy some provisions for the train journey. Changing money was not possible anywhere, but fortunately they took Egyptian pounds in the small store we found. I bought some sardine cans again and some hard white bread, biscuits and dates. I could also fill the water bottle and buy a couple of local cola-type sodas. That I again found sardine cans; I realized much later when I read about Napoleon waring in Egypt at the end of the 18th century. Even though he himself never came this far south, he realized that he needed easily transported field provisions for his soldiers. Sardines ended up in tin cans with a small key to roll up the lid. And the tins still looked like that in 1971 in Wadi Halfa. Ever since then, I have been amazed that such a key has never found its way to any Swiss army knives - to my knowledge, and I have searched several Victorinox shops in Zûrich. Nowadays, however, the can and the key are history, so the Swiss need not worry.

Tomorrow it would be September 12 and I had been on the road for two months and had now crossed my Rubicon.

Kassala

The train started with a jolt and we slowly rolled out of Wadi Halfa. We had been waiting for six hours.

When we arrived at the station after a dusty truck ride, the train was already there and we bought tickets and boarded - and waited. When it finally moved, it was dark and full of people and some had to stand in the aisles with their luggage. The luggage racks were full of our backpacks, the locals' sacks and bags. There was a toilet of a kind at one end of the carriage; a room with a hole in the floor and a large clay pot full of water to wash with after one had done one's business. You could close the door, but not lock it. No toilet paper, of course, but by now I had realized I needed to always have a roll in my luggage. Indispensable, especially as I felt. There were only two faint, naked light bulbs hanging from the ceiling, barely lightening the carriage. We sat on wooden benches, two and two opposite each other, or three if you crowded together, which most people did. So everyone from the boat got a seat; I sat with a Sudanese family, or Nubian perhaps is the right word.

We were in the Nubian province in northern Sudan, Africa's largest nation by area at the time; a country that in 1956 became the first independent one in Africa. A country that only ignorant and indifferent imperialists could have created. A country with a Muslim northern half and a black African southern half whose people "physically and culturally are as different as Chinese and Norwegians," as Richard Dowden writes in his fine book *Africa: Altered States, Ordinary Miracles*. (The name Sudan is said to come from Bilad as-sudan, the land of the blacks, in Arabic.) The British, of course, didn't care about that, as they had their own imperialist interests to guide them. Today the country is divided in two different ones after years of war and famine.

The family in front of me was pitch black, almost blue, dignified and beautiful. They had five children, the oldest of whom was about eight years old and so pretty that it was hard not to stare at her. She also looked curiously at the Swede sitting opposite her. They didn't speak any English so communication was difficult, but we smiled and nodded and got along reasonably well under the circumstances. I realized that when we get off, we shall never see each other again. The curse of traveling, and perhaps also the charm. Writing this I wonder where they are now? What is the girl doing today? She is an adult - if not dead; 50 years have passed, and 2002 the average life expectancy was 17.7 in Sudan, according to Wikipedia. If alive she is probably the mother of several children. Does she remember the pale-faced boy with the long blond hair who sat smiling opposite her on a train out of Wadi Halfa in September 1971? No, of course not. But I remember her, at least with the help of my diary.

The night was eventful. We saw young Sudanese taking down their bags and crawling up onto the luggage racks to sleep. This also gave everyone more room on the seats to stretch out. Don and I found a shelf and decided to take turns. I got the first shift and crawled up. Initially I was a bit worried that I would fall down. But the train moved slowly and stopped frequently, as the desert was flat and the tracks were essentially straight. No curves or hills. I slept well until three when Don woke me up. Now it was his turn to lie down and I got his seat for the rest of the night. But when I climbed down in the dark, I missed the backrest I wanted to put my foot on. I fell, hit the floor and landed on an old man sleeping in the aisle. He and everyone else in the carriage began screaming and shouting. But no one was hurt, we were both fine. I apologized but he was furious and yelled angrily at me. This however led to that several people who had slept on the luggage rack now decided not to, as they thought I had fallen off the rack. So now there was more free shelf space and I could climb up again and sweetly fall asleep.

We met up with the Nile again the next morning, after having cut through the Nubian Desert to Abu Hamed - I saw on my Michelin map No. 154. Had I then known anything about the Karmah-, or Kush civilization, as the Egyptians called it, from about 2500 BC and the pyramids and ruins it left behind down the Nile, I might have got off here, and travelled to Dongala and the third cataract for all its pyramids and temple ruins. The Nubians were rich and had been plundered of slaves and gold by Egyptians for centuries (Nubia is thought to come from the ancient Egyptian word for gold: nub). During the 20th century, Egyptologists have argued about how much of the Pharaonic civilization is based on Nubian culture. The issue is sensitive, as it has to do with the extent of how black Egypt's ancient high culture was. That it later became so, however, is undeniable. In the 7th century BC, King Pianchi of

Kerma, the capital of Kush, invaded Egypt and installed himself as pharaoh, creating the 25th dynasty, which ruled for almost 100 years and was thus a black Nubian dynasty. The Kuch nation reached its peak, incredibly rich and ruled over an area stretching from Khartoum to the Mediterranean Sea. Today there are more pyramids in Sudan than in Egypt!

I was blissfully unaware of this when we, now in a half-full train, rolled out of Abu Hamed on the morning of September 13. In Abu Hamed we had been able to buy some food and drink 'chai,' as tea seemed to be called in all other languages. There was always plenty of tea wherever we stopped. And we often did. Mysteriously sometimes in the middle of a flat nowhere. In the seemingly deserted landscape, we still saw dromedaries from time to time. At first I thought they were wild - there were no people around - but I had never heard of wild camels. Soon I noticed that their front legs, or one back and one front, were tied together so that they could only take small steps, enough to move forward, but not to gallop away to freedom.

The train soon became crowded again. Not that I disliked children, but these large families with children who all seemed to be crying and squealing were stressful. And my stomach was still upsetting me and I also felt feverish. I tried to read and daydream and stare out at the flat landscape. But it was difficult to enjoy in the heat, the noise, the stale smell from the toilet and the sand blowing in from the open windows.

Suddenly my face got wet; was it raining? No, the sky was still naked and blue. Then I saw a little girl vomiting out of a window in front of me and realized what had hit me. I was already dirtier than I had ever been and this intestinal shower certainly did not improve my appearance. Leroy sat opposite me and couldn't help but laughing at my misery. With water in the urn in the toilet, I could wash away most of the vomit on my face, hair and clothes, but I felt miserable.

When it got dark, Leroy, Don, Jim and I climbed out and onto the roof of the railway wagon. We had noticed that young male Sudanese did this and Leroy investigated and convinced us. There was plenty of room up there. I found a free spot in the middle of the carriage roof and crawled into my sleeping bag, as it soon became really cold. A little anxiously I held one arm around a ventilation pipe. But the train was very slow, so there was actually none or very little risk of rolling off the

44

roof. I managed to fall asleep for a few hours to the slow rhythm of the train, even though the luminous sky was magnificent.

At two in the morning we arrived in Khartoum and did not really know what to do. But we managed to find two cars that for a reasonable sum drove us all to the city's hostel. There we managed to wake up a couple of young boys who worked at the hostel and who didn't mind at all that we awakened them. Instead, they were fantastic and welcomed us and we were even able shower before we gratefully and clean crawled into bed. It was pleasantly cool so we all slept very well.

A deafening thumping on the hostel roof woke me up the next morning; it was pouring down: a tropical torrent the likes of which I had never seen before. I also felt worse: high fever and vomited a bit. But I managed to get into town when it stopped raining and waded to a pharmacy where I bought Nimerol - I see in the diary. I swallowed a few of them, according to the pharmacist's instructions, and then crawled into bed for the rest of the day. I lay there sweating, trying to sleep some and drink as much as I could. Food was out of the question. I was, however, mostly worried about being left alone when everyone else departed for Kassala.

We were all going to East Africa and there were now lively discussions about how. Most people wanted to go via Ethiopia, which meant going to Kassala. You could get there by train or truck. The latter would take a day and a half and cost US$ 5 and the train two to three days for US$ 2. Getting to Asmara in Ethiopia from Kassala was not possible by land, this was now clear to everyone. The flight went once a week and the next one was the following Thursday. Quite impossible to get to if you took the train; it was now Tuesday. Leroy, Jim and Don therefore left with a truck that evening; they might make it.

Although I was used to traveling alone, I now had had company since Cairo, gotten used to it and felt comfortable and safe in it. Especially in my current physical condition. I felt more like a small, pathetic child than an adult world traveller. Mike and Debbie were kind though. They bought me a plane ticket for next week's flight and yogurt and promised to wait for me. Now we had just over a week, which felt good.

The next day some people left by train to Kassala. I stayed mostly in bed also this day. I was cold and sweaty. In the afternoon I felt well enough to go into town with Mike and Debbie to the Ethiopian Embassy. I needed to extend or renew my entry visa that I had obtained in Stockholm. It had now expired. But they refused; I would have to buy a new one. I decided to ignore that information and hope that I could fix it in Kassala or at the airport. At least now I had a plane ticket.

Not only Mike and Debbie were kind but also the people in Khartoum. We hitchhiked in town wherever we went and the first car always stopped and were friendly and curious about who we were, where we came from and where we were going. Often they would offer chai or food. We were also left alone when we walked the streets; a welcoming change compared to northern Egypt.

Before I fell asleep that night, I took lots of pills given to me by all the others in the hostel, without having the slightest idea what it was I was swallowing or how the pills reacted together. Twelve pills I wrote in my diary that I washed down with some coca cola. They all said that their tablets would help against fever, stomach ache and dysentery and I chose to trust them all. Feeling depressed and desperate, I really did not want to be left alone when everyone else took the train to Kassala the next day.

And miracles do happen! I was the first out of bed the next morning after waking, as usual, by the prayer caller's "Allahu akbar." I felt completely restored. Today I don't understand it. It was of course insane to take different kinds of unknown medication in that way. But I was young, stupid, desperate and probably also quite strong.

Together with Mike and Debbie, I managed to see some of Khartoum that day as well. We went over to Omdurman on the other side of the Nile. Mike and Debbie had read up and could tell me about the battle here on September 2, 1898, when the British slaughtered more than 10,000 Sudanese in a rebellion against their colonial power. A superior British army with machine guns mowed down the Sudanese long before they could inflict any damage on the British. Hardly honourable, as Churchill wrote in his account of the battle in which he participated at the age of 24. Of course, General Kitchener was still welcomed as a hero later in London. "Not the finest moment in British history," Mike declared.

Khartoum wasn't really a beautiful city, as flat as the Nubian desert, scattered endlessly and without character everywhere, I wrote in the diary. But the riverbank was nice and we found a café where we could sit in the shade and have some food and enjoy the traffic on the Nile, the palm trees' rustling in the wind and the muezzin calls from countless mosques. In Khartoum, the Blue and White Nile meet. The former comes from the Ethiopian highlands and carries 6/7 of the Nile's water, while the White comes from Lake Victoria. It should supposedly be possible to see the rivers running side by side here in Khartoum: The White's greyish water and the Blue's brownish green. But I did not see any difference, instead I ordered a banana shake. Since Cairo, I had drunk these as often as I could. Thought it was good for my stomach, if not it was at least good and cheap.

"How come you are traveling in Africa?" Mike suddenly asked me as we sat in the shade looking out over the Nile.

"I actually don't know. But I have hitchhiked a lot in Europe and wanted to move on. I thought about India but just about everyone else I know goes there and often for the wrong reasons. I wanted to do something different. I also have friends of my parents in Tanzania I hope to visit. What about you, what are you doing here?"

"We weren't meant to go to Africa at all," Debbie replied. "We were in Greece and met a couple who had been to Kenya and convinced us that we should go down there. Initially we were supposed to go to Israel and work on a kibbutz."

"We still hope to do that when we have been to East Africa," Mike added.

"I hope to travel around Africa and eventually end up in Morocco," I said.

We were the only white people in the café; all the others were jet black, almost blue, and majestic in their galabyias. Often they were marked with scars on their faces. Both men and women, although the latter were as few in the streets as in Egypt. The scars were deliberate and rather beautiful. Later, I came to understand that it was the facial markings of different peoples, revealing which ethnic group you belong to. I came to see it in almost all of Africa and have understood that it is an old tradition. Herodotus wrote in the 4th century BC about the facial markings he observed among Africans in Egypt   .

That evening I could finally eat and enjoy a meat stew before we went to the train station; I liked the food better here!

The train to Kassala was said to take up to three days. And it started well. When the train with me, Mike and Debbie rolled out of Khartoum after a few hours delay, the carriage was not even full, and no families with children. The first night was filled with singing. A group of Sudanese students entertained us almost all through the night. One of them sang the verse and the others joined in the chorus. They sang beautifully and we all enjoyed it in the dark carriage. Yet I managed a few hours of sleep on the luggage rack.

To begin with, we travelled along the Blue Nile and its green scenery. In Sennar we would leave it and turn east towards Kassala. Which we did on the second evening. Again it became flat, black and a rocky desert, but the next morning it was greener again after El Hawata; we were approaching the Ethiopian highlands. But it was slow going. Often the train stood still in the seemingly empty desert, without us understanding why. The students told us that it had probably rained ahead of us and the rails could have started to move. At each station we stopped we stayed for half an hour up to two or three hours. I wrote in my notes that I had cycled faster to Kassala! A bit annoying but really, I was in no hurry. We would make the flight on Thursday and this way we could stretch our legs, leave the train and find something to drink and a bowl of meat stew to eat, which seemed to be the standard dish of the Sudanese street kitchen, and it was good. A bit tricky for Debbie though, who was a strict vegetarian. But it was important to stay close to the station. Suddenly the train whistle blew and it took off. It was however so slow that we easily caught up and jumped on the train.

Now there was a lot to look at when we had left the desert. I see in my diary that I have noted several beautiful and for me of course unknown birds. Nowadays, as a pensioner, I have become a relatively passionate bird watcher, so I am delighted to read that even at 19 I at least observed flying faunas. I can deduct from my notes that I saw herons and vultures; the smaller birds and birds of prey I mentioned are more difficult to guess at.

We also became acquainted with other somewhat less pleasant flying creatures. At a small station before Gedaref we ended up in an Old Testamentish swarm of locusts. As soon as we stopped, the carriage was swarming with large green-yellowish locusts. A big thick cloud that descended over everything in the carriage. Every surface in the car and on us humans was soon covered with locusts. They were the size of a thumb and not difficult to brush off, but it was not pleasant. When we went out to buy something to eat and drink, they were everywhere. Our shoes crunched as we walked on the locust-covered ground and our hair and clothes were constantly attacked. Strangely enough, I didn't find them as repulsive and disgusting as the equally large cockroaches I encountered in every place we stayed. We recognised what a nuisance the locust swarms must be to the locals. For us backpackers, it was simply another adventure to tell when we returned home one day. We soon moved on and left the locusts behind, even though the wagon was full of them, mostly dead by now though.

The second evening we sat and talked to the singing students who were very curious about us and we hardly got to ask them anything. They were on their way to Kassala for some field studies, that much we understood. They came from the University of Khartoum and were, of course, all male. We asked if there were girls at the university. "Yes, but not many. Often their parents don't want them to continue their studies. It's sad, but it will probably change with the modernization of our country." We all hoped so. They were not so curious about Sweden while they asked Mike and Debbie lots about New York. Understandable.

Another guy sitting by himself told us that he was studying engineering at the American University in Cario but was now on his way to northern Ethiopia to fight for six months in the Eritrean Liberation Army (ELF). Then he would return to Cairo and his studies again. From Kassala he would hike into Ethiopia to the mountains north of Asmara.

"Can't we join you, so we don't have to fly to Asmara," we asked.

"No," he laughed. "It's dangerous and well in Ethiopia, how would you explain how you have entered the country? They would immediately throw you in jail. So better if you fly, I think."

We agreed with him.

I had hoped to sleep out on the roof the second night, but it was impossible. It thundered and rained quite often and a lot. Mostly in the distance, but also on our train, so everyone stayed inside. I slept on a luggage rack again. And rather well as it was cool as usual in the desert.

The closer we got to Kassala, the fewer we became in the carriage. Mike spent most of the last day on a luggage rack sleeping or reading. Debbie the same over two seats and I mostly sat at my usual place by one of the windows looking out over the now slightly rolling and green scenery. We often saw large herds of dromedaries, which here did not seem to be tied to their legs in any way. Often they galloped at full speed, afraid of the train. A strange sight. More fun to watch, however, was when they ran before galloping, with their legs on the same side on the ground, swaying from one side to the other. The ship of the desert. We understood that it was greener than usual now, thanks to the rains and it was beautiful. When the train stopped in the deserted landscape, which happened often, there were always children running from the horizon. And if there was a small village nearby, women would come running towards the train to sell bananas, tea, oranges, nuts and dates on trays they carried on their heads. It was hard to grasp how the trade worked, but the students helped us and soon we managed ourselves. As a consequence, and not a pleasant one, the wagon got messy when everyone threw food scraps and all other rubbish on the floor all the time. Now, just before Kassala, after almost 50 hours, it was not a pretty sight. And Danish newspapers were everywhere. All the food you bought at stations was wrapped in Danish newspaper. Did the Danes give their old newspapers to Sudan? Strange foreign aid, I thought, and couldn't quite understand it.

Kassala's train station was way out of town; together with the Eritrean guy, Nazenat, we took a taxi into town. Mike, Debbie and I found one of the two hotels in town. The more expensive one. The cheaper one, where a room cost 15 piasters, was full of our friends from Khartoum who were all staying there. They hadn't made last week's flight. Our hotel was also full but we each got a bed on the hotel's roof terrace for 25 piastres, about half a dollar. And it was comfortable. Cool, almost cold. But Debbie and Mike were cold as they had sold their sleeping bags in Athens before flying to Cairo; they were going to travel in hot Africa! Therefore didn't need any sleeping bags, they had naively argued. They regretted it now and came to do so even more in Ethiopia.

Around four that first night we woke up to rain so we had to move into the hotel and the staff arranged our beds in a corridor. The next day they gave us a large room together.

Debbie, jag and Mike on the roof terrace of the hotel in Kassala.

We stayed five days in Kassala waiting for the flight, coming Thursday, so had time to explore the town. Then it was a small town (today it is said to be home to nearly half a million people) and a pleasant one, even if not a beautiful town, but the Taka Mountains rise majestically on the horizon towards Ethiopia and give the town a dramatic backdrop. Chiefly it was flat though and now, after the night's rain, wet and muddy. But it drained away quickly in the sandy soil. We found nice cafés and restaurants where we became regulars. I was now also fully recovered from the fever and stomach problems so could participate fully.

We discovered a bakery where they made wonderful bread, like pita bread. Soon we learned when they were freshly baked and every morning, we bought a couple that we tore the inside out of and put banana slices in instead. They melted a little as the bread was still warm from the oven. Then off to our regular café for breakfast, which every morning came to consist of orange juice, yogurt and the strong Sudanese coffee, to the banana rolls. An excellent start to the day.

Now I was reading Steinbeck's *The Grapes of Wrath*, which Debbie had lent me. It was instantly epically captivating and hard to put down. I often sat on the terrace of the hotel or in our favourite café and read. But we also strolled around and explored the city and its surroundings. There was a small river running through the city, the Gash or Mereb River, which in the rainy season now was full of rapid water. Sometimes we met young men, dressed in white outfits, and a beautiful leather belt with a knife and a big sword. They looked wild with a hairstyle reminiscent of Jimi Hendrix when he forgot to brush his hair. Nazenat, the ELF-soldier from the train, who we met from time to time, told us that they belong to a nomadic tribe of the Beja people, who live in the mountains but during the rainy season come down to the greener surroundings of Kassala. They looked quite dangerous and I did not dare to photograph them but bought a postcard with them and sent home to Harpsundsvägen 3.

We also visited the Khatmiyyam Mosque, built in 1840 but partially destroyed during the Mahdist war at the end of the 19th century. However, still beautiful in its simplicity compared to mosques in Cairo, and important for the largest Sufi order in Sudan: the Khatmyyasufis.

The hotel we stayed in was next to the Ethiopian consulate and one day I went there to again try to extend my visa. But I was told the same. I had to buy a new one. I didn't feel I could afford that. And when they told me that I could get a visa at the airport in Asmara, I decided to wait and hope for an extension in Asmara.

I also spent some time with Leroy. Mainly because he was a bit crazy and funny. He was from Australia, spiced every sentence with the f-word and had hitchhiked from Bali to Egypt, via India and Afghanistan, so an experienced traveller it was fun to listen to. He turned 29 one of our days in Kassala - 10 years older than I - and we celebrated him as best we could in one of the town's modest restaurants. He had managed to get hold of some marijuana in town so we all got reasonably high that night.

One day I followed him up into the mountains. We took a taxi to the basis of Taka range and started our trek. It was nice to hike a bit and do something other than sit and read. We had water, bread and bananas with us and expected to be on the move all day. It was beautiful to get up and be able to look out over the city and how the landscape spread out to the west. We encountered several of the nomadic people with swords but they took no notice of us. Nor did they want contact when we addressed them. They just stared curiously at us and disappeared behind a mountain ridge before we caught up with them. Tricky guys! Also here I noted the beauty and variety of the bird fauna, including my first marabou stork.

Once back at the hotel, I took a nice, warm shower. Best shower since Cairo. All showers after Cairo had been cold, but here they were luke-warm. The water was heated by the sun in a large tub on the roof. Wonderful. I took several showers a day here, as Kassala was both hot and dusty.

In the evenings we usually got high, as Leroy was generous with his grass. We would sit in our favourite coffee shop and discuss and laugh. Many of the others, especially Mike and Debbie, were interested in the spiritual. I instead tried to argue for a rational, materialistic view of re-ality, like the rational Marxist-Leninist I pretended to be. I don't remem-ber how well I succeeded in the marijuana fog, but I see in my notes that I enjoyed it.

When we got to our hotel room one evening, Mike asked me if I wouldn't mind going for an evening promenade: "We would like to have some time to ourselves," as he put it. I understood and took my Stein-beck for a walk in the quiet and dark Kassala. The café was still open so I sat there and read for an hour or so, with a cup of tea. When I got back to the room, Debbie was already asleep and Mike smiled and nod-ded a grateful goodnight.

On Thursday, September 23, it was time to fly to Asmara. Mike, Deb-bie and I heartily thanked the hotel staff who had certainly been kind and accommodating. Nothing to complain about. Which I paradoxically thanked them for by stealing one of their blankets, a thin, green check-ered cotton blanket. I managed to do it great justice though, as I carried it with me throughout Africa, as well as on later trips to America and Asia. My snuggle blanket! Linus has his and now I had mine! It was per-fect when it was too hot to crawl into the sleeping bag - which is why I stole it. But I was a little ashamed.

This would be my first flight. I had never flown before and was nerv-ous, something I tried to hide but didn't succeed with too well, as the others teased me. We were now 15 Westerners who had connected from Khartoum. We all took a small bus at nine o'clock to the airport. Which was not much of an airport. It consisted of a small hut with a couple of uniformed and armed guards, an orange and white wind cone and a flat grass field that served as a runway. No place where I could extend my visa to Ethiopia. The quality of the airport hardly made me less nervous. Nor did the fact that no plane was waiting for us or appeared to be arriving. It should have left at 12.30, but not until five o'clock a DC-3 for 32 passengers landed. There were about 30 of us now. By then we were very hungry and thirsty as we hadn't brought anything to eat or drink. Not even tea was available at the "airport." But food and drinks were promised on the plane.

Asmara

The food we were offered was lemonade and buns. Not exactly what we craved, but we voraciously devoured it all. After 50 minutes we landed in Asmara, Ethiopia. My first flight went smoothly but now I was really nervous to face the passport control. I didn't have a valid entry visa, mine had run out. Hopefully they would not stop me from entering the country, but give me a tourist visa, or offer to sell me a new one. To my great relief, however, they just stamped my passport and gave me three months in the country, as if my entry visa was still valid. Unexpected, but I did not mind at all.

Now I was in Ethiopia, or Abyssinia as it once was called, though Asmara today is the capital of Eritrea. A remarkable country; it is one of the oldest nations in the world and has the second largest population in Africa, after Nigeria. Homer mentions it in 700 BC in the *Iliad* and already in the first song of the *Odyssey*: Poseidon is with the Ethiopians, the "people who live at the edge of the world." And Herodotus, 300 years later, calls it "the outermost of all countries." This is how far south knowledge of the world extended in antiquity. It was the same with the Romans. Ovid's knowledge ends with the land of the Cephs, as he calls Abyssinians at the beginning of the fifth song in the *Metamorphoses*.

I knew nothing about this when we found a clean and cheap hotel where the rooms cost 1.50 US$ per night. Mike and Debbie wanted their own room this time, so here I ended up sharing a room with Kathy and Patrik, an American couple carrying around a cassette player, which was okay too. I could enjoy some Dylan and John Lee Hooker. Why I didn't take a single room, my diary doesn't reveal, but probably I was stingy – or they didn't have another room.

What I did know at the time was that Ethiopia had never been colonized during 'the scramble for Africa.' But it had been at war with the Italians a couple of times. First in the late 19th century which ended with an overwhelming victory for Ethiopia in 1896. The next time the Italians showed up, they were more successful and the fascist regime conquered the country in 1936. In 1941, however, they were repelled by allied forces and the country became free again.

The Italian influence was nonetheless noticeable in Asmara in 1971.

The architecture in the city centre looked, and I guess still does, completely European and the city was once called Little Rome. Everywhere there were trattorias, often with Italians behind the counters serving fantastic coffee and Italian ice cream. What distinguished them from those in Italy was mainly the obligatory portrait of a bearded Haile Selassie, weighed down by a chest full of medals. The streets were paved and had sidewalks – enormous change from anything we had encountered since Cairo. The first night I also had a good pasta with a glass of milk, a beverage I didn't know I had missed. Nor that I hadn't heard church bells since leaving Europe. Here I was reminded of that when the city's churches and cathedrals rang at noon. The fact that the city had churches and cathedrals was not only due to the Italians. The country has been partly Christian since at least 300 AD. With that, the country also got a written language, Geez, while few other societies in Africa had a written language before Islam or Christianity arrived. Geez is today the liturgical language of the Ethiopian Orthodox Church, while the official language is Amharic. They also have their own timekeeping system, which caused problems for us when we had to catch buses. The day does not start at midnight but at six in the morning. The calendar is also different from our Gregorian one; it is based on the Coptic Church's calendar which is constructed on the resurrection of Jesus instead of his birth. I never managed to understand the almanac, which didn't matter much. But it was different.

So was the cold. Asmara, which in Tigrinya, the language spoken in northern Ethiopia, means 'the four villages that give harmony,' is 2350 meters above sea level and the nights were really cold. I slept well.

I awoke my first morning in Asmara to both prayer callers and church bells; not a bad alarm clock, a "jubilant ecumenical duet," as Kapuscinski calls it. And it was cool, and early, so I stayed in bed for a nice while. I had slept in both shirt and pants and had not taken the usual shower before bed. A bit different from previous nights on the continent, and nothing I minded at all; nice to not having to sweat, which I now had done regularly since Alexandria.

The first thing the five of us did after a trattoria breakfast was to change some money on the black market, which turned out to be a bit tricky. The hotel had told us where we could find the local black market. In a corner of a small square, we located a cool guy in sunglasses who promised to help us. He took us around a few corners and down a small alley and into a café, where he told us to wait. Soon he returned with another young man in just as dark sunglasses and they led us to a bar nearby where we walked through a big room with pool tables and into a smaller and shady room where they also played pool and also cards at some tables. The games on all the tables stopped when we entered and it became completely silent. We looked at each other and wondered what would happen next. I was glad that I was not alone in this precarious situation and guessed that the others felt the same way. We didn't dare to say a word. The two guys in shades steered us into a small side room where a large black man in even darker sunglasses met us. He looked scary but laughed and joked so we relaxed a bit. He asked what we wanted to exchange and when we said we had traveller's checks, he insisted that we did not write the dates on the ones we wanted to exchange. He pulled out a large bundle of the local currency, birr, or Ethiopian dollars as it was called then and gave us a double rate compared to the official one. We were then escorted back to the square and, of course, got out of there in one piece.

Kathy and Patrik went back to the hotel while Mike, Debbie and I took a bus to the US military base, Kagnew, just outside of the city. Mike and Debbie hoped to buy some literature. And they did. We picked up about ten second hand novels, mostly by Kurt Vonnegut, an author I was unfamiliar with at the time. Mike and Debbie, however claimed that he "is one of the best writers in the US today. You absolutely must read him, especially his *Slaughterhouse Five*." I promised to do so. We also had some coffee at the base, with American donuts.

In the evening we celebrated Mike's 24th birthday. Debbie had bought him a sketchbook and a beautiful leather belt. I gave him the Hohner harmonica I had brought from home. I was just an amateur blower while Mike was a musician and played in a bluegrass band at home. The harmonica found a better address.

The next morning we immediately ended up at the local military headquarters. We had taken a bus out of town to start hitchhiking south towards Aksum and Addis Ababa. There was a military post where the city ended and as soon as they saw us getting off the bus with our backpacks, they waved us in and put us in a jeep to the headquarters. Patrick and

Kathy were already there, as were Jim and Don for the same reason.

It turned out that we needed a permit to travel south, whether we took a bus or hitchhiked. But they couldn't help us and took us all to the Immigration office. There we waited in a big hall with fluorescent lights and echoing walls for more than two hours. The official in question was still busy. It didn't matter much, as long as we finally got a permit. None of us were in a hurry, but some of us were becoming irritated.

But finally, the responsible official received us and firmly announced that tourists must fly to Addis Ababa. "Due to the current situation and the civil war in the Eritrean province, we cannot have tourists on our roads. And certainly not hitchhikers. You could be kidnapped by the guerrillas. That would create international mayhem, something Addis absolutely wants to avoid."

We pleaded loudly and referred to Ethiopian embassies we had visited who had assured us that we would be able to travel on the roads in the country without problems. He became a bit hesitant, told us to wait and left the room. After a while he came back and told us to go to his boss. Here we were told the same but with persistent pleas we managed to persuade him to arrange certificates so that we could travel to Aksum. It was only in the Eritrea province that a certificate was required. He told us that sometimes European mercenaries come down to fight with the ELF, so they don't want Europeans on the roads. We promised not to take up arms. We just wanted to get to Kenya and thanked him emphatically.

They drove us back to the military headquarters where they already were informed and wrote out three certificates for us. They were very nice and even drove us to the roadside post where we had first tried to hitchhike.

Together we all got a ride to the next small town on the back of a large truck. While the others disappeared south on another truck, Mike, Debbie and I had a good omelette lunch in a little shack. As we hiked out of the village after the lunch, we were joined by about 20 little boys. They apparently found us hilarious, laughing at us and wanted to talk and touch us. They had no English and we no Amharic so we couldn't do the former but we did greet them all. Soon a police car stopped and wanted to see if we had permission to travel here. I showed them our certificate – a document I found in a box in the basement and have next to me as I write this (what one saves?). When I presented this paper they became friendly, wanting to help us in every way and even saluted us. They sent the kids away and wished us good luck. Next lots of long-horned cattle, watusis, and sheep completely surrounded us. This however meant that trucks had to stop and we had a chance to ask for lifts.

A truck promised to take us to Aksum. Mike jumped into the passenger seat and Debbie and I climbed up onto the bed of the truck. It turned out to be a nice, and cold trip. We had to wrap ourselves in clothes and blankets. The scenery was rolling green and there were small villages and farms everywhere. The truck soon became full of other travellers, including Jim and Don, but mainly Ethiopians heading south. They had to pay for the lift, not so we Europeans, odd, I thought. But we did not get to Aksum. At 18.00 the roads were closed in the province because of the war and we were stopped in a roadblock in a small town; Adi Quala my map informed me. We found a small hotel where a bed cost 1 birr a night.

We overslept the next morning; all the trucks that got stuck in the roadblock the previous evening, had already left when we turned up. We slept well in the cold, curled up in sleeping bags and wrapped in two blankets provided by the hotel – Mike and Debbie of course only in several blankets. We ended up taking a bus to Aksum.

In Aksum I met a group of Swedish MPs, 15 of them, who were on a study trip to Ethiopia. It was nice to speak some Swedish again. They were here to look at the remains of the great Aksum Empire. A rich trading nation from 100 B.C. until the 10th century. It was mainly and initially a Jewish kingdom, but under King Ezena II it converted to Christianity in the 330s. It acted as a trading partner between Rome, the Arab world and India and was considered one of the four most powerful empires of the 3rd century, along with Rome, Persia and China. It has left behind several famous obelisks, also here in Aksum.

We saw nothing of that but continued in a jeep to a small village without electricity, Haida. It was on the edge of a large rift, with a beautiful view of the green valley. We were in the Ethiopian highlands. Here and all the way from Aksum, I had noticed the rich bird life: a lot of birds of prey and some crow-sized red birds, as well as bright blue ones that flashed by in the intensely green landscape. Lovely.

Before dark we, Debbie, Mike and I, tried to find a place resembling a restaurant. The small hotel we stayed at offered no food, just beds and a few blankets in a couple of rooms separated by plywood walls that almost reached the corrugated metal roof. A candle was also given to us. Having walked the whole road through the little village, we thought we had found a place to dine and asked if there was anything to eat. With our sign language an old woman understood and offered us to sit on some stools around the only table in the room. She pumped up and lit a pump gas-oil lamp that shone incredibly brightly before she turned it down. An amazing piece I had never seen before, but came across throughout Africa. The woman laughed all the time and promised to cook up a spaghetti scramble. Which she did brilliantly. I wrote in my diary that it was the best spaghetti I had ever eaten. She also produced three beers for us. Magical, especially as we soon realized that it wasn't a restaurant at all, but we had forced our way into her home after asking around. I don't know what we paid but I hope and believe it was decent.

The next day we thought we would make it to Gonder, but it was impossible. It was rumoured that a bus to Gonder would leave at 11am, but because of the different time system, we were unsure when this would happen. We sat at our hotel next to the road - the whole village was stretched along the one main road - hoping that some traffic would happen south. Nothing. Instead, we fanned flies that seemed to have practically taken over the village. They swarmed like dark clouds around you, and the children in particular, who, standing curiously watching us, were covered in them without seeming to care. I had managed to get hold of a fly whisk, knotted rope on a stick, which now came very handy. I sat and waved it back and forth around my head. The flies here were different from the ones at home, where they can annoy and buzz in windows. One or two might wake you up too early if you haven't managed to get rid of them before going to bed. But here they were spoiled by garbage, death and waste and the amount of people. In this village, at least, life seemed to belong to them; they ruled, set the agenda, even if people tried not to pretend that they were there. But of course they didn't succeed. The children in front of us were full of flies all over their faces, crawling into the corners of their mouths, their eyes and trying to get into their nasal cavities. And if someone had a wound, which most seemed to have on their bare legs and arms, it was a feast for the aggressive flies.

The children's hairstyles amazed me. The boys were shaved in the most imaginative hairdos: mohawks, crosses or circles. The girls' hair was braided all along the top of their heads down to their ears and then fell beautifully over their shoulders.

At four pm a bus actually materialized; the first vehicle of the day heading south. We waved it down and after an hour we ended up in Adi Arkai. There we spent the night and for the first time I ate sour injera bread with an extremely strong meat stew. A dish that came to dominate my entire stay in Ethiopia. Perhaps not the greatest culinary experience, but good. And the grey pancake-like injera was really necessary to neutralize the colossally spicy stew, no matter what was in it, although there was always meat of some kind.

Following day we took a bus to Gonder. A breathtaking journey up winding roads with fantastic views of deep, green valleys where now a bright yellow flower dominated and bloomed everywhere. So even though it was cold and a bit scary on the twisting and narrow roads, it was a wonderful trip where I sat and daydreamed and gazed out over the spectacular scenery.

At one point the bus stopped and all passengers were asked to depart. Then it continued with only the driver over a serpentine curve that stood on pillars over a deep ravine. When the bus without approximately 2700 kilos of passengers had successfully crossed the curved bridge, if I can call it that, we passengers had to walk across it and board the bus and the journey could continue. I wondered what would have happened if the bridge had collapsed under the bus!

Now on the Ethiopian plateau, again more than 2000 meters above sea level, there was less vegetation. The landscape was flat and all the land was cultivated, and in a primitive way. After an ox or a horse or a donkey, the farmer ploughed his field with a wooden plough, or walked double folded and harvested with a cutter. Everywhere cattle grazed and even horses, which seemed to be wild - but that could hardly be so? Then the plateau suddenly ended. On the west side it dropped in a steep, deep, precipice, the Rift Valley, while it slowly sloped down on the east side; we were on top of a ridge. And then we arrived in Gonder.

Gonder is the fourth largest city in the country, at least today, with a population of over 300,000 and with a rich history. I realized this when we visited several palaces in the city. Gonder was once the capital of

Ethiopia. It became capital of the empire after the emperors in the 17th century spent the rainy seasons up in Gonder and near Lake Tana. Emperor Fasilides built the first palace after which each new emperor apparently felt compelled to build his own palace, according to *Africana, the Encyclopaedia of African and African American Experience*, a massive and heavy book of more than 2000 pages, which today, when I write this, is my main source of facts from my African library here at home.

The Fasilidae Palace is the most famous and it was exotic and surprising for a 19-year-old ignorant hitchhiker from Högdalen to visit. It reminded me of a European medieval castle, so I realized that there was history here that I had no idea about. At the Fasilidaes Baths, a religious festival seemed to be taking place. Beautifully dressed people were singing and chanting what sounded like prayers. Here I bought an Ethiopian stone cross to hang around my neck on a leather strap. I came to wear it quite carelessly during all the years I hitchhiked around the world. I still have it somewhere, though it's been a long time since I wore it - I'm now a little more sceptical at wearing religious trinkets.

In Gonder, which was a relatively modern town with lots of small shops offering a wide range of products, I bought a flashlight and a lighter: necessities, I had realized. I also bought a roll of nice and soft toilet paper. The Sudanese ones had been hard and even difficult to tear into pieces. There was never any paper in the toilets we visited and I wasn't about to start using only hand and water. But I had continued drinking tap water even after my water purification tablets ran out in Kassala. I realized that it could not be avoided. Plastic-bottled water had thankfully not made its appearance in these parts of Africa yet, and drinking the local sodas, which, although always available, did not work, was costly and rather disgusting. I hoped that my body would get used to the local water and thus far I hadn't been sick. So far so good.

I also had my shoes shined. That hadn't happened since Stockholm, so it was needed. A young boy did it for me. He had chased and begged us as he saw my shoes were of leather and indeed in need of cleaning. I gave in. But it made me uncomfortable. The first time a boy knelt down in front of me and shined my shoes. It bothered me. Mike and Debbie just thought I was silly.

"All over the world you find these shoeshine boys," said Mike. "Often it's their only opportunity to make money; shouldn't they be allowed to do it?"

"You're probably right but I'd rather shine them myself and it feels wrong with a guy on his knees in front of me, who ought to be in school right now. The world should be a better place, so he wouldn't have to beg to shine a rich European's shoes."

"Sure, but it will be a long while before the world gets there, if ever; I doubt it," Mike said.

"And now you can't polish yours yourself," Debbie said with amusement. "So why not let this boy do it? He'll be grateful for the opportunity, make some money and your shoes will look good, right?"

And my shoes certainly became spectacular; they had never been so shiny and I would of course have more people shine my workers shoes from Gamla Brogatan in Stockholm before I got home. They were the only shoes I had with me so I had to take care of them.

The hotel we stayed in was a luxurious establishment compared to the ones we have stayed in since Asmara. Electricity and running water, windows and a small desk with a lamp and a wardrobe for clothes. The dinner we found, for half a US dollar, was also extraordinary. Debbie and Mike finally got their vegetables. It was hard to be a vegetarian in these parts. Everywhere meat was the order of the day and fish on the menus was something we hadn't seen in the restaurants we frequented since Cairo. So while I had a steak with vegetables, they had a cauliflower stew with vegetables. Mike could cheat sometimes and eat meat but Debbie was hard core and sometimes it was just white bread or naked spaghetti or rice or injera for her. This resulted in her sometimes being very tired and weak, and a bit bad-tempered.

Both were of Jewish descent, from New York, and I guessed fairly typical East Coast Jewish intellectuals of their time. Black-haired and slim. Mike with long hair and beard and dark glasses and often with a big generous smile. Debbie a little smaller, more fragile, a little cross-eyed and determined. Both sharp, if a little hippy-dippy, which I suppose we all were. But we had fun together, got along well, even though they, like all the other hitchhikers I met, were older than I was. In 1973 I visited them for two weeks on their farm in Maine where they lived on Mike's music and the macrobiotic food they grew. We had a great time then too, but that's another story.

The next day we boarded a bus that would take us all the way to Addis Ababa. It took two days with an overnight stay in a small town on the way. There we converged with the bus going north, so the simple hotel, where we slept four to a room, was obviously for bus accommodation. Dinner was again spaghetti; it was either that or injera with meat stew. We sat up into the late hours talking about the travel experience with the Europeans from the other bus heading north. Already at five the next morning we were awakened, far too early and left after a simple breakfast.

The most remarkable part of the trip was seeing the Blue Nile Valley at Bahir Dar. Suddenly the plateau ended and it plunged steeply downwards. It took the bus almost two hours to get down and then up again to the other side of the gorge. There was not much water in the river which otherwise presents a spectacular fall. This was the small Abbai River, whose source is sometimes considered to be that of the Blue Nile. The river, thus here called Abbai, flows into Lake Tana, and on the other side out to become the Blue Nile. Most sources today consider Lake Tana to be the source of the Blue Nile.

This I read about in Alan Moorehead's *The Blue Nile*, a book I bought second-hand in Addis Ababa. I still have it, as well as his *The White Nile*, which I found in Nairobi. In them, of course, he tells of Europeans' pursuits for the source of the rivers. That people had lived around them and the lakes for ages was of course not so interesting. Still, it was exciting reading: in the blue book especially about the travels and ravages of the conceited Scotsman James Bruce as he wanted to be the first to "discover" Lake Tana in 1770, when in fact two Jesuit priests had already visited and documented the lake for Europe in the early 1600s.

In Addis, I read in the local press that the Swedish prime minister, Olof Palme, had just visited Tanzania under celebrated and successful circumstances – something that later would have pleasant consequences for me. But before that we found an inexpensive hotel with hot water. A shower cost a birr, but was wonderful: our first shower since Asmara. It had simply been too cold for cold showers. I also exchanged money but without any shady circumstances like in Asmara. Now I had spent 2,000 SEK in 2½ months, although some of it still in my wallet in the form

64

of Ethiopian birr. 8,000 SEK left at home. I see in my notes that I calculated that so far, October 2, I had spent an average of 26 SEK (about 3US$ a day). Not too bad considering that it included a month in Europe. If I continued like this, I could stay away for 385 days on the 10,000 SEK I had saved! It turned out to be 365 days.

Addis Ababa became the capital of the country in the 19th century. It was Emperor Menelik II's wife, Taitu Betul, who founded the city in 1886 by some hot springs when her husband was away on military manoeuvres. Addis Ababa means 'new flower' in Amharic but was nonetheless not as pleasant as Asmara or Gonder. A chaotic and hilly city full of poverty. More beggars than I had experienced anywhere before, who often were blind or grotesquely mutilated. At the same time, one saw palatial villas behind well-guarded walls of broken glass. A strikingly conspicuous class difference. Three years later, in 1974, Haile Selassie was overthrown in a military coup. Things didn't get much better after that, with a rabid Soviet-backed junta, known as the Derg, ruling with a particularly Stalinist iron fist. Today, the country is better off with a Nobel Peace Prize-winning president.

I wish I had gone to Harar when I was in Addis. An intriguing 6th century city with a medieval circular wall. It was for many years a forbidden city for Westerners and the fourth holiest city in the Muslim world. When the Scottish explorer Richard Burton visited it as the first European in 1855, it was an almost presumptuous adventure, as it was said that when the first white Christian stepped inside the walls, the city would fall. It did not. Burton was able to stay for ten days before returning to the coast. But I would also have liked to visit Arthur Rimbaud's house. He stayed in Harar on and off between 1880 and 84 as a representative of a French trading company. In 1971 I had not heard of Burton or Rimbaud staying in Ethiopia, although I had certainly read some Rimbaud. His poetry was required reading if you were a teenager interested in literature. But I did not know that he had lived in Harar. Paul Theroux visited Harar in the early 2000s, which he writes about in his largely dreadful travel book *Dark Star Safari*. Theroux discovers that what is now billed as the poet's house was actually built after Rimbaud's death in Marseille in 1891. Still, it would have been exciting to visit, even if the house in 1971 did not function as the Rimbaud Museum Theroux describes. So instead, I left Addis Ababa the next day.

Yabello

The bus to Dilla cost seven birr and was supposed to leave at six in the morning, so I was up before the sun. The bus station was, as in most major cities in Africa, seemingly chaotic and fascinating; it worked in a way that was utterly incomprehensible to me. But I was helped. As soon as I showed myself, I was attacked by screaming boys wondering where I was going. When I told them, the most persistent one dragged me to one of the buses and threw my backpack on the roof where another young boy shoved it down with all the other luggage. I got on and thought it was time to go. But it wasn't. I didn't see a driver so asked a fellow passenger when he thought we were leaving. He shrugged: "When the bus is full." "But it was supposed to leave at six?" He shrugged again. So, we just had to wait.

Kapuscinski has described this phenomenon in his book *The Shadow of the Sun*. It is "a kind of lifeless waiting," he writes. When people in Africa get on a bus, there is a silent state of "deep philosophical sleep." I, of course, had no such peace of mind, although I had become accustomed to the fact that time is really about people here: once they have filled the bus, then we leave. So I accepted the situation and gazed fascinatingly at the commotion of the bus station. The sun was up now but it was still cold and damp. People were well dressed; the most common piece of clothing was a blanket thrown over the shoulders. There was smoke and steam in the misty morning air as it grew brighter. Along one side of the bus stop there were small shacks selling simple, but probably good food, but also plastic bags and other stuff that might be useful on a bus trip.

I was alone now. Mike and Debbie had decided to hitchhike. All three of us felt that it was time for a break; we started to get on each other's nerves a bit. Now I was traveling alone for the first time since Greece. It would probably be fine too, I thought. I had started to read Vonnegut's *Slaughterhouse-Five*, which after the first chapter promised to be fantastic and exciting company.

At quarter to nine, the bus finally rolled out of the bus station. Now I was heading down in southern Ethiopia that so many had warned me about travelling in at this time of the year. From what I had heard though, it was only after Dilla that the roads would become difficult. Initially, the bus drove upon a nice paved road. But soon the asphalt ended and immediately the road turned into a rough, slippery dirt road. On a downhill slope, the bus veered off the road down a ditch, thankfully slowly. We all had to get out while the driver and his assistants tried to get it back up on the road. A lorry eventually arrived and stopped to help. After a laborious struggle with ropes and chains and a winch, the lorry managed to pull the bus out of the ditch and soon it came gliding down the road and we were able to board again.

The highland's landscape had now turned into deep green forest, perhaps jungle. I hardly knew the difference between a forest and a jungle, but wanted it to be a jungle: more exciting. In any case, it looked impassable. As did the road now. It was just a muddy, wet stretch of land that only differed from the rest of the landscape in that nothing grew there.

In Awasa, Mike and Debbie got on board laughing when they saw me. They had been hitchhiking but hadn't gotten any further and decided to take the bus. So now it was the three of us again, which of course was fine. And at seven in the evening we arrived in Dilla where we found simple accommodation.

After an omelette breakfast the next morning, we went to the local bus station. There we learned that there were no buses south from Dilla during the rainy season, only jeeps taking passengers. We asked around and found a Land Rover that later would drive to Yrga Chafe - the last village with a gas station before Moyale, my map informed me. We got to Yrga Chafe relatively smoothly even though the road was not the best. But it would get worse. At the market in Yrga Chafe we found a new Land Rover that was going to the next village, Agere Mariam. It would cost four times what we had paid to Yrga, even though the distance on my map was barely a quarter of what we had just covered: 27 km according to my map. But there was no room for bargaining, so we paid, sat in the open bed of the jeep and waited. There were apparently two jeeps traveling together and it took a while for them to fill up with passengers.

Both drivers were relatively young men, maybe 25 years old and better dressed than everyone else. Jeans, nice leather jackets and even proper leather boots. Both were quiet under their N.Y. Yankees caps, but their two helpers, or sidekicks, were all the livelier. Two young boys, still in their teens, running back and forth, negotiating and persuading people to ride with them and no one else. They were successful: we became about 15 passengers in our jeep made for eight passengers. And now it began to rain

I got a seat but could not move at all in the packed crowd and had a bum in my face all the time, which soon however was not my main concern. Before long I realized why we were two cars and why it cost so much. The dirt road was completely flooded. It was virtually impossible to see where it was going. Sometimes we were about to tip over to the left, sometimes to the right as one pair of wheels disappeared into deep water or a mud pit that the driver had no idea of as we just slid through flooded mud. Everyone screamed and howled every time it felt like we were about to capsize. I was terrified. Mike and Debbie seemed steadfast; we didn't say a word, just looked at each other with a mixture of misgivings and horror. I regretted sitting as I couldn't move. If we turned over, I was stuck. Mike stood up and Debbie and I soon managed to push ourselves standing. Now we could somewhat parry when it seemed like we were going to turn over. Sometimes, when it looked completely impossible even for him, the driver would veer off into the bushes and trees and leave the road, only to return later.

At one point we came upon a truck that was stuck and leaning in an impossible and worrying way, trapped in the deep wheel ruts and mud. Our two jeeps decided to try to pull it out. We all had to get off and it felt liberating to stretch legs and thrilling to see the jeeps pulling the big truck out, skidding this and that way with a seemingly terrified driver at the wheel. But miraculously it was successful and I realized that these jeeps were no ordinary cars. And we moved on. A little later we came across a large tanker that was stuck. Apparently something in the truck had broken a couple of days ago and they had sent a guy to Addis to get spare parts. Two men had now been waiting here for a couple of days! We gave them some food, wished them good luck and that the spare parts would arrive soon. The tanker blocked the whole road but our Land Rovers easily drove around them. But I wondered how on earth the truck we earlier had pulled free, which was behind us, would get pass the tanker.

Now I had made sure to stand at the edge of the jeep's bed so I could jump off if it tipped over. Which I did, scared to death a few times, and

I wasn't the only one. At one point the entire left front wheel came off and rolled down a slope. We came to a sudden and tilting stop. I managed to throw myself off together with some others. An Ethiopian boy had the misfortune to end up screaming in a cactus. It took as long to remove all the thorns stuck in him as it did to attach the spare wheel. The one that rolled off was found and attached to where the spare had previously been.

And we slowly plodded on. The dirt road was still hopeless and largely invisible. I jumped off a few times more when I thought we were going to turn over; this was possible because we were moving very slowly. Landing in a mud or water puddle didn't bother me; I was already soaking wet and muddy from the constant drizzle and muddy terrain. It was simply impossible for the driver to guess what was hiding under the surface of the puddles. I was now standing so I could look ahead and be somewhat prepared for how the car would pitch and roll and tilt. It was awful; I was truly terrified the whole time, and grateful that we were two jeeps driving together. It felt a bit safe. Truly amazing that the drivers and the jeeps managed to get through. Obviously not the first time they drove down this invisible road. They were incredibly good at parrying and avoiding the worst holes as much as possible. Four-wheel drive together with low gear obviously coped with the most impossible roads.

When we finally arrived in Agere Mariam after seven hours over 27 km of mud and pools of water, I sincerely thanked the drivers for getting us to Agere alive.

I began that evening's diary entry with: I am alive! While we had been warned, ever since Cairo, that the roads in southern Ethiopia would be virtually impassable this time of year, I could never had imagined this wet and muddy hell of a dirt road. Now I hoped that the worst was over, which we were promised as the country would become drier the closer we got to Kenya. I have since been on many safaris in a Land Rover in East Africa, and been sliding through muddy dirt roads, often stuck and punctured, but there is still nothing that can compare with the nightmare between Yrga Chafe and Agere Mariam in mid-October 1971.

We found a small cold hotel next to the market and also a modest restaurant where, as usual, a viciously strong meat stew with sour injera bread was served. As so often in these simple restaurants in Ethiopia, there were young women who served the food. But here that was not all that was offered. Two extremely beautiful young girls came up to us men after having served the food and both poked a finger in their noses with a challenging and inquisitive look. Although the approach was unfamiliar to us, we understood and thanked them for the offer, but no thank you. Instead, we greedily ate the food before we wandered off to our simple hotel in the eternal drizzle. It felt wonderful to crawl into the sleeping bag, even if the room was damp and raw.

The next morning, after a white-bread-and-tea breakfast, we planned to travel with the truck we had pulled free the previous day, but luckily, we instead came with a Toyota jeep to the next village, Save. A little better road and we were only 12 passengers. Almost comfortable.

In Save it was market day. The village and marketplace were full of people and animals. A lot to look at for someone from a southern sub-urb of Stockholm. It seemed that people from different ethnic groups had gathered at the market to sell, buy or exchange. Some women were beautifully adorned with lots of arm and neck rings and the men often carried spears or rifles and some were almost naked, in spite of the ra-ther cold weather. Others were more westernized, while the animals just looked like any other animal.

We found some more white bread, bananas and also a Toyota jeep going to Yabello, 83 km south. We climbed onto the rear passenger bed as they said they were leaving soon. It was then twenty to twelve. Noth-ing happened, which did not surprise us, but we did not dare leave the car; what if it suddenly left without us? So, we sat on the jeep and watched and waited. When we asked, they always said that yes, sure, we're leaving soon. But we didn't. When the market started to empty of people and animals, there were more of us in the jeep, which was of course what it was all about. They had to fill it with as many people as possible to make the trip profitable. At five in the afternoon we set off. And at nine in the evening we arrived in Yabello.

But it wasn't a pleasant trip. It rained the first few hours and although we pulled a tarp over us where we sat, it often blew off so we all got soaked. Not only that. Most of the Ethiopians in the jeep were men and drunk; they had probably spent some of their earnings from the market in one of the simple taverns around the market place. They sang and

70

shouted and teased us all the time. At first it was a bit funny, soon tiresome and then really annoying. Gradually, however, they disappeared and finally there were only seven of us left: quiet and peaceful. The road was also a bit better, even if we sometimes slowed down and slid through waterlogged parts of the dirt road. But the countryside was now drier, more savannah-like, and dromedaries started to appear again. Here people did not ride them but used them only as pack animals, I soon realized.

In Yabello we stayed in yet another simple hotel. We, or at least I, ate the same meat stew with injera in the light of the usual pump lamp. It spread a fantastic light, so nothing to complain about. There was no electricity in these villages, so outside it was pitch black with an overcast sky, no stars or moon. As if a black sack had been pulled over reality. A darkness I had never experienced before. Outdoors people spoke to each other without seeing one another, barely seeing the hand in front of you. A flashlight was good to have.

I have a nasty faecal accident in Yabello. After dinner, for the first time since Addis, I am in serious need of a toilet. Something I welcome, while at the same time dread, considering where we are and what I suspect the toilet will look like. But there is nothing doing so make my way in the dark to the toilet offered. I find it in a shed outside the restaurant. It consists of a carpentered room with a tin roof and a stone floor with a hole. The stench is unbearably pungent and I can only breath with my mouth. The hole is located in the middle of the room and just over a meter from the walls on all four sides, so I cannot reach and use the walls when I squat. In addition, the floor is full of both loose and solid shit left behind by previous visitors. They have ignored the hole or simply missed it. I crouch down carefully. I am used to squatting by now, but I usually need to support myself against a wall. Here I am not able to. The tricky part is also making sure that my pants do not rest in the soggy shit on the floor. A difficult balancing act and of course I lose balance and end up on my arse when I suddenly feel cockroaches tickling my butt. I sit flat over the hole and have to use my hands in the faecal sludge of the floor to get up. At least I manage to avoid the solid shit. But not my pants. I swear several Swedish sacred oaths but finally manage to get my business done. Afterwards, I can actually wash myself some in the restaurant where they have soap and running ice-cold water.

I have no idea what my pants look or smell like. But Mike and Debbie say nothing, and neither do I. Since I am wet from the day's rain, there is probably no trace of my mishap.

The next day I had almost forgotten the accident as I could not see any visible trace on my trousers. It made me glad but also confused me a bit; had I dreamt it all? No, I hadn't; yesterday evening's diary notes were very explicit about last night's calamity.

We were now joined by Patrik and Kathy and their music player. They had had the same terrible experience between Yrga Chafe and Agare Mariam. Together, we soon ended up on the back of a truck. Above the packing we could make ourselves quite comfortable, although there were more and more of us. When we finally arrived at Mega, it was packed with people. It was however, in light of previous jeep lifts, a pleasant trip. The view from the truck bed was wonderful and it was nice to sit and daydream and look out over the increasingly dry countryside, often to music from the cassette player. I have a photo from the truck where we are all wrapped in blankets. Mike has a little boy on his lap looking into my Instamatic 50; it looks quite nice.

The country was more desolate and wilder than anything I had hitherto seen in Ethiopia. Rarely did we see any people, and if we approached a small village, we always smelled it before we saw it. One character in the truck had a rifle with him and was obviously a bit bloodthirsty. Every time we saw gazelles, which we did from time to time now, he knocked on the cab to make the truck stop. He jumped down and threw away a couple of shots, but missed every time. Fine, we thought.

I saw termite mounds here for the first time in my life, fascinating constructions. Then it started to rain as it got dark, so again we ended up under a tarpaulin. The truck also got stuck several times but always managed to move on. It wasn't the first time they made this journey either.

At eight o'clock we arrived in a dark, cold, grey and rainy Mega. The rooms we slept in and the food we ate (meat stew with injera), everything was soggy. Then we five Westerners sat and listened to American music in the simple damp and cold room that served as a restaurant. I was wearing double socks, a short and a long-sleeved sweater, plus a shirt and then my jacket, plus the blanket from Kassala around my head and neck. We couldn't bear to talk. Mike tried to read Vonnegut in the dim light while the rest of us quietly sang along with Crosby, Stills, Nash & Young. The few other guests ogled quietly and curiously at us. Outside, the clouds hung menacingly over the low rooftops while the village road seemed to drain away in the perpetual rain. Tomorrow we hoped to get to Moyale and Kenya.

After the usual breakfast of white bread and tea, we got a lift with a truck that would take us to Moyale the same day, the driver assured us. And if not, he promised to provide food and accommodation. We didn't believe that at all. But we managed to haggle a little on the price. At eleven we started and arrived in Hidi at six pm. By then we had had two punctures. There were whistling thorn bushes everywhere in these areas and the thorns, which can be a decimetre long, can apparently also eat into truck tires. We stayed in Hidi that night. I again ate meat stew with injera, which I had come to really like. The others instead found an old lady who made a spaghetti sauce for them. The driver did of course not pay for the food, but we could sleep on top of his truck bed. We all climbed up and slept quite well above all the tobacco it was loaded with.

Flat tyre in southern Ethiopia.

And then it started to rain again. We pulled a tarpaulin over us and perhaps managed some sleep before it cleared.

The following day commenced as usual with white bread and tea. The driver promised again that today we would definitely reach Moyale. But we did not. Even if we this time chose to believe him, but that didn't help. First of all, the truck was full; about 30 passengers soon crowded on top of the tobacco and it became crowded and grumpy. And of course, another flat tire today as well. Just before Moyale - we could almost hear and smell the town - the truck came to another punctured stop, and the driver announced that we would stay the night here, as it was getting dark. We objected, but to no avail. The locals took it all in stride and even had some food with them. The five of us hadn't been that farsighted. But the driver, who, although he had a tendency to make wild promises, was actually a nice guy, gave us some bread, dried meat, carrots and water. All dinner we had that night. Then some crawled under the truck to sleep, while most of us, including us palefaces, climbed back up onto the truck. There we huddled together and managed to sleep reasonably well. No rain this night.

The next morning, October 9, we finally rolled into Moyale, the border town with Kenya.

74

Moyale

In Moyale, I would encounter unexpected, highly unwelcomed and very trying complications with far-reaching consequences. When we left the truck, we first found a restaurant for an appreciated breakfast. Here they had eggs with the white-bread-and-tea. Then we all marched off to the border out of Ethiopia. I was a little worried that there would be problems, even if I had a stamp that gave me three months in the country. The border post consisted of a small hut and a road barrier that was down. In the hut sat two young men, each with a rifle, who excitedly came out when a group of dirty Europeans came trudging. With great curiosity they asked how we had fared down from Addis. We told them that it often had been terrible and that we were very happy to finally be here. They laughed and cared more about us than our passports, stamping us out and wishing us good luck in Kenya. Relieved, we walked through the small valley between the villages to Kenya's Moyale.

This is where it all began. At the Kenyan Embassy in Stockholm, I had been assured that as a Swedish citizen I did not need a visa for Kenya, which is why I had no visa for Kenya in my passport. But according to the border officer in Moyale: "Only nationalities from the Commonwealth do not need a visa." I explained and pleaded and begged. "Can't you give me a visa here then?" No, I had to return to Addis Ababa and get a visa at the Kenyan Embassy there. The thought of going back up to Addis in the cold wet weather and on the dangerous and terrifying dirt roads brought tears to my eyes. And then back down again! No way! The other four tried to comfort me and appeal to the immigration officer. To no avail. But we got him to call his bosses, who unfortunately confirmed that he was right. Unconceivable.

I had to leave Kenya. I said a miserable and sad farewell to Mike and Debbie and Kathy and Patrik who took a bus to Nairobi at two pm. I hiked unhappily and very, very lonely back through the valley to Ethiopia. There was no one at the border checkpoint, which was probably my good fortune. I had left the country and had no new visa for Ethiopia, so grateful that I was able to sneak into the country again. I checked into a cheap hotel and sat down to my diary. Enormously depressed. What was I going to do? The mere thought of traveling twice more on the muddy and flooded roads between Moyale and Dilla really made me feel sick. And of course the tears came; I was the loneliest person in the world: abandoned and utterly disconsolate in the vastness of Africa!

I sat for a long time writing in my diary. I felt so utterly miserable that I was not even homesick. A great emptiness filled me: hollow; it was as if a great grey blanket or cage had been lowered over me - and only me. But eventually I managed to turn my self-pity into anger: I became furious, pissed, which actually pleased me and I decided to find the shower that the hotel had promised. Shower and wash my hair and change some clothes, that ought to cheer me up a bit.

In the shower I was naked; I hadn't seen my own naked body for a week, had not undressed or changed any clothes, not even underwear since Addis. I had slept in my clothes, even in the hotels, all the way down here because of the damp cold. Now that I saw my pale body, I realized it wasn't only mosquito bites that itched. Discovered that I was lice-bitten and I pinched a flea off my neck. Not so nice, but hardly unexpected considering the beds and trucks we had slept in and on. And even if the shower only was lukewarm, it was intensely pleasant to scrub my filthy body, and then to put on clean underwear and an almost clean shirt and pants.

The next day was a Saturday so I decided to wait until Monday and then cross over to Kenya again and to the post office where I should be able to call the Swedish Embassy in Nairobi. I knew I was in the right! At the police station in Ethiopian Moyale I spoke to the local police officers who were sympathetic and promised that I could stay until Monday, but I had to leave my passport with them. This I did somewhat reluctantly. Monday morning I could pick it up again and leave Ethiopia for good. Whether it would be possible for me to travel up to Addis again if I had to, they could not answer. That was up to the border patrol. And the border post was closed until Monday.

Now I just had to wait for Monday. I was reading Thomas Mann's *The Magic Mountain*, which I had traded for a Vonnegut. His *Slaughterhouse-Five* was a fantastic book - which I would later in life teach several times in high school. Mann's thick novel would keep me busy for a while. On Saturday and Sunday I was still allowed to stay during the day Kenya's Moyale, but not overnight. There were slightly better places to eat and

76

cleaner in Kenya than in Ethiopian Moyale. I also met other travellers who all felt sorry for me, which made me feel a bit better. They all said that my embassy would surely fix it on Monday. I regained some spirit. At the same time, I began to reconcile myself to the idea of returning to Addis, if I had to, and if I could. The next minute I was just as down-hearted again. Addis? No way in hell!

When it darkened, I had to walk alone back through the valley to Ethiopia again. I really felt sorry for myself! The nights I slept uneasily in the same hotel, after several pages of Thomas Mann by the light of an equally lonely candle.

On Monday morning I checked out, collected my passport from the police and left Ethiopia for good - I hoped.

At the border post in Kenya, I met the same official as on Friday who was now irritated and refused to even talk to me, telling me to get out of the office and the country. I flew into a temper and shouted back in beautiful Swedish. Something he completely ignored. So I went to the post office where they helped me use a radio phone to call the Swedish Embassy in Nairobi. When I got through, I explained my dilemma and also asked if they could pay for the expensive call, which they promised to do. They also promised to contact the immigration office in Nairobi and ask them to inform Moyale that Swedish citizens do not need a visa for Kenya. So, I was right. But the fact that my embassy confirmed it was of course not enough for the conceited ass in Moyale. He still re-fused to let me into Kenya, saying that he needed new directives from his superiors.

At least, when he realized that I had spoken to my embassy, he changed his attitude, calmed down, listened to me and promised that I could remain in Kenya during the days while he waited for instructions from his superiors. I sat down in the shade on the veranda of the same eatery I had been hanging out at during the weekend. Ordered an ome-lette and pulled out Thomas Mann. They played *My Boy Lollipop* with Millie Small on the radio the whole time. It stuck in my head for days. I also wrote an aerogram home, but didn't tell them all the details of the horrible trip from Addis, or the tricky situation I was presently in.

I kept reasoning back and forth with myself; if I after all had to return to Addis, there was of course nothing else to do. But then I thought: what the hell! Now I knew I was right. If he wouldn't let me into Kenya, maybe I could sneak in across the border? It should be easy, but probably not so wise if I later would be stopped by the police. Teary-eyed and swearing, I promised myself not to give up. Then I turned to *Der Zauberberg* in English to alter my thoughts.

When dusk arrived, fast as always on these latitudes, I checked with the passport office again but no new information, so I had to go back to Ethiopia and sleep in the same hotel again. They were kind at the Ethiopian border control and let me spend another night there. And that was the end of my Ethiopian dollars.

The next morning saw me again hiking with my backpack through the valley to Kenya. Once there, I immediately got hold of my 'friend' the passport officer. He was amiable again but had not received any new instructions. I asked him to call his bosses in Nairobi. No, but to Marsabit and his immediate boss he promised to call. Back at the same diner and veranda, I had the same breakfast as yesterday, listened to Millie Small, and read about Hans Castorp's extensive adventure at the Berghof Sanatorium in Davos. But I found it hard to concentrate, the anxiety was gnawing away at me; the whole thing was really starting to get on my nerves, to say the least. Now several people in Kenya's Moyale had taken an interest in my fate. They had noticed the blond youth sitting all day on a shaded veranda reading and had begun to wonder why. Rarely does any traveller stay more than one night in Moyale, if at all; everyone hurries on to Nairobi. So what was I up to? Several people were checking in on me and feeling sorry for me, which felt good - even if it didn't alter my situation.

I also discover for the first time in my life that I am white. I had never thought about that before. Growing up in a suburb outside of Stockholm, there were not many dark-skinned people, if any, in my neighbourhood. And since Alexandria I had always been in the company of other Caucasians. Here in Moyale, I was the only paleface, and on the veranda, it became obvious that I was different; I was the other. At the same time, I represented the 'centre,' rich Europe and the West - I was a European man! I realized something for the first time in my life: how important skin colour can be. Wherever I went, people stared at me. Some laughed, children sometimes got scared and ran away, while young people wanted to talk. The latter meant that on the veranda in Moyale I often had curious and pleasant company.

There were also other hitchhikers passing through Moyale, that I spoke with, wondering if they had visas. Among them was a Dane about to leave Kenya after a month in the country. He did not have an entry visa, as Danish citizens did not need one either. I asked him to follow me to passport control. There we showed the Dane's passport:

"Look here, as a Dane, he doesn't have an entry visa but got a tourist visa when he came from Tanzania, at the border there. So it's not just Commonwealth citizens who don't need a visa. It's probably the same for Swedes as for Danes," I said.

"Of course he doesn't need a visa when he leaves the country," the official replied.

"Oh, please. He has entered Kenya once, for crying out loud, and without an entry visa."

"It's none of my business. All I do is stamp him out."

That was as far as we got. Relentless and irritated with me, he insisted that everyone except Commonwealth citizens must have an entry visa, ignoring the fact that the Dane clearly did not. I angrily walked away and sat down again on my porch, now not only depressed but really furious. But it didn't help much.

When evening came, I did not really know what to do. I was not allowed to stay in Kenya and had no birr for hotels in Ethiopia. At the restaurant I had met a group of hitchhikers heading north, but they were now too late to enter Ethiopia. The border post was closed for the day. I had seen the ruins of a burnt down house in the valley between the borders and suggested we sleep there.

It turned out to be a nice night and I could forget my predicament for a few hours. The ruin offered both rain and some wind protection and we made a fire that we kept going all night. One couple was from Australia, a German who had now been traveling for seven years. Impressive. The other three were from the USA. Nice conversations. I prepared them for the flooded roads to Dilla, while they said that my embassy would surely fix it, otherwise I could easily sneak into Kenya without getting my passport stamped and then fix it when I got to Nairobi. Maybe they were right? We turned in but slept rather irregularly as we were all worried about the fire dying. We knew that there were both lions and hyenas in the area.

The next day, Wednesday, looked pretty much the same as the previous one. I confronted the border officer who still had not received any new information, sat on the same veranda, ate the same food, read the same book and listened to the same *My Boy Lollipop*. In the afternoon I called the Swedish embassy again and they were surprised to hear from me. They thought it had been sorted out and promised to talk to immigration again. But nothing happened that day either.

That night I had to sleep alone in the ruin. I had no other option. In Kenya I was not allowed to stay overnight and no birr for hotels in Ethiopia. However, I guessed that one more night in the ruin would be fine, even if I was alone. I had no matches, so before I left Kenya I found a box in a small stall near my favourite restaurant. My lighter sometimes malfunctioned and I wanted to make sure I could start a fire. There was some wood left over from last night and I easily found more dry branches and quickly made a fire, with some old Danish newspapers. A fire I really wanted to keep going all night, so there wasn't much sleep. The worry about the fire was mixed with excitement: lying alone under the open sky, with a crackling fire in the East African night and listening to its sounds. And there were plenty sound although I didn't know what I was hearing. Maybe lions? Certainly hyenas. Still, it satisfied some of my dreams of adventure I had had in my room on Harpsundsvägen. At the same time, I was of course still worried about my situation; I constantly felt sick when I thought of south Ethiopian cold, wet roads and tried to put them out of my mind, which was not always possible, even though I now felt sure that I was right and that things would work out in the end. Still, there were many things that disturbed my sleep. I probably fell asleep in the early hours because the sun woke me up and by then the fire was long dead. It had gone well; no lion had eaten me as far as I could see.

As I entered the passport office for the sixth day, 'my good friend' finally had news. He had received a telegram instructing them to let me into Kenya, but without stamping my passport. The uniform stopped me, otherwise I would have hugged him and given him a big kiss. But probably just as well I didn't. It turned out, he told me, that his people in Marsabit had thought that I didn't have a passport. Was apparently what the Swedish Embassy had said, how they could have gotten that idea.

Their second conversation had apparently sorted it out. But Immigration in Marsabit was not entirely satisfied. As soon as I arrived in Nairobi I had to visit the Immigration office and meet a Mr. Kibaki. In my ecstatic relief, I didn't think much about this, instead I hoped that I, without any visa stamp in my passport, wouldn't be subjected to police check before Nairobi.

Overjoyed, I had breakfast at my regular eatery where everyone congratulated and hugged me. I had now been stuck here for six days and felt truly finished with Moyale and ready for East Africa. As I sat there, now enjoying Moyale, Leroy and Jim arrived on motorcycles. When they saw me, they stopped, joined me and had an omelette with coffee each. I told them about my adventure in Moyale and they told me that they had bought the bikes in Addis and intended to sell them in South Africa.

"But how on earth did you get through the roads after Dilla?" I asked.

"Fuck yes, it was tough and took a hell of a lot of time, but it was actually easier for our bikes to get through than for cars," Leroy said. "And we could sleep outside wherever the hell we wanted and drive in the dark too, so ok. But it will be fucking great to get to Nairobi tonight."

"What have you done with Don?"

"He flew home from Addis," Jim said. "Longing for home and tired of traveling."

"The bastard chickened out," Leroy laughed.

"Strange and a bit sad for him," I thought. When we finished eating, they left, but we promised each other to meet up in Nairobi.

I had heard about a Land Rover to Isiolo that was supposed to leave soon. It did not materialise until seven in the evening. By then I had been joined by an Irishman, David, and a New Zealander, Alex. We had both lunch and dinner before setting off. We drove all night and it was relatively comfortable as there were only eight of us in the passenger seats. The dirt roads were not nearly as bad as in Ethiopia, without being good; we had to hold on all the time to avoiding bouncing around like tennis balls. An hour after leaving Moyale we were stopped by a large male lion standing in the middle of the road in the spotlight. Magnificent and a worthy welcome to East Africa, I thought, also remembering the nights in the ruin under the open sky not far away. Soon after that encounter we came across Leroy camped next to the road. He was in his sleeping bag in the open air, with his bike parked on the side of the road. Jim had not wanted to stop, but had gone on by himself. All the Kenyans in the car got animated. "You can't sleep here! There are lions and hyenas around here and they will eat you!" We told him about the lone male we had seen but Leroy just shook his head and laughed. After some more parleying, when the driver offered us all coffee and biscuits, we moved on. I hoped I would see Leroy again...

The sun was rising as we approached Marsabit and suddenly the driver and all the Kenyans wanted to stop for sleep, after driving all night! We protested, saying that they had promised we would reach Isiolo tonight. And why hadn't we slept during the night, when it was dark? But the driver of course ruled and there was a two-hour nap just outside the city before we drove on again.

Now we were in Marsabit National Park and we saw lots of game: including reticulated giraffes and Grevy's zebras, both more beautiful than their relatives in southern Kenya, but also ostriches, antelopes, monkeys and hyenas. It was as if Kenya immediately wanted to welcome me with much of what I had dreamed of, with much of the fauna it offered; perhaps it was apologizing for how it had treated me in Moyale? In a bush we saw two large elephants and one with giant tusks. Later I realized that it was probably Ahmed, Kenya's, indeed all of Africa's most famous elephant we saw, with the country's largest tusks. He had presidential protection and his own bodyguard the last years of his life. He died in 1974 at the age of 55 and his tusks weighed 67.2 kg. He is now stuffed in the National Museum of Kenya in Nairobi.

We also met two of the country's most famous ethnic groups, the Turkana, who live in northwest Kenya around Lake Turkana and in neighbouring countries. They were simply dressed in dark sarongs but richly adorned with lots of necklaces and bracelets. I found the Samburu warriors even more handsome. The Samburu are related to the Maasai of southern Kenya and northern Tanzania. Like them, they live on their large herds of cattle and are therefore equally nomadic. It was exciting to meet them and impossible to avoid as I almost met as much curiosity here as they would have done in Högdalen.

We arrived in Isiolo at half past two in the afternoon after passing through Samburu national park. A drier landscape and rhino I have written in the diary that we saw. In Isiolo we found a really good restaurant where we had a steak with French fries and boiled peas. Very good, if a bit expensive. I felt I deserved it. Apparently the standard of restaurants was better here than in Ethiopia, at least the menus offered more variety. Simply a more well-off country it seemed. Then we all three went out on the road to try to get a ride to Nairobi. Here it should be possible to hitchhike again as there was a lot of traffic. We split up and I was quickly picked up by a Ford Taunus. First private car I travelled with in Africa. It was nice to sit in a comfortable, soft and proper car seat. The driver, an older Kenyan who was going to Nyeri just south of Mt Kenya, was friendly and generous; we stopped at a rest area under the country's highest snow-capped mountain, near Nanyuki. We had crossed the equator, he told me, and now I was in the southern hemisphere for the first time in my life. He offered me beer, coffee and a ham sandwich that he had brought with him. He told me that the NFD (Northern Frontier District), which we now travelled through until very recently had been closed to travellers. This because the so-called 'shiftas,' Somali bandits have controlled the entire district. "Now it is safer but it is still unsafe to travel in the northeastern NFD, and attacks still occur." Me, I told him a bit about my hardships in Moyale.

"Kenyan bureaucracy can be a pain in the ass. I have a small farming business, growing flowers whose seeds, I sell to Europe. And I have to pay bribes all the time or I don't get my goods shipped. Often the money goes to the president's relatives."

"That sounds terrible," I said in surprise. "Why don't you just refuse?"

"If I do, my stocks are delayed and hence ruined. But I shouldn't complain. Things are going well and I can support my family, which is now quite extensive: five children, plus my parents and my wife's parents."

When we arrived in Nyeri, he drove me to a Hindu temple where I could sleep on a simple wooden bench for free and was even offered a vegetarian dinner. However, I was full. But I accepted a lukewarm shower.

The next day I quickly got a ride on a truck to Nairobi.

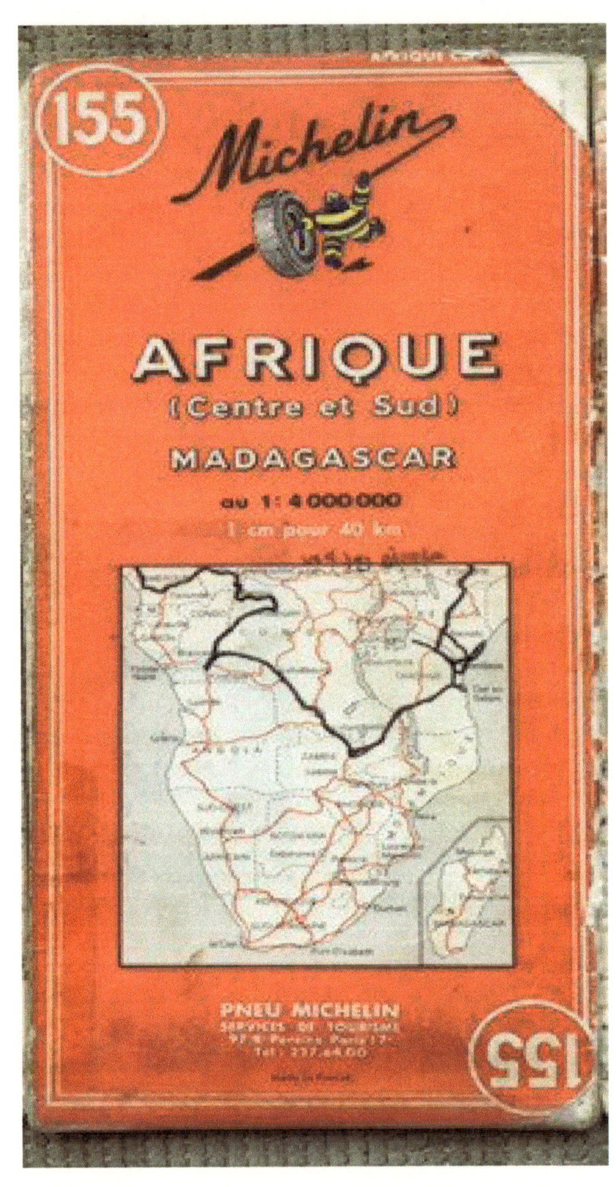

Nairobi - Bangui

Nairobi

Finally I sat in a café in Nairobi, in Kenya, in East Africa and it was time to change map, from Michelin 154 to 155. I drank my first Tusker beer, which I thought I deserved. It would not be my last, even if I did not drink many during the three months I came to spend in East Africa. Too expensive. But later in life there have been several. This is a part of the world I have returned to many times. I lived for two years in Limuru, north of Nairobi, in the late 1970s, with a girlfriend I had met in San Francisco; I would return for my own literary research and lectures to both the Universities of Nairobi and Dar es Salaam, go on a trip to Bukoba in Tanzania together with students of mine, celebrate my 60th birthday with my family on a safari trip in northern Tanzania and Zanzibar, and visit my youngest daughter who was studying her second year of high school at the Swedish school in Nairobi. Lots of East Africa, and I have not regretted a single day of it, but usually claim it is the best part of the world.

In October 1971, I was full of anticipation, not knowing how much Kenya in particular would come to mean in my later more adult life. Now it was time to get to the hostel. I did so with a bus that took about half an hour. It went up towards Limuru, through the coffee fields to the tea plantations. In the diary I wrote that the area around the hostel looked like a wealthy residential area in England. It is part of the so-called 'white highlands,' which extend all the way up to Nanyuki. The part of Kenya that British farmers confiscated, stole from the Gikuyu farmers who had been farming there since the 16th century, when they in turn stole it from a now vanished hunting people, the Dorobo, according to Jomo Kenyatta's anthropological classic *Facing Mount Kenya*.

The hostel consisted of a simple, rather large brown wooden house with a small kitchen, three bedrooms with four bunk beds in each, thus eight beds in each room. Next to them was a larger living room with a big table in the centre, some battered armchairs in one corner, and a small desk in another. Outside, the plot was fairly extensive with deciduous and coniferous trees, which served as a camp site. Most people chose to sleep outside, even if they didn't have a tent. This cost two

Kenyan shillings (KES) (you got 8.5 KES for one US$ on the black market). If you slept outside, you could still use the small kitchen, the toilets and the two cool showers - which everyone did.

My first night was great. Mike and Debbie were there and pleasantly surprised to see me walk into the hostel: "You made it, Erik! Wonderful," Debbie hugged me. "Yes, but it was tough." And I told them about how difficult it had been and how I still had no visa, but had to present myself at immigration tomorrow. Several familiar faces appeared, including Rick, a black American I last met in Khartoum. Instead of traveling east by train, he had gone south by boat up the Nile to Uganda. Jim and Leroy were also there with their motorcycles. So, Leroy wasn't devoured by a lion either.

We built a fire in the garden and Mike got hold of a guitar which he played admirably well. There was singing and music well into the small hours. I had spread my rain poncho on the ground, and then my sleeping bag, which I crawled into and lay there listening until I fell asleep with my gas-mask-shoulder-bag as a pillow.

The next morning I trimmed my beard, or rather my 19-year-old scraggly facial hair with the scissors on my Swiss Army knife. Not too successful, but I probably looked a little better; I wanted to be as presentable as possible when I visited the immigration office. I took the bus downtown but Mr. Kibaki was not in on that day. I promised to come back on Monday. Instead, I went to the Hilton in the same building and sat down to write cards to Sweden, including one to Gun in Skillingaryd - as I had promised. I then tried to hitchhike up to the hostel without success, always tricky in a city, so tock the bus again.

Down the street from the hostel was Arthurs, a small café with an additional duka, as the small shops throughout East Africa were called and usually owned by Asians. Arthurs served cheap and good food. A dinner cost four shillings (½US$). If you did not cook your own food, you went here morning, noon and evening, which many people did, and here I ate fish and chips my second evening in Nairobi. Then Leroy offered marijuana when we gathered around a fire again and everyone got elevated to Mike's brilliant guitar playing.

The climate in Limuru was pleasant thanks to the altitude of 2240 meters above sea level. The days were like a warm summer day in the

86

archipelago of Stockholm and the nights were cold like an autumn evening in the same archipelago. A teenager from Stockholm enjoyed himself, in other words, and slept well in his sleeping bag under the high crowns of the trees. The flies were also few and reserved, nor were there any mosquitoes in the evenings as in the archipelago.

Sunday I remained at the hostel, which meant a lot of Thomas Mann at Arthurs with good and strengthening Kenyan instant coffee in hot milk.

On Monday I went straight to the immigration office. This time I did meet Mr. Kibaki. A Mr. who turn out to be rather unsympathetic to my situation. I tried to explain the misunderstanding between me, the Swedish Embassy and them; I have a passport, which of course I presented. But before he would stamp it, he wanted to see a plane ticket out of the country:

"Do you have a ticket back to Sweden?" he asked.

"No," I said.

"Ticket to another country? So I know you will leave Kenya."

"No, I am traveling overland by bus to southern Africa. Tomorrow I'm going to Moshi in Tanzania to visit friends of my parents."

"Ok. How much money do you have?"

I showed my remaining traveller's checks: 130US$.

"Insufficient!" he declared and stamped "Deported Immigrant 7 days" in my passport. I had to leave the country within seven days! This shouldn't really be a problem, I reasoned rather naively, as I was going to Moshi tomorrow.

I then visited the Swedish Embassy close by. There I got to read some Swedish papers. My football team, Hammarby seemed to be hanging on in the first division, and Palme was being praised in East Africa for his recent visit. It looked like Sweden was doing well even without me. A young, interested official wanted to hear what had happened to me in Moyale and promised to compose a letter from the embassy and send it to the immigration authorities so that it would hopefully not happen to anyone again. He wished me good luck and thought that things would work out as long as I got to Moshi. In Moshi I was to meet Sten and Lilian from Jönköping. They worked in the cooperative business in Tanzania and Sten had worked with my father in Coop in Småland, south of Sweden.

But I didn't make it to Moshi!

I made my way through Nairobi early the next morning and at 9 am I got a lift with a Canadian couple who were going to Moshi. They both worked as teachers at the University of Dar es Salaam - a university with which I would have a lot of collaboration later in life. The road down to the border town, Namanga, is also the road to Arusha in Tanzania and Amboseli National Park, below Kilimanjaro; a road I have been down many times. This my first time I remember as the most breathtaking, with animals everywhere and Kilimanjaro majestically in the background. At one point there were 23 giraffes standing in our way and refusing to move. But as we became more honking cars, they gracefully strode in under the acacia trees.

In Namanga I easily left Kenya but was not so fortunate at the Tanzanian border post. The immigration officer saw the stamp indicating only seven days in Kenya in my passport and asked why. I explained as best I could, whereupon he also wanted to see a plane ticket, or my money. Of course, I had no more plane ticket or any money now, so he stamped "Refuse entry" in my passport.

Please, help me Lord! What is happening? Was it never going to end? And it would take quite some time before it did. I still have my passport and sit with the stamps in front of me as I write this. These days they don't give me the creeps, but back then I was becoming desperate.

I said goodbye to the Canadians and marched back to Kenya. Of course they wondered why I returned. At least they let me back into the country - I had six days left! However, I had to promise to immediately return to the immigration office in Nairobi and absolutely leave the country within six days. I promised everything; they even produced a document to this effect, which I had to sign and later show in Nairobi.

There is always a lot of traffic between Nairobi and Arusha, so I quickly got a ride up to Nairobi again. Once in the city, I found out the address of the American Express in Mombasa and wrote to my parents that they had to send 2000 SEK there immediately. I had no plans to visit the immigration office again, nor to leave the country within six days. During the ride up to Nairobi, I had devised a different strategy. I would go down to the coast and wait for the money on the beach of the Indian Ocean. Once I had the money everything would be fine, I convinced myself, even if not so successfully, but I couldn't think of anything else.

When I walked through the gate of the hostel in the afternoon, there was a bit of a commotion and I had to tell them what had happened to me in Namanga. Some laughed, others felt sorry for me. They all agreed that the best thing would be to wait for the money in the sun by the sea under the palm trees. There is a nice hostel north of Mombasa, I was told. I spent this evening alone at Arthur's; I had no desire for company that night. I felt empty and desolate. Would it never end? Would they deport me when one day they inevitably discover that I have overstayed my seven-day visa? Or what? But I somehow managed to suppress these gloomy thoughts and soon crawled into my sleeping bag under the tall pine trees. After a few hours it started to rain so all of us who were outside had to move to the concrete floor of the house. It was not nearly as uncomfortable as it sounds. I had now slept uncomfortably many nights already; the most important thing was really that it was dry – and cheap. Sleep I was obviously able to do anywhere and everywhere.

The next day was Kenyatta Day, so Rick and I went downtown to experience it all. The celebrations took place in Uhuru Park in central Nairobi. And we were not alone. But we pushed our way through the crowd for a nice view of the festivities. It seemed to start with a big military parade to some rather catchy marching music. Then several dance groups, all representing different Kenyan ethnic groups, came dancing by. Dazzling performances. I stood in awe at all these beautiful people and music. Then it was time for the President to give a speech.

Jomo Kenyatta, or Mzee as he was known, was the country's first president, from independence in 1964 until his death in 1978. During what the British call the Mau Mau rebellion, and the Kenyans the War of Liberation, he was imprisoned for seven years. Later he was able to return to Nairobi and become the country's president, father of the nation, and his grim appearance was found on all banknotes and portraits in all business premises and official buildings – when writing this his son Uhuru Kenyatta is president.

At the time of Jomo Kenyatta's death in 1978, I was in the country, staying with some friends north of Mombasa, and I remember the whole country holding its breath in anxiety: what would happen next? But it was a peaceful transition. Daniel Arap Moi of the Kalenji people became president, thus avoiding political conflict between mainly the Luo and Gikuyu peoples. Something Kenyatta had foreseen when he appointed Moi as vice-president and his successor. Kenya is still one of the very few countries in Africa that has not experienced a military coup. Moi's tenure as president, however, became a miserable time for the country. Like his predecessor, Moi favoured his family, friends and tribesmen who, like him, enriched themselves at the expense of the people of the country. But in an almost admirably creative way, he also looted the treasury of everything he could lay his greedy hands on, like some other notorious kleptocrats on the continent, such as Nigeria's Abacha and Congo's Mobutu. In particular, the so-called Goldenberg scandal in Kenya illustrates the shameless behaviour of the dictatorial thief Daniel Arap Moi (see Richard Dowden's *Africa* and Wikipedia). Kenyans, but especially the Gikuyu, were outraged. But Moi, who controlled the press, police, media and military, did not allow any opposition and imprisoned all those who protested, including the country's eminent writer Ngugi wa Thiongo, who has written several great novels, also about Moi's misrule.

Now Jomo Kenyatta stood before me. An impressive man, on this occasion dressed up in a leopard hat and cloak, sturdy and with a much more elegant fly whisk in his hand than the one I had bought in Ethiopia. He began in English and it was a patriotic speech that everyone politely applauded. But then he switched to Swahili, which got him and the audience going. The stern-speaking president was now transformed into an entertaining orator who had the audience laughing, cheering, singing and dancing. What it was all about I could only guess, but it was obvious that he was a good rhetorician who could captivate his audience. The next day I read in *The Standard* that one of the issues he addressed was whether to hang thieves in public, which the audience had apparently shouted in support of. Here I had to refrain from stealing blankets!

The next day I set off for the Indian Ocean. It was slow going. After two short lifts, I was picked up by a Kenyan who was going to a Sikh temple for their free lunch. Naturally, I accompanied him and got a good vegetarian lunch. There I met an American who had a lift to Voi that I could join. The journey there went through Tsavo National Park and we were several times stopped by elephants that loitered over the road. There were traffic signs warning about this in the same way that we in Sweden warn about moose. Maybe I should have stolen a sign warning of elephants, as tourists sometimes steal our warning signs for moose - but I didn't dare, given what Kenyatta had said yesterday.

I have travelled between Nairobi and Mombasa many times since, but never have I seen as many elephants as in 1971. There are several reasons for this, including poaching to satisfy the disgusting ivory cravings of simple-minded Asians, but also climate change, which has caused years of severe droughts. The World Wildlife Fund's latest report, *Living Planet 2020*, notes that populations of wild mammals: fish, birds, reptiles and other vertebrates have declined by almost 70% since 1970.

What the hell are we doing?

From Voi we both took a bus to Mombasa, where we arrived after dark. The American disappeared to a hotel and I found a Sikh temple. They had a guest room that I was directed to. The room was maybe eight square meters, a window to the courtyard and of course a door. Three wooden benches were all the furniture. But it was more than enough for me. They also served a good dinner and a warm shower. All free and very welcome as Mombasa is unpleasantly humid and hot. The jeans were sticking to my legs and shorts were now the only option. In Nairobi it had often been too cold for this. After a few hours of sleep, another hitchhiker arrived for a night on one of the benches. After a few polite phrases, we silenced and tried to fall asleep. But it was difficult; hot, humid and millions of cruel mosquitoes that all wanted to suck my blood. A horrible night.

In the morning we had a light breakfast together and he told me that six months ago he had met Christ after years of doing drugs at home in the US. Now he was working as a teacher with two friends (who also joined for the breakfast) in a small village below Mt Kenya. A nice breakfast and they gave me their addresses in case I'd be in the area.

After breakfast I found the American Express and informed them that I had money coming. They advised me to also visit the major banks in Mombasa and ask them to notify Am Ex when and if they had received my money. After that I hitchhiked up to Kanamai, about 25 kilometres north of Mombasa, and the hostel there. The last bit from the highway I had to walk. Admittedly, it was beautiful with orange groves, banana plantations and swaying coconut palms, but hot, hot and nothing on my head (I had lost my safari hat from Luxor) and my backpack was now starting to weigh a lot with all the books I had collected. It was soon time to send home a package of books I wanted to keep.

Leroy and Jim at the hostel north of Mombasa.

The hostel was fantastic. A fairly large house under the ubiquitous coconut trees with a lovely shaded veranda overlooking the Indian Ocean. A simple kitchen was provided and a small restaurant if you did not want to cook yourself. Five decent rooms with three bunk beds in each. Clean and tidy with fantastic hot showers and there was even paper in the toilet, which also had a toilet seat; long time since I had seen that. About 30 meters from the veranda was the Indian Ocean; you constantly heard the waves rolling in on the beach. A sound that rocked me to sleep every night. But the hostel was strict; a German managed the whole place with the help of a bunch of young Kenyans he pushed a little too much. I didn't mind, but Leroy, who like Jim, was staying here when I arrived, didn't like it at all. Leroy also disappeared up to Malindi the next

92

day. Both were in almost the same predicament as I was. They had sent for money that had not yet arrived and they weren't really sure if any actually would arrive. I was; mom and dad I could depend on. The question was rather how long the postal service and the bureaucracy in Kenya would delay things. (Imagine how easy it all would be today!)

But instead of worrying more than I needed to, I enjoyed the atmosphere. I had longed for this too. Tropical beaches with coconut palms overlooking a turquoise ocean. I sat in the shade on the veranda and read more T. Mann, or swam and took long walks along the beach. Food was also a delight; eggs for breakfast, fruit salad for lunch and fish for dinner. Here I could wait for the money indefinitely.

There was a Christian seminar in the hostel. Half of the people staying there participated and they were served food in the dining room. One evening I was invited to have dinner with them and it turned out that one of them had studied theology and worked in Gothenburg for three years. He was now serving as a priest in Mombasa and attending the seminar. Festus, as he was his name, was enthusiastic about meeting me and speaking some Swedish, which he did quite well. It became a great evening in their company.

The following day I spent a lot of time with Festus. When he heard about my visa problems, he immediately promised to help me; he had a relative working in the immigration office in Mombasa.

"But you have to come and stay with me in Mombasa tomorrow, when the seminar here is over."

"But..."

"Yes, absolutely. If I am to help you, which I must as you are from Sweden, you must stay with me. The least I can do for you."

And so it happened.

Before Mombasa, I still had another day on the beach and several lovely swims in the ocean. Just outside there was a coral reef where you swam among multicoloured fish that I previously had only seen in *National Geographic*. There were also moraine heads sticking out of coral holes; they did not look as attractive and on the way out to the reef there were lots of sea urchins to be avoided.

After dinner we sat and discussed religion. It turned out that Jim was raised in a deeply Christian home in New Mexico and knew *The New Testament* almost by heart. He liked Jesus, but said he was just one of many prophets in the Middle East 2000 years ago, but exceptional for his message of love. Actually, completely unthinkable in a time and environment where there was constant religious struggles. And that his particular message emerged victorious from all these religious battles is incomprehensible, especially considering the terribly violent god of *The Old Testament*. The others around the table, including Festus and a German pastor sitting with us, agreed to some extent, but for them Jesus was of course the son of God, so they couldn't quite swallow Jim's whole argument.

The following afternoon I followed Festus to Mombasa. He lived modestly in a two-room apartment with a kitchenette. After a simple dinner for 1.50 KES at a nearby restaurant, I slept very well on a simple bed Festus borrowed from a neighbour, despite the humid heat and all the cockroaches that crawled everywhere in the apartment. The next day was Sunday and service in Festus' Lutheran church and I of course attended. The liturgy was in Swahili and Festus' sermon seemed to go down well; the congregation applauded. It was very different from what I had experienced in churches in Stockholm, even though it was the same denomination. Here there was much more music, singing and a friendly atmosphere.

The German pastor from the previous night joined us and we spent the rest of Sunday strolling around Mombasa. We quenched our thirst on the magnificent veranda of the Castle hotel in town. An old colonial retreat with white pillars framing the beautiful veranda full of greenery.

The next day they both accompanied me to the immigration office. We met Festus' relative and I explained myself and presented my passport with the fateful stamps and the document with my signature. I was very nervous. But thanks to both Festus and his German colleague, whose name I don't remember, confirming that they would take care of me, I was given a new document allowing me to stay two more weeks in Kenya, but still no visa stamp in my passport. I also had to show up and report to the office every three or four days. Sad I thought, as I didn't want to stay in Mombasa more than I needed to. But I figured the money from home would certainly arrive within a fortnight.

I spent a few more days with Festus and we had a great time together. We laughed and discussed: lots about religion.

"It is important to know which religion people belong to and which church. It is almost the first thing I ask people I meet. It's crucial," Festus argued.

"But I, who am not a Christian, have no religion, but rather agree with Lenin that it is an opium for the people. What do you think of me?"

"Of course you are a Christian. You've been confirmed, haven't you?"

"Yes, but it was hardly a matter of conviction, rather tradition and that my parents expected it, even though they are not religious."

"That I want to help you is the Christian way to act; you have problems that I think I can help you with. Plus I get to practice my Swedish," he laughed.

Today I might have expressed myself in a more nuanced way, but I was a child of the left-wing movement in Sweden. Instead, I would probably have pointed out that while faith is an individual aspect of one's life, all religions are man's understandable attempt to explain the incomprehensibility of why we live. The fact that religions around the world look so different has to do with their historical and material and geographical context. All are, of course, equally 'true.' Moreover, life is too short to worry about the afterlife, which seems to be the main concern of most religions. Strange, given that we know nothing about the afterlife, which, on the other hand, is perhaps why we worry; but things were fine before I was born, so they will probably be fine after I die. Instead, we need to make sure we live as well and peacefully as we can in the little time we have.

But I could be wrong.

Festus emphasized the importance of religion in East Africa and told me about all the evangelical churches that were springing up everywhere. Later, I read in Richard Dowden that evangelical churches in Africa is the largest growing religious movement in the world. I also experienced this all over sub-Saharan Africa. People were often curious about which church I belonged to, and Dowden writes: "I have met only two people in Africa who do not believe in God." Christianity, Festus now argued, is crucial for the success of Africa. And judging by how missionary schools earlier completely dominated education in sub-Saharan Africa, he had a point. Today they are not as dominant. But when the continent was liberated, virtually all primary schools were missionary.

Festus also told me about his family, who were living in a village near

Kilimanjaro. He had only one wife and was against polygamy, which was common in the country, especially among Muslims. He had three children, whom he did not see very often, as they lived with their mother and her parents. But he went there with money every two weeks. The next day he also disappeared and I was left alone in his small apartment for 24 hours. That went well too.

Monday morning, I was awakened, as so often in Africa, by the roosters in the area, but here also by the call to prayer in the nearby mosque. The coast is mainly Muslim due to the trade with the Arab countries since the Middle Ages, not least with slaves. I first went to Am Ex and asked if any money had arrived. No. Then to the immigration office for a report and then I hitchhiked up to Malindi. Festus knew my plans and I promised to return in four days.

In Malindi I met Leroy, of course. Jim had also driven here. They liked Malindi better than the hostel in Kanamai. Nice to meet them again and it also meant more marijuana smoking. This time it was not Leroy who offered but Declan, an American who had bought 10 kg of marijuana in Uganda in the belief that it could be sold in Kenya for a handsome profit. Now he could hardly give it away. Instead, he sat here and offered it generously around the fire we had built on the beach. Before dusk, we admired the flight of frigatebirds as they hunted and stole fish from other birds. Skilled fliers and thieves, and easy to recognize, even though they often flew extremely high, with their angled wings and long straight tail. Something I learned there and then. We all slept well on the beach under the palm trees.

Malindi was then a relatively small town, nice with some larger hotels along the beach north of the city centre. We stayed south of the Vasco da Gama monument, where only fishermen lived and there was a small hotel that most hitchhikers frequented. The Portuguese explorer arrived in Malindi and met the local sheikh here in 1498. The sheikh gave da Gama a guide to India who knew about the monsoon winds. This is remembered by the pillar that stands on a promontory south in the city.

I returned to Malindi many times, most recently in 2004, when it had become a rather unattractive city, completely overdeveloped and loud. A bit scary, at least after dark, unless you were hiding behind the walls of the international hotels. But then, in late October 1971, it was more like a small sleeping fishing village, especially south of the monument. In other words, a lovely place to while away the time until money arrived from Stockholm.

And so I did, and worried. If no money came, the 90 US$ I had left would soon run out. It would not be enough to travel far or to satisfy the authorities. What would they do then? Send me home and let my embassy pay? I knew this had happened to others.

I climb a coconut palm in Malindi.

Yet I slept unashamedly well in the sand under the palm trees to the winds in the palm trees and the sound of the waves. But it was important not to lie directly under a palm tree: I didn't want a falling coconut in my head. During the days, I could leave my backpack at the nearby hotel, which for some reason was always full of Italians, and stroll around the city but mainly along the beach, forgetting my precarious situation. I was intrigued to watch all the fishermen bring in their catch. Lots of fish that I had never seen: shark, tuna and other exotic fish that you could then order in the simple restaurants along the ocean. One evening we grilled fish over an open fire and a couple of Italians who joined us from the hotel brought rice and salad. I also learned to body surf here in Malindi. Something I then came to do wherever in the world I ended up in waves. Great fun!

On November 1, I took a bus back to Mombasa and presented myself at the immigration office. Then off to Festus', who was happy to see me and in the evening we went to a free movie theatre. But first we had to eat: "Friendship must be fed," Festus laughed. It was a simple but tasty stew at his house, and then a movie. A truck pulled up in a meadow and unfolded a screen and then we all sat in the grass or on some of the few chairs and benches they had provided. A terrible movie about some spies being chased all over Europe by dangerous communist agents. But there was plenty of action, and pretty ladies in very little clothes added to the adventure for the young male audience who laughed and cheered throughout the movie.

The next day my money finally arrived. 155 pounds sterling in Barclays traveller's checks. Fantastically relieved, I then went to the immigration office. I had to wait there for a couple of hours, but I didn't care. Everything would be fine now! And after lunch I finally got a visa that allowed me to stay in the country for two months. Now it was time to celebrate! But first I went and bought some clothes at an open market where they sold better second-hand clothes: a shirt and a pair of shorts and a pair of decent leather sandals.

In the evening I found a small café where I drank a Tusker before Festus came home. Then we went downtown and I bought us a slightly better dinner than what we usually ate. For dessert we had good fruit salad at small street stall. Festus was genuinely happy that my visa problems were finally over. It had been almost a month since I first arrived in Moyale. A month of nagging worry and anxiety. I was now relieved to say the least and thanked Festus warmly for his help. Without his relative in the office here in Mombasa, it would probably not have been possible. He got a big teddy bear hug - Festus that is. Then we went to a real movie theatre and saw another action movie, this time with Jim Brown and Raquel Welch. It wasn't much better than the previous free flick. However, the audience in the theatre did not agree with me. They shouted and hooted loudly when Jim crushed all the bad guys and whistled when Raquel showed up sparsely clad.

When we got home around midnight, the apartment was even more full of cockroaches. But there was nothing we could do about it. We crawled into bed and fell asleep sweetly.

The next morning I took a warm farewell with hugs and promises to keep in touch. I also took a picture of him in front of the house he lived in, but for some reason it didn't turn out well, so cannot include it here. Festus had been wonderfully helpful and we stayed in touch for years after that. He was a man with such admirable qualities that you really wanted him to like you.

Moshi

Finally, I was going to make it to Moshi.

I quickly got a ride with a truck to Voi. There I turned south while the truck continued west to Nairobi. An Indian couple going to Arusha, and therefore through Moshi, soon picked me up. After the usual initial introductions, they told me how difficult it was to be an Indian in Kenya these days. They were both born in the country and owned a garment factory and a couple of shops in Mombasa. The government kept restricting their economic freedom. They were no longer allowed to send money to relatives in India, and if they wanted to leave the country, they could not take all their savings with them, only a statutory small portion.

"Admittedly, things are worse in Uganda, where Idi Amin simply throws all the Asians out of the country after having stolen all their possessions. But in Kenya it is not much better. The Africans are simply jealous of us, because we are good businessmen while they are lazy."

I nodded and listened with interest. They realized that I didn't know much about it all. But I now understood why it was always Asians who wanted to change money on the black market: a way for them to get Western currency.

The road went through Tsavo West and we saw, among other things, eland antelopes. But at a great distance. They are shy, which is probably because the Maasai hunted them and they therefore learned that people should be avoided. Wise animals. Of course, we also saw giraffes and elephants; they are hard to miss.

At the border in Taveta, I got nervous again. What would happen now? But it went without a hitch and I was granted a visa for a three-month stay in Tanzania. And soon we were in Moshi. A city that began as a German military base in 1893. At the time of writing, Moshi is said to be home to just over 200,000 people. But in 1971 it was more like a large village stretching along a long main street, although the railroad had already reached here from Dar es Salaam in 1912.

The first night I ended up at the YMCA. A very nice place, albeit expensive: 28 shillings a night, including breakfast. But it was worth it. They had a big pool that mirrored Kilimanjaro. There were also mosquito nets in the room and access to a hot shower! So the next morning, before breakfast, I had a lovely swim in the pool below Kibo, as the highest well-known and majestic peak is called. The YMCA is a large white building right at the entrance to the city. And it's still there; I stayed there again in 2002. I don't remember what it cost then, only that I was not as impressed, although the pool and breakfast were still okay, but the quality of the rooms had deteriorated considerably. Above all, the mosquito net was full of holes, which of course lead to me not sleeping at all.

On my second day in Moshi, I looked for the local COOP office, where I knew Sten Eriksson was working. I found it and him and I was expected. Dad had written them and informed that I was on my way and would be in touch. It was decided that I should move to their home immediately. I was given my own room in a villa with a beautiful flowering garden. A long letter from my mother with lots of information about what was happening at home was also waiting for me. Nice to read, even if all the information was not so pleasant; my brother and his girlfriend had broken up under bad circumstances apparently.

In the evening we ate meatballs, potatoes, brown sauce and lingonberry jam! While the Swedish troubadour Evert Taube sang on the turn table. A very agreeable evening.

In the soft and warm bed, I could then finish Thomas Mann's *The Magic Mountain*. It had been heavy reading at times, especially the long passages in French, which of course I simply skipped. A lot went over the head of the 19-year-old adolescent. I have later reread it, of course in Swedish, in connection with literary studies at the university and then enjoyed it much more. Now I would instead embark on *The Lord of the Rings*, the entire trilogy, which I had been carrying since I first packed my backpack. I had read all the parts in Swedish during the first year of high school and, like everyone else, had been completely captivated. Now I was looking forward to reading it again and in Tolkien's own idiom.

Sten and Lilian belonged to a fine cooperative generation, as did my parents. Sten and my father had worked together in Jönköping, where my father opened the first COOP supermarket in Småland in the early 1950s - and my brother and I were born. Sten and my father had stayed in touch since then, even though our family ended up in Stockholm via Södertälje in 1958, with my father pursuing a cooperative career in the capital, and Sten internationally. None of them would voluntarily shop at the privately own grocery stores, ICA (neither do I if I can avoid it!), insured themselves with Folksam, refuelled the car at OK, travelled with Reso, lived in Familjebostäder, all cooperatively owned companies. And of course they, almost reflexively and without reflecting voted for the Social Democrats. A noble generation that built the welfare of Sweden and believed in cooperative ideals; today I wonder where those ideals have gone. Is it only old fogies like yours truly who stubbornly advocate common ownership in these market liberal-fundamentalist times?

Sten, Lillian & Poppi in their garden with Kibo in the background.

The next day I stayed in the house and its garden, where of course Kibo could be seen every morning and evening when the clouds did not obscure its crown. A view one never tires of. I wrote a long letter home, one to my sister in Zûrich and several aerograms to friends in Högdalen. Then we sat in the living room in front of a fire and talked after another delicious Swedish dinner.

102

They were now done with Tanzania after living here for four years and were both over 60 - but younger than I am today - whereas I then saw them as very old indeed. For Christmas they were moving home for good. They had already started to pack somewhat. I was a bit surprised that they had two young men helping out, one in the house and one in the garden: "Do you have servants?"

"More like domestic help. We had no such plans when we moved here," said Sten. "But it is impossible for Europeans living like this not to have help in the house. We are looked upon as employers, where there are job opportunities. If we didn't have Joseph and Juma, we would have a queue of young men looking for work here all the time. And unemployment is high in Tanzania."

"Besides, it's too hot for us, at least in the garden. Nor can we manage an East African garden. So Joseph is both necessary and good. We will miss them both," Lilian added.

"What are you going to do with Poppi?" I asked. Their labrador.

"We have found a family we know here who will take care of him."

"Are you looking forward to moving home?"

"Yes, we are getting a bit tired. But we will miss Tanzania. All the friends and colleagues. And the amazing generosity, kindness and joy of the people here. Sometimes you wonder why; despite Nyerere's promises, things don't look very promising for the country. People here are a bit resigned, don't think they can influence what happens in Dar."

"What would be needed, do you think?" I asked.

"I think they have to allow more private initiatives," Sten said. "Unfortunately, you can't just rely on cooperatives and communally owned companies. Just look at how much richer Kenya is, where foreign ownership is allowed. But yes, the class differences there are bigger and more noticeable."

"It will also be nice to have some cold," Lilian added. "Even though we will surely miss the warm weather when we sit in Jönköping and freeze."

The next day I went to Arusha, which is a larger city and regional capital. I wanted to buy some Christmas gifts that Sten and Lilian promised to bring home and post in Sweden - as long as it was not too big. I bought some Maasai paraphernalia and a small wooden bust. Then I stocked up for the planned ascent of Kilimanjaro, including tuna cans, fruit, chocolate and nuts.

Climbing Africa's highest mountain was not something I had planned to do. But in Nairobi I had met several people who told me that it was really just a long walk. Sten and Lilian also encouraged me, even though they had not climbed it themselves. They knew many people who had, and all had said it was a magnificent, even if a cold, adventure. I decided to give it a try.

After an early breakfast the following day, I set off with a lighter backpack, just the clothes I thought I would need, sleeping bag, some food and drink. I took a bus to Marangu where I had a good cup of coffee and biscuits at the Kibo hotel before starting the hike up at 9:30 am. 80 kilometres from Marangu to Uhuru peak and back was what I was looking forward to. It would take five days. Three different cabins to stay in. In 1971, Kilimanjaro was not yet a national park so there were no restrictions, or gates to pass through. Six years later it became a park with strict rules on how to ascent the mountain. You had to have a guide and you could absolutely not do it alone. Now lonely Eric could climb it without any impediments.

Initially, the walk went through large banana plantations and small villages. In a small shop I bought some more biscuits and bananas. After the banana forest, the rainforest took over. There are five climate zones on the mountain and this is the so-called forest zone. Green and impenetrable. The path was so far passable by jeep and after a couple of hours I met a tourist officer on his way down in his jeep. He told me that it cost 5 shillings a night if I wanted to stay in the lodges on the mountain, so I paid it there and then and got a receipt. I found it affordable. But he did not mind that hiked alone.

It took me just over four hours and about 15 kilometres to reach the first lodge, Bismarck hut, or Mandara as it is now called. There I met a fellow who apparently ran the place, who told me that a couple of Americans had spent the night here yesterday and were thus a day ahead of me. Soon he disappeared down in a jeep and I was alone. At sundown I sat on the veranda of the cabin and enjoyed the view of the Lossogonoi plateau with lakes shining in the moonlight and some smaller volcanic peaks that, like Kilimanjaro, shot up on the savannah. Just before it got dark, a young Australian girl and a Canadian came down. The latter was really frustrated. He had climbed several peaks in Europe and America, but not this one. While he had come down with altitude sickness and was vomiting and feeling sick, his girlfriend from flat Australia, who had never climbed anything but a ladder before, had easily hiked up to Uhuru Peak. He found it hard to swallow and went to bed early as he still felt sick. The girl and I sat up for a while and she told me that the descent was the worst. Then I slept well after a simple meal they shared with me.

Gabrial and Dennis leaving the rainforest on our way up Kilimanjaro.

The next morning, I was joined by a Canadian and an American. They had driven a car almost all the way up to Mandara and had therefore made it up here before 10 o'clock. The three of us decided to join forces for the rest of the mountain. After a cup of coffee, we started our hike together and it was initially quite steep up through the rainforest. And suddenly it ended and we were in the grass zone. At first it was more savannah-like grasslands, which soon turned into heaths. Here we encountered lobelia and giant hogweed. Strange and partly beautiful plants; the latter only occurs on the mountain slopes of East Africa. The vegetation on East Africa's high mountains is unique because of the daily shifts in temperature; it is winter at night and high summer during the day.

The Canadian, Dennis, and I had the same pace so we could chat and walk along, while the American, Gabriel, was slower with somewhat clumsy coordination. We often stopped and waited for him, which we didn't mind as we were hardly in a hurry. We would get to the Peter's or Horombo hut anyhow. It took four and a half hours. It is located at about 3700 meters above sea level. Back then it was a simple cabin with a few wooden bunks, today there are several cabins and a proper tent site. Here we met a lone Australian who was on his way down. Together we prepared a relatively good and warm dinner, as Dennis and Gabriel had brought a Primus cooker with them. But it was hard to fall asleep. I had all my clothes on, including hat and mittens I had borrowed from Sten, but despite this I was cold in the sleeping bag and worried about what it would be like in the summit cabin.

On my way across the saddle towards Kibo

The second morning, after I might have fallen asleep without realizing it, we made porridge and coffee. This was the last place we would find water, we knew, so we filled our bottles. Then it was off. At first it was steeply uphill before we reached the so-called saddle at 4500 meters altitude, between Mawensi and Kibo. We could even see the Kibo hut gleaming in the sunlight. But it was a long way to go. Now the landscape was flat, dark sandy, full of large lava rocks. It was a pleasant walk in the dry, cool air in blazing sunshine. After three hours we reached the Kibo hut, which is 4720 meters above sea level. If I was going to get altitude sickness, now was the time. I knew that. But I didn't feel anything yet, nor did the others. The cabin itself was in terrible condition. The wind blew in between the wall planks and it was not possible to close the door properly. But we made a simple, hot dinner again and went to bed early after sundown. We had to get up early in the dark the next morning. As I crawled down fully dressed in my sleeping bag, I looked enviously at Dennis and Gabriel sneaking down in their underwear. They obviously had better quality sleeping bags!

At two o'clock we were woken to Dennis' little alarm clock. No, that's not correct, I didn't wake up, I was awake. I had been so terribly cold that sleeping had been impossible, just lying and shivering in my thin sleeping bag. It was now several degrees below zero, even inside the cabin, and my clothes and sleeping bag were not at all adequate for this temperature. I was therefore happy when the alarm rang and it was time set out. First we drank a cup of coffee on melted snow water. Good and invigorating. Then we started the ascent with flashlights in the dark. But we were lucky, a half-moon shone and we could turn off our flashlights. It was slow going. Here the oxygen was less than half of what it is at sea level. It was 50 ant steps in zigzag, pause, then 50 more ant steps. Gabriel fell behind again but we saw him all the time and when we got to Gilman's point, 5685 meters above sea level and 960 meters above the Kibo hut, we waited for him. By then the sun had risen over Mawensi and we could see the whole of southern Africa. Of course we wanted to continue to Uhuru Peak, 5895 meters above sea level and the highest point in Africa. Together the three of us walked carefully on the glacier and along the crater to our right.

The name Kilimanjaro is said to come from the Swahili for hill, kilima, and jaro, which would mean white, shining. But its etymology is uncertain, and perhaps rather uninteresting. Ptolemy, in one of his writings, mentions a snow-covered mountain among the "cannibals of inner Africa," which is the first time, I understand, that the mountain is mentioned in writing. From a Western perspective, the first person to discover the mountain was a German missionary, Johannes Rebmann, in 1848. But it took a while before anyone believed him: snow at the equator? Nonsense!

The Chagga people who have lived south of both this and the adjacent Mount Meru since the 11th century, of course have several ontological stories about the mountains' origins that predate the first white man's discovery. They called the mountain Kibo, which apparently means snow, and still live on for the highest peak.

The first people we know of to climb Kibo were a couple of Germans with their then only 18-year-old chagga guide, Kinyala, on October 6, 1889. Since then, hordes of people have done it. Also by motorcycle and regular bicycle – but surely not all the way to Uhuru peak! Normally it takes five days up and down this trail from Marangu, but the record is just under five hours; how the hell did that happen? Must have been from the Kenyan side. The route I took is the most common and is now considered a tourist highway. But it is not to take lightly. It is mainly altitude sickness that can put a stop to the enterprise.

At the top.

All three of us survived and reached the top of Kibo, at Uhuru point just before seven. The view was magnificent all the way down to Cape of Good Hope - or so we thought. I have a photo of me at the top and it looks like I have all my clothes on, looking stuffed, yet I was freezing until the sun warmed everything also at the top. The Uhuru peak was then just a pile of rocks with some flags and a few plaques. Today it looks a bit different! Something you can see if you google it.

Soon the clouds rolled in. But that was also beautiful, with the sun shining on the cloud carpet below us and other smaller volcanoes on the savannah peering up out of the carpet. We photographed each other and then turned downhill.

It took 50 minutes down to Kibo hut and it was painful. As the Australian girl had said, going down was worse than up. Having to break all the time hurt my toes and knees. When we reached Kibo we were quite exhausted. We rested and ate some carrots, nuts and chocolate before we started trudging across the saddle again. It went well, but soon it was downhill again. It took almost three hours to reach the Horombo hut. There we had an hour's break with some food. They heated a soup I also had some of. Did me well. Then I wanted to move on. Gabriel and Dennis chose to stay in Horombo, but I wanted to go down to Mandara so as to be able to sleep proper in a warmer night. Even though my feet and knees ached, I went on alone through heather and savannah and then the rainforest. I had no water with me as I remembered we had crossed several small streams on the way up. Now, on my way down, they were all gone: had some villain dammed them higher up? It was a thirsty walk. I had broken a stick to help me along and used it so intensely that my palms were bleeding. But I kept going. My knees screamed with anger and my toes were soon completely numb. But of course I couldn't stop. I swore and dug reserves.

Just before six, I finally stumbled into the Mandara cabin. Completely exhausted, shaking and crying. When I took off my shoes; my socks were bloody from the torture I had put my toes through. In the hut there was a large party with porters and a guide who all were going up the next day. They duly felt very sorry for me and offered me a generous meal. Then I went to bed.

I slept for 13 hours! I have never done that before or since – I think. Anyway, it did me good and the walk down to Marangu was slow and almost pleasant. Now I could enjoy nature again. I also wondered why I had climbed Kilimanjaro. It was certainly not on my mind when I took the subway out to Skärholmen. But the mountain is there to be climbed! Today I am of course glad I made it, especially since I no longer remember the pain, only the adventure and the glory.

I have visited Moshi and especially Amboseli Park several times since then and it has been very obvious how much less snow and glacier there is on Kibo. Almost 85 percent of the ice has disappeared during the 20th century. Of the glacier that existed in 2000, about 40 percent has now disappeared in 2020, we can read. It is believed that at this rate, Kibo's majestic white crown will be completely gone by 2050. Tragic, even if it doesn't affect the people living below Kilimanjaro, as there is enough rain on its slopes to keep the soil fertile.

Apart from all the birds, including lamb vultures (I think) on the saddle, I saw no animals. There were supposed to be buffalo and elephants on the slopes and I was probably glad I hadn't seen them. Wilfred Thesiger, British adventurer and author, climbed the mountain in 1962 and on the glacier, he saw five wild dogs following him and his party. What they were doing up there is a mystery. Otherwise, the most famous animal on the mountain is the frozen leopard that was discovered on the glacier sometime in the 20th century and immortalized by Hemingway in his short story *The Snow on Kilimanjaro*. There is a famous photo of it from 1926 and the place where it was found has since been called Leopard Peak.

Kilimanjaro is also considered to be poor in vegetation. The Swedish botanist Olov Hedberg has researched the flora of the East African mountains and found that only 54 species grow above 4000 meters on Kilimanjaro, which is apparently unusual enough to consider the mountain as plant-poor. Something I certainly did not notice, rather the opposite.

Back in Moshi, I stayed three more days with Sten and Lilian. I rested, licked my sores and finished Tolkien, which of course I liked just as much now as when I earlier read it in Swedish. I also washed clothes, bathed in a hot tub, ate good Swedish food and had nice conversations. They were truly kind; I felt welcome, enjoyed myself and thanked them sincerely when I moved on. When they arrived in Sweden, they phoned my parents, who got a live report on how I was doing. This pleased my mother and father.

The next time I was in Moshi, a few weeks later, I ended up staying with Charles and Jack, two American Peace Corps members. When I hitchhiked here from Dar es Salaam, Charles joined me on the road in Korogwe. After half an hour we were picked up in the same car and then I followed him home. They lived in a simple house with two rooms in the African part of Moshi. The toilet and kitchen were out in the yard where they interacted with the families living around them. It was mainly the children who wanted to play with them all the time. In six months they had learned enough Swahili to survive on their own here. Not another white person as far as the eye could see. I liked it here, stayed for five days and tried to pick up some Swahili.

Jack worked for the YMCA and was setting up a pottery workshop on the slopes of Kilimanjaro. Charles was teaching English at a school in Moshi.

Jack and Charles at home.

On my second day with them, which was the first day of Advent, I visited Sten and Lilian and they offered me lunch and were curious about everything I had done since I was last with them. They had finished packing and were flying home the following Saturday. Done with Tanzania.

I was not. Staying with Charles and Jack, I spent time with the families in the compound, went shopping at the market and cooked in the simple kitchen with my Peace Corps friends. We also visited the small local library and in a bookshop in town I bought a large map of Kilimanjaro, which I later sent home and it still hangs framed on the wall behind me as I write this. We were also invited to spend several evenings with their American friends who lived in a stylish villa in the same area as Sten and Lilian. There we were treated to good food, cigars and brandy, and also, I remember, Rod Stewart's latest album: *Every Picture Tells a Story*, which we listened to all evening. A Swedish couple also joined us and we sat and smoked weed and listened raptly to Rod's latest. A record I can still listen to, even if I am now a bit bothered by the too persistent and simple drumming on every track.

These people were teachers or paramedics or, like the host couple, worked at COOP (knew Sten). They talked about dinners and parties with their friends in Moshi and Arusha. A different life than the one I had met so far in Africa and certainly different from the Peace Corps members I stayed with. Kim and Jason, with whom we stayed, had two small children so it was understandable that they lived as they did, with a cook, gardener, nanny and a young girl who always seemed to be cleaning.

One night Charles, Jack and I were babysitting for them. They left some marijuana and whiskey which we finished together with more Rod Stewart. Two American girls also joined us and we cooked lots of good food and it was a very pleasant and late evening. I laughed so hard my stomach hurt also the next morning and I was hung over most of that day. The closest to a real party I'd been during the trip.

In the middle of January, I was back in Moshi again. On the evening of January 15, 1972, I knocked on Charles' and Jack's door. But they were not at home. However, neighbours who had keys recognized me:

"Jambo, habari gani?" "Nzuri sana." And I was let in and found the same bed I had previously occupied. "Asante sana." Late in the evening Charles and Jack showed up and were pleasantly surprised to see me - I think, or so I wrote at least in my notes.

The next evening I drank pombe for the first time at a small pub nearby, a beer brewed from millet. Quite strong, but hardly comparable to a Czech pilsner, or even Tusker. In any case, we got a bit tipsy and then went over to Jason and Kim again, where there seemed to be a party every evening. A Swedish girl and two Tanzanian colleagues of Jason were already there and it became another long and fun night. A lot of political discussions about the future of the country. I mostly listened but could see that Charles and Jack were the ones who appreciated Nyerere and his Ujamaa socialism the most. The two Tanzanians were not as convinced.

I needed to change some of my clothes before moving on. At the market in Moshi, I tried to sell a pair of brown, too tight and bell-bottomed jeans (I had put on weight!). But no one wanted them. On the street, however, I found an Indian who bought them for 35 shillings. I then used that money in the market and bought a pair of baggy corduroy pants. Just right for the climate. I sewed an inner pocket on them for my passport and money, although it was usually fine to keep them in my shoulder bag. Here I also got my shoes shined after having had them in a plastic bag for a long time on the coast. When I unpacked them, they were green with mold.

I stayed several times in Moshi, a city I liked very much and got to know. My first stay, including the Kilimanjaro hike, was with Sten and Lilian and then all the time with Charles and Jack. The latter two always made me feel welcome and I thoroughly enjoyed every stay with them and their lovely neighbours, as well as the dinners at Kim and Jason's I was invited to. Those were days I now remember fondly and wonder what Charles and Jack are doing today? After I left Moshi one last time, I have unfortunately had no contact with them. Sad and silly, but nothing to do about today.

On January 18, 1972, I left Moshi for the last time and started my journey home, you could say, although I was still heading south towards Zambia and it would take almost six months to get back home.

Dar es Salaam

After climbing Kilimanjaro and staying with the Erikssons in Moshi, I hitchhiked to Mombasa again. It was slow going but eventually I arrived. I had not eaten since I left Moshi so promptly found a restaurant where I started with a favourite: samosa. Then I had meat stew with chapati. Delicious! The Sikh temple's guest room was full, but I could sleep on the floor and it turned out to be a blessing. Previously I had slept on one of three benches in the guest room, sweating and being tortured by mosquitoes. But on the floor it was slightly, but still noticeably, cooler and the mosquitoes did not care about me, so I came to sleep on the floor every time I stopped in Mombasa henceforth. The concrete floor was of course hard, but so were the benches. I put the rain poncho on the floor, then the sleeping bag as a mattress, the blanket from Kassala over me and used my shoulder bag as a pillow. Cozy as hell. And gratis!

I needed to send a book package home before going on to Dar es Salaam; my backpack was getting ridiculously heavy. But the post office was closed for the weekend, and now it was Saturday, so I ended up staying on the floor in the Sikh temple for three nights. This meant quite a lot of promenading around in the city. Also looked for something to read in the book stalls I saw, but found mostly junk. Instead I gave myself a haircut, which was fun, and I came to look quite hilarious. The barber had never before cut a hair like mine, he claimed. Everyone in the salon was cheerfully curious about my hair and some even collected the relatively blond curls which ended up on the floor below me. But it was cheap. I also visited the old Arab quartiers of Mombasa, which was crowded and full of children who were terrified when they saw me: even with my new haircut! Also found my way to Fort Jesus next to the old town, at the far end of Mombasa Island.

Ibn Battutta is said to have visited the city in 1331 and it is known that there was a port here as early as the 12th century when Arab traders founded the city. Vasco da Gama was the first European in 1498, initiating Portuguese interest in the city. In 1593, they built Fort Jesus in an attempt to capture and hold the city. They were after the lucrative Indian Ocean trade. But the Portuguese were not very successful; the Ottoman Sultan of Zanzibar regained control of the city and its trade until the

British incorporated it into their empire in 1887. Today the fort remains a ruin and tourist attraction,

I have never liked Mombasa. Too hot and humid and ugly. But as a harbour and a hub for all the tourist destinations on the Indian Ocean from Malindi to Diani, it is important, although this has become less so since Muslim fundamentalists in Al-Shabab have terrorized the coast. In 2014, when I last was in Kenya to visit our youngest daughter at the Swedish school in Nairobi, it was only on the Diani beach and further south towards Tanzania that tourists could enjoy the sun and sea. The city's deep Kilindini harbor (a port I, together with my British/Kenyan girlfriend called at on the Polish cargo ship 'Zygmunt August' from Rotterdam, on a July day in 1977) and the railway up to Nairobi guarantee that Mombasa will never decline in importance.

This was something I didn't care much about at the time. Instead, I looked for a good place to eat. At an Indian establishment close by I was offered a big plate of meat and vegetable stew and a couple of chapatis for 2 shillings. That was my dinner every night; lunch usually samosa. After both lunch and dinner I would buy a fruit salad at one of the many fruit stands in town. Breakfast was my own that I ate at the temple: milk, plus bread with jam. Then I always found a good cup of instant coffee in a glass of hot milk. Something I can still drink. The same goes for the banana shakes that were served for 25 cents on the streets.

As I was stuck for a few days I washed some clothes; the temple had washing lines from where one was fairly certain clothes would not disappear. There were walls and gates to the temple that they closed at night, although they were never locked from what I noticed. This waiting for the post office to open on Monday and my relative disinterest in the city made me homesick in my boredom. It gnawed worryingly in my stomach all the time. I tried to fight it off but it was difficult. I was also alone for the first time in a long time. I took out the Dan Andersson volume and sat in the shade in Uhuru Park and read aloud to myself. In particular, I read "Vårkänning" (Spring feelings) over and over again until I knew it by heart. Don't know if it quenched my homesickness, but it is still a beautiful poem.

A young Kenyan sailor sat down next to me on Saturday afternoon while I was reading. Charles, he introduced himself as. He was in trouble and wanted my advice and help. He had been robbed of his passport and money and now needed 40 shillings to get a new passport and re-enlist. Could I help him? In the end I gave him 6 shillings as he had managed to scrape together the rest elsewhere. I saw him a couple of times during the weekend, which enriched the days.

At the Sikh temple I was not alone either. On the last night there were four of us in the guest room again. Everyone but me slept on the benches. They did not believe me when I claimed that it was noticeably cooler and mosquito-free on the floor. The most peculiar character was a Japanese who showed up Sunday afternoon. He just threw his stuff into the room and then disappeared into Mombasa to document his visit with his camera. He later told me that he was traveling around the world but never stayed more than one night in each place. He only photographed every place and then moved on. Now he was going up to Cairo and then Morocco before Asia again and finally back to Japan. A strange way to travel, I thought. He didn't allow himself to be influenced by the journey, by the places he rushed through, didn't take his time: "didn't give an ounce of his integrity to the journey," as Nicolas Bouvier wrote in his fine travel book: *The Way of the World*. What rewards can one derive from such rushing? Didn't we travel to expose ourselves "for things to happen and change; otherwise you might as well stay at home," according Bouvier.

I was also fascinated by the Sikhs. I didn't know anything about their religion, but I understood that hair was important, at least for the men. Inside the temple you could see them washing their hair and understand that they never cut it. Long, black and beautiful. That made me jealous. Especially since I had now cut off large parts of my sun-bleached curls.

It was finally Monday, which I started with malaria tablets. The post office was now open and I could mail a package of 4.5 kg of books, which cost 28.50 shillings. My backpack became liberatingly lighter. Nice. Then I visited Festus, who hadn't been home over the weekend.

"Erik, how wonderful to see you again!" It was a fond reunion. His wife and youngest daughter were with him. He asked me what I had been up to since we last met and I asked him what he had been up to since last we met. We had coffee and laughed and had a great time. His wife was sweet and his daughter cute, but a little sceptical of me. Festus and I were in correspondence for several years after this last meeting.

I ended the evening, like all these Mombasa evenings, by sitting in

Uhuru Park and enjoying the crowds, drinking coffee and maybe a banana shake and writing in my journal. Meeting Festus and his family had certainly cured my homesickness; I have friends here too! And tomorrow at 6.30 am I shall take a bus to Tanga, a harbour city in northern Tanzania.

The bus journey was memorable. In Lungalunga, (great name) just before the border with Tanzania, the bus broke down. The driver and his two helpers tried every trick in the book to get it going again, but the bus refused to cooperate. The driver then followed an oncoming bus back to Mombasa to get a new bus. This took five hours. It rained almost all the time but we passengers, who were a half-full bus load, could at least sit inside the bus and wait. No one had food or drink with them, or at least I didn't.

The new bus that arrived had seen much better days. It was a run-down city bus with loose seats in its rear half. The dirt road was bumpy and potholed as usual, so the seats were thrown back and forth, up and down, this and that way, making a devilish racket. I asked if I could sit on the roof, but it was not possible. Prohibited by law, the driver claimed. When we arrived in Tanga after two hours, and a smooth border crossing, my ears were ringing from the chairs' bouncing about in the rear of the bus. Terrible. I couldn't find a cheap hotel to sleep in either. A nice guy I met promised to help me find a cheap bed and dragged me all over town without success. So I ended up on a beach, or rather next to a small strip of sand by a stream down to the harbour. There was no beach in this seaport. And no sleep. The night was hot and humid and mosquitoed. When it finally lightened, I found out that I was practically in an anthill. And right behind a graveyard full of tombstones. Nice one Erik! Luckily no one had seen me and I was quick to get out of there.

It was relatively easy to find the way out of Tanga and the road south towards Dar. At some small street stalls, I managed some breakfast. But this didn't make it easier to get a ride. Instead, after a few hours of thumb waving, I gave up and took a bus to Segera, where the road from Moshi and Arusha meets the one from Tanga. There was more traffic here and soon I was sitting in a Peugeot with an American missionary from Texas, now living in Arusha. We spent a few hours talking about Nyerere's politics, which he thought were insane and irresponsible, about Christianity, which he had a very pragmatic and practical view of, while expressing disgust over Catholicism. He was probably a Lutheran. The best part of that ride was the sandwiches, cookies and coffee he offered when we stopped for a break. And in Dar er-Salaam he drove me all the way to the Windsor Hotel, where I knew I should stay; all the backpacks in Dar did.

There I shared a room with two other guys and the bed cost 7.50 shillings a night (you could get 11 shillings for a dollar on the black market in Dar). One of them was a British bookworm, Justin, and the other a Tanzanian who only slept in the room; didn't see much of him at all. Justin, on the other hand, stayed in his room and read all day. He had lots of books on a shelf by his bed and I could borrow whatever I wanted. I picked *The Magus* by John Fowles, which he highly recommended. We talked literature and had a good time together the days I was in Dar. I was also able to take a hot shower for the first time in a long time; the otherwise excellent Sikh temple in Mombasa did not offer anything like that. But there was water rationing in Dar so it took time and three different bathrooms with showers to clean up. Then I felt great.

The next day I suddenly heard someone shout: "Erik!" It was Jim who was in Dar to ship his motorcycle home. We had not seen each other since Malindi, so there was a lot to recapitulate.

"What have you done with Leroy?" I asked.

"That bastard is still in Malindi. He plans to stay there as long as he can and make a living by selling marijuana."

We both shook our heads but also admitted that we liked the crazy Australian a lot. Jim himself would soon fly to Paris and then cruise around Europe for a while before going to college in California. I gave him my brother's address if he happened to go to Stockholm. He had finally got the money he had been waiting for, but not so Leroy, as far as Jim knew. None of them would make it to South Africa.

I visited the Swedish Embassy a couple of times these days where I could browse through several *Dagens Nyheter* (my daily paper in Sweden), which was always nice. It was also cool and lovely at the embassy, as it is of course equipped with air conditioning. Otherwise, Dar is as hot and humid as Mombasa, but a much nicer city.

Here I also saw a strange behaviour, which is perhaps typical for East

118

Africa? I don't know. Suddenly a guy came running like a madman on the sidewalk in front of me. I moved out of the way, also for the crowd of people screaming after him: "Catch the thief!" Soon he was caught and they attacked him with punches and kicks. After a while, a police car arrived and pulled him into the car, bleeding all over his face. The next day it happened again. This time the thief spotted a police car, ran to it and jumped in, grateful to be arrested rather than lynched by the mob chasing him. Apparently, one shouldn't steal in Tanzania either.

Dar es Salaam began as a small fishing village, Mzizima, but in the late 18th century Majid ibn Said, then Sultan of Zanzibar, built a summer residence here. Attracted by the sheltered harbour; the port soon developed and he renamed the town to its current name, which means port of peace/sanctuary. In 1887, however, the German East African Company took over the port and the town. They also built a railroad and it became the capital of the colony, and remained so when the British captured the city during World War I in 1916. Nyerere later wanted to move the capital to the more central Dodoma, but there was no money for that at the time, but in 1996 Dodoma officially became the country's capital, although Dar still serves as its de facto financial, administrative and political capital.

Kapuscinski describes the city well in his book, *The Shadow of the Sun*, how it consists of three parts. Closest to the sea is the nicer part; Oyster Bay north of the harbour, where of course the Europeans and the rich Tanzanians live in large handsome villas with quiet servants. Further in, the Asian neighbourhood takes over. More crowded, although there is a lot of money, lots of shops that offer everything you might need. The Windsor Hotel was located here. The third part of the city, which Kapuscinski calls the African, is made up of mud huts and simple shacks with corrugated iron roofs covering the muddy ground in a myriad of alleys.

Quite far to the northwest is the country's premier university, which I came to lecture at in 2002. More peculiar, however, is that now when I was in Dar in 1971, I was closer than ever to the Ghanaian writer Ayi Kwei Armah. He was then a professor at the University of Dar es Salaam. Of course I knew nothing about this then, or who he was. But I bought his first great novel here from a street vendor: *The Beautyful Ones*

Are Not Yet Born. I spent almost 15 years studying this and Armah's other novels before I completed my PhD in 1999 on his novel's narrative strategies. I have never met or had any contact with him, as he is notoriously silent about his own literature, but I know that he has read some of what I have written about his novels and essays. Back in November 1971 I could have visited him; perhaps we bumped into each other in town?

What I did encounter were many Swedes. I knew that Sweden had a good and close relation with Tanzania, and Olof Palme had recently visited, but I was surprised that I could buy Swedish crispbread and hear Swedish at almost every street crossing.

I also saw Chinese everywhere. They were all dressed the same: baggy blue pants, white shirt and baggy blue jacket. They were in the country building infrastructure and had both engineers and workers with them. I thought that was a bit strange; why couldn't they offer jobs to Tanzanians?

Something else that I also marvelled at was the old Swedish newspapers I found all over town. In Sudan they had been Danish. The Swedish ones were used in the same way here: whatever you bought was wrapped in old Swedish daily's. Also a strange form of development aid, I thought in my diary.

Tanzania was in need of aid. And Sweden favoured the country, and may still do so even though its aid has been reviewed, as they say, because of undemocratic tendencies in the country. But in 1971, Tanzania received a lot of aid through SIDA (Swedish International Development Authority). Nyerere's Ujama socialism was popular among social democrats in Sweden. It was an African socialism where the adjective African was more important than the noun socialism, according to V. Y. Mudimbe in his *The Invention of Africa*. It was more of an African communalism, where Nyerere wanted to create a new society based on traditional African family structures. It may not have been economically successful, but unlike many other post-colonial countries in Africa, Nyerere managed to avoid conflict and fightings between different ethnic groups. This is remarkable as such conflicts often predate colonialism and were not taken into account when the colonial powers divided the continent between themselves in Berlin in 1884.

After a few days in Dar, I finished *The Magus* and returned it to Justin.

120

Then I borrowed J. B. Priestley's *The Good Companions*. I was not kind to Justin here; I read it slowly so that I could take it with me when I left Dar. Callous of me. Justin wanted it back but didn't push it as I was only half way through when I went north. However, I promised to send it to him. But for some reason I forgot and the book is still on my bookshelf and I remember liking it a lot. I also managed to find a second-hand copy of Tolstoy's *Anna Karenina* for 4 shillings in a small bookshop. So now I had some good reading to look forward to when I went north again at the end of November 1971.

Serengeti

One day in early December I was sitting in a small village, Makuyuni in Tanzania, hoping a car would pass by. I had hitchhiked from Arusha and got off where the road to the Ngorongoro Reserve and the Serengeti begins. I knew it would be difficult to get a lift to and in the Serengeti, but I had also heard that people had managed, so I wanted to give it a try. It was already exciting.

The countryside after Arusha was beautiful. It had rained after the annual short rains, so the savannah sloping down from Mount Meru was green and lush; the season of flowers had arrived! As soon as I left the city, I also encountered wildlife. At first, mostly zebra and Grant's and Thomson's gazelles. The latter two of course named after British explorers (James Grant and Joseph Thomson). I was also fascinated by the Maasai. Now I was in their country.

Makuyuni was a small village of about 15 houses and I sat by the roadside reading Tolstoy in the shade of a large baobab tree. A tree that is hard not to fall in love with. In Swedish we also like to call it the monkey-bread tree, apparently because baboons like its fruits. Its thick trunk and primitive appearance can be seen everywhere in sub-Saharan Africa. It is said that it can be up to 2500 years old. Not the one I was sitting under though; it didn't provide much shade either, as it was almost empty of leaves. On the other side of the road some young Maasai stood leaning on one leg, supported on their long-leafed spear and looking curiously at me. After a while they came over and peered even more intensely at the Swede with the long sun-bleached hair. They tried to communicate with me in both Maa and Swahili, but after "Jambo! Habari gani?" all I could offer was Swedish and English. We resorted to pointing and laughing. They obviously thought I was an odd character, which of course I was in Makuyuni, as they would have been in Högdalen.

The Maasai are, as Melanie Kipury writes in her book on their oral literature, "probably Africa's most famous, or infamous, group of people." When traveling in East Africa, it is impossible to avoid them, especially now in the 21st century when many of them have left their traditional pastoral life to make money elsewhere, especially on the coast where tourists congregate. When I spent a week with my family in Zanzibar in 2012, there were Maasai guards at the gates of almost every hotel, and the same on the Diana Coast two years later. And everywhere you found them selling their jewellery. The equally 'exciting' Turkana and Samburu communities are not nearly as 'corrupted' by the tourist industry, although they are actually even more fascinating from a Western exoticizing perspective.

Still, it is impossible not to write about the Maasai in a text like this one. Something the Kenyan writer Binyavanga Wainaina agrees with in his wonderful satire *How to write about Africa*, where he ironically insists that Maasai must be included in any depiction of Africa. The encounter in Makuyuni was the first time I met them. But over the years in East Africa, and especially during my travels in south-eastern Kenya and the Maasai Mara Reserve, I have often met and interacted with them, visiting several manyattas, or 'bomas,' as their villages are called, enclosed by so-called 'enkang,' walls of thorn bushes to keep out predators at night. Visiting their small houses, 'enkaji,' is now offered to all safari tourists in both Kenya and Tanzania. They make a lot of money from this.

In 1971, however, this was not as widespread. And many of the young men were still naked under their red blankets, 'shuka,' and covered in red ochre and their hair braided and covered in red mud. Their earlobes were enlarged, which fascinated me, especially when they hung the earlobe above the ear. It looked funny. These young men were the only ones with hair, otherwise all Maasai heads were shaved: nothing between them and the sky! I was amazed at how beautiful the women were. I wondered if Swedish girls would be as pretty with shaved heads?

Like some other peoples, the Maasai believe they are God's chosen people. "Equal are God and the Maasai," as one of their many sayings goes. And Christian missionaries have rarely been able to convince them of Jesus' sovereignty. They are said to have emigrated down from southern Sudan and since the early 19th century settled where they mainly live today in northern Tanzania and south-eastern Kenya. This part of East Africa was long free from both Europeans and Arab slave traders because they all feared the Maasai, as did everyone else in East Africa.

After a while of comical communication with the young Maasai, I got a ride in a narrow and bumpy truck to Mto Wa Mbu. Like most small villages, this consisted of one street where all the houses were located. Around it, paths went out into the dominant banana plantations. In a small restaurant I got a chapati with meat stew and really good water. Then I continued, even though the afternoon was late. But I got a short ride to Karatu. There I spent a memorable evening.

This village boasted a small hotel, which gave me a tiny room with walls almost reaching the ceiling, but there was a mosquito net over the bed. They even helped me arrange a lift the next morning with a Land Rover going into the Serengeti, as long as got up in time. Which of course would be no problem, I thought, unaware of what the evening had in stall for me.

After checking in, I went and sat under another tree; the only one that was free. Under all the others, men - no women - were sitting conversing. I was the only European in the village, as far as I could see. And I felt great where I sat reading *Anna Karenina*. People passing by or sitting under other trees all greeted me as if I was a normal ingredient in the village as they were. I responded politely as I had learned to do: "Jambo! Habari gani?" I felt part of it. Happy and carefree.

Things even improved at sundown when I discovered that I could take a lukewarm shower at the hotel. They even lent me soap and a towel. I also got to go to the toilet properly for the first time in a long time: a blessing. The hotel had a small restaurant and a very lively bar. I had another meat stew with chapati and then sat down to read on the veranda outside the bar in a very dim light. Tolstoy had really captured me and it was hard to put the book down. But then a young man invited me in to the bar for a beer, which of course I could not refuse. It turned out that he was a police officer and his name was Walter.

"I heard you were from Sweden, so I have to buy you a beer," said Walter. "Your prime minister was just in Tanzania and you support us Tanzanians more than any other country, so the least I can do is buy a Swedish citizen a beer."

Soon we were squatting over a table in the bar, both with a Tusker. We had two beers each before he insisted that we move on to his brother's bar, where we would meet the village mayor and police chief. And so we did. More pilsner were devoured in an even smaller and darker bar in an alley behind the main street.

They were interested in Sweden and why we are so generous with aid

124

to Tanzania. I tried as best I could to explain that Nyerere's Ujama socialism appeals to Sweden and especially to the Swedish Social Democrats. I, for my part, was curious about the Serengeti and all the national parks around it and whether they were Maasai. Something even I thought I saw in the dim light that they were not. They laughed.

"No, we are not Maasai, thank God." They actually disliked them: "Cocky and treat their women like donkeys."

"Do you ever go on safaris and see all the animals?" I asked.

"No, it's for the tourists. We can't afford it; it's very expensive, even for us Tanzanians. But it's good that we have these parks so the wildlife survives. We also make a lot of money from it. But most Tanzanians have never seen a lion."

Soon all the beer made us inebriated, and today I can't really read what I wrote in my diary before going to bed at. A memorable evening for which I ought to thank Olof Palme – if I could. They were full of praise for him after his visit to the country. Today I wonder if I would receive the same friendly treatment just because I am Swedish. I don't think so. Sweden has abdicated as a country of solidarity. Now the blue-brown parties in government instead insist that we should use aid to force refugees back to the countries they have fled from. Appalling, and Palme must be turning over in his grave at Adolf Fredrik's church.

The next morning I woke up a bit hungover and far too late. I had missed the Land Rover I was supposed to get a ride with. After some coffee and bread, I sat down on the outskirts of Karatu. At 11 am I got to follow another Land Rover belonging to an oil company; it was going to Seronera, Serengeti's administrative village. Just after Karatu we came to the gate next to the Ngorongoro Reserve. They thought I belonged to the car, so I didn't have to pay entrance fee and the driver didn't say anything else, nor did I.

After the gate, it was upwards on a red clay, laterite road that most resembled a washboard. I was surprised that he was going so fast. But soon I understood why; you have to drive fast on the top of the grooves. If you slowed down, the car bounced up and down on the corrugated road and it became a very unpleasant experience. In any case, I still thought we went too fast through a dense rainforest up to the Ngorongoro Crater. But we stopped on the edge of the crater, where we got out at a lookout point. And I could actually see herds of elephants down in the giant crater.

In the Serengeti, I managed to convince the entrance guards that I was living and working as a teacher in Moshi, so only had to pay residence fee; a 10th of what tourists paid (which of course wasn't possible when I revisited the area with my family in 2012: very expensive, but worth every penny!). I paid for two days that I hoped would give me the wildlife experience I had dreamt of.

Down from the crater and it turned into savannah again with lots of animals everywhere. I stared so I almost got a headache: zebra, wildebeest, gazelles and several lions already on this journey to Seronera. And two large herds of buffalo, one of which we slowly drove straight through. "They are the most dangerous of all animals in East Africa," declared Peter, who was driving.

He dropped me off outside Seronera and told me there was a campsite a few kilometres away if I just followed the road. Optimistic and very naive, I threw my backpack on my back and started walking. At first I felt a bit cocky walking alone on the savannah and seeing all these animals around me. But soon there was a group of about 20 buffalo standing in the way and staring at me very curiously. I turned around, remembering what Peter had said. Instead, I sat down under a tree beside the road hoping a car would come and give me a ride. There were no cars. I started reading Tolstoy again. Even in Serengeti I couldn't tear myself away from the adventures of Anna Karenina, Levin and Count Vronsky! But I often looked up from the book to make sure no hostile animals were approaching.

After an hour or so, a first car arrived and it was two young men from The Serengeti Research Centre. They promised to drive me to the campsite. But when they realized that I had no tent, but intended to sleep on the ground in my sleeping bag, they turned around. The campsite was just an open space where you could pitch a tent, nothing else. Thus available also to all of Serengeti's predators. "You can't sleep without a tent or at least a camp bed with a mosquito net. If the lions don't get you, the hyenas probably will."

So I was soon back in Seronera, where there was nowhere for me to stay. It was recommended that I try the closest safari hotel. A hotel you could see from Seronera, about a kilometre away. Instead of taking the

126

road there, which was a big detour, I cut straight across the savannah this time, guilelessly unaware of any danger. Soon I walked right through a huge baboon herd of at least 30 animals. They slowly and politely moved, giving me a passage way through them, while staring at me both angrily and curiously. At the time I felt no concern or fear, but I have realized later that it was insane. If they had wanted to, they could have torn me apart as easily as anything, although it is not often that they attack people. But a lonely guy from Stockholm they could easily have made into mincemeat. I have often, especially later when I lived in Kenya and went on safaris a lot, thought about how stupid I was in 1971.

Well, I survived and once in the safari hotel, I was informed that they wanted 44 shillings per night, which far exceeded my budget. I wondered if they had something cheaper. And it turned out that they did. I got a simple room for 5 shillings, including breakfast, where local drivers and guides to tourist groups slept and ate. I was very pleased with that arrangement. Dinner I ate inside the hotel's café. A club sandwich and a Tusker. Enough for tonight. Now the only question was how I would get around the park and see some game.

The next morning, however, I realized that I was in the right safari hotel. The place had a gas station. Early in the morning, several cars came to refuel for the day's excursions. It was just for me to walk around and ask. Today, I can wonder at myself, that I had the nerve to attack complete strangers and force myself on them when they had spent so much to visit Serengeti. But the most unfavourable answer would be a no, I figured.

An American couple in a Land Rover, however, took pity on me. They lived in Tanzania and had been to the park before. Something that surely made them more likely to let me accompany them. They also knew the park a bit. So soon I was sitting in the back of an open jeep that slowly travelled across the savannah and we saw so many animals that it is impossible to describe, which is not really necessary as everyone has seen countless nature films from Serengeti and the world's most famous migration. The savannah was now also covered with mainly wildebeest and zebras, as they this time of the year have migrated south from the Maasai Mara in Kenya. We made a morning tour, then they drove me back and went to have lunch at their hotel. At half past three they showed up again and I joined them for an equally nice afternoon drive. Most memorable, perhaps because I have a beautiful photo of it, was probably a leopard lying on a branch above us, staring with its intense eyes straight down at us.

We saw lots of lions, as you do in Serengeti, and elephants, buffalos, some black rhinos, giraffes, hyenas, a cheetah family and of course countless wildebeests, sometimes covering the entire field of vision, zebras, impala and gazelles. At a so-called hippo pool we saw both crocodiles and countless hippos. We tried to get close to the eland antelopes but couldn't. Equally fascinating were the birds: of course ostriches but also the strolling secretary bird, the glossy starling, kingfishers, several weaver birds with their typical nests at the hippo pool, vultures that always showed the way to carcasses and lions or hyenas, the beautiful crown crane, saddle-billed stork, ibis, crowned lapwing and blackbirds, ground squirrels and guinea fowl, black-winged vultures and several eagles and the majestic African fish eagle, as well as the hideously ugly marabou stork with its bald, slightly reddish head; there are said to be up to 400 breeding bird species in the Serengeti!

In his and his son's book *Serengeti Shall Not Die*, Zûrichard Grzimek writes that in the mid-50s they counted 370,000 large mammals in the

128

Serengeti. That sounds low considering that more than a million wildebeest are said to migrate between the Serengeti and the Maasai Mara
every year. I wonder how many they would be able to count today, when
we read that one species becomes extinct every day and that two thirds
of all animals will soon be gone!

We turned back at dusk. Then the savannah became even more beautiful
with all the umbrella trees, acacias reflected in the blazing horizon. They
photographed even more. I took four pictures during my entire stay in
the Serengeti! And today it is a bit touching, almost, how little I photographed. The next time I was in the Serengeti, in 2012, the five of us in
the family took over two thousand pictures. And of course, in colour.
All my pictures from this year in Africa are in black and white - and few.
It had to do with the cost. Film was expensive, even for an Instamatic
camera. Instead, I bought postcards throughout Africa, mailed them or
sent them home along with books.

When the Americans left me at my hotel, I thanked them profusely. I
didn't really have words for how grateful I was for one of the best days
of my life. Then I never saw them again.

I got to eat dinner together with guides and drivers in the small Tanzanian compound at the hotel. I should have done so yesterday as well. Very tasty and I did not have to pay; they said it was included in my hotel fee. I knew that was not true, so they probably paid. And everyone was nice. They wondered how I had ended up staying there. And how on earth I had gotten there, seeing as I didn't have my own car. I told them everything I could and they laughed at my reckless walk through the baboon herd. A lovely evening in good company.

Then I went back into the hotel and ordered a shandy and sat by a fire they had built on the lawn in front of the restaurant. Around the fire Americans and Brits and Germans and other loose safari people had gathered after their dinner, telling stories of their day's safari adventures. Nice too. I was quiet, listening and watching the shadows of animals that lurked on the other side of the fire.

The next day was Tanzania's Uhuru Day: 10 years this December 9 since the country became independent. This was not noticed much in the safari hotel. Instead, everyone in the hotel was excited by the night's commotion. A lone buffalo had been attacked by a pride of lions close to last night's fire. I had not noticed anything as the sheds where I was staying were on the other side of the hotel bungalows. But all the other guests had been up most of the night watching the spectacle. It had taken time for the lions to kill the buffalo. When I got there after a quick breakfast, they were still there along with vultures, jackals and hyenas all waiting for their turn. I also tried this day to get a ride out into the park, but without success. I settled for what I had seen the previous day and sat down and watched the cadaver show with a good cup of coffee.

The manager of the hotel, who had let me stay with the drivers and guides, soon came and asked if I wanted to go to Seronera and see the Uhuru celebrations there. Which of course I did. And it was exciting. I was the only white person, which was fun at first, but soon became awkward. They absolutely wanted me at the stand of honour with the park's top brass. I felt very uncomfortable, but had to accept it and was soon able to relax and enjoy the show. Not unlike the National Day celebrations in Nairobi with speeches, dances and music, but on a smaller scale.

Later in the afternoon there was a bus to Arusha which I took and got a good window seat to once again enjoy the flora and fauna through the Rift Valley.

Lamu

Back in Mombasa. Two days to Christmas Eve. I arrived late last night with a truck from Voi. The driver chewed cat the whole trip and offered generously. I had never tried it and was curious. It tasted bitter but with a little sugar it was fine. We chewed, talked and spat until we arrived at midnight. Once at the Sikh temple it was impossible to sleep, so I just threw my backpack in the room and went out on the town. I walked elevated and resolutely on the quiet and empty streets for hours to wind down.

Back then you could walk even at night in Mombasa without being beaten and robbed. Today it is not advisable. There is a reason Nairobi is called Nairobbery, and it is not much better in Mombasa. But in 1971 I was able to stride through large parts of the city unharmed, in an energetic cat-rush until three am, when I quietly and tired slipped into the temple and finally could fall asleep.

The following day I went to Malindi again. First with a lift up to Kilifi and the ferry across the strait. There, as usual, I bought cashew nuts from one of all the vendors who ran between the cars in the line up to the ferry. The truck wasn't going any further, but in the queue, I was able to ask around and a German in a Mercedes promised to take me to Malindi. He was a strange character. He knew almost no English, only a few phrases, which was strange as he worked in the country. Unclear then with what. Despite five years of school German and a sister in Zürich, I did not understand everything he said. However, I realized that he had a peculiar view of the peoples in East Africa. He called them cannibals and was apparently genuinely surprised that they were wearing clothes. As I write this, it sounds as if he was making fun of me, but reading my diary it doesn't seem so - or he managed to fool me completely - not unlikely.

Suddenly, halfway between Kilifi and Malindi, we stopped, we had run out of gas. He had not checked how much gasoline he had in the tank before leaving Mombasa. Foolish, and also this indicated that everything was perhaps not operating well between his ears. But sometimes you have to tolerate stupidity too, I thought.

We stopped a jeep that helped us with enough gasoline to get to Malindi. As strange as he was, and despite my poor German, he apparently enjoyed my company enough to invited me to lunch at one of the best hotels just north of Malindi. It turned out that he was the manager of the hotel and gave me a great feast: several dishes to which we drank beer, gin and whiskey. While we were eating, he started commenting on the girls serving: "Have you seen what great asses they all have?" Something that was actually true. I had noticed that here on the coast the women even reinforced their bottoms with, as it seemed, extra cushions under their dresses. But that wasn't what the German wanted to draw attention to, but that they were "wonderfully voluptuous and nice in bed." I tried in my faltering German to shift the conversation to the weather and the food, although the girls were certainly good-looking. I've always loathed that kind of masculine, locker-room-jargon about girls, despite spending many hours in changing rooms around soccer and ice hockey games. It's simply stale and undignified. But the food was good and afterwards I thanked him politely when he drove me into town.

The evening became memorable as well. I spent it after a simple samosa dinner with good coffee at a simple dance tavern. It was full of lovely East African dance music. Here I fell in love with this music. I have been listening to the brilliant, sometimes monotonously endless guitar loops ever since, and am doing so now as I write this: a CD called "Kenya Special" with bands like The Mombasa Vikings and The Rift Valley Brothers. The Ghanaian, Congolese and Senegalese dance music, as well as that of Zimbabwe, is better than East Africa's, I find today, but everything swings wonderfully. It was also then difficult to sit still and just watch. But I, the only "mzungu", white individual in the establishment, didn't dare to ask anyone to dance, even though several of the girls were fantastically beautiful and moved across the floor as if they were part of the music. But suddenly one of them came over to me and asked me if I wanted to dance. Surprised and terrified, I still said yes. I've always loved dancing and the opportunity to do so in a small bar in Malindi was too good to pass up, even though everyone was staring at the only blonde in the room. As usual, it took a while before I could forget about everyone else and just dance with my partner. But soon also I was in a trance and we swayed around like everyone else and everyone forgot that I was not Kenyan. Sometimes they played music I recognized; James Brown, who was almost deified in East Africa, and Stevie Wonder, whose 'Sir Duke' they played several times to my delight. A song I still associate with that enchanting evening in Malindi. After we danced ourselves to exhaustion, I offered her a Tusker and we sat down at my table. She then asked me if I wanted to follow her home, spend the night with her. When I politely declined the generous offer, she took her beer and went back to her friends.

Instead, one of the young fellows serving sat down with me. He was wearing a nice t-shirt with a Toulouse-Lautrec print of can-can girls. "What happened with the girl? You were dancing so well together."

"Well, she wanted me to go home with her but I wasn't interested." He laughed and told me that she was a 'working girl.'

"Yes, I got that." Then I asked him if he liked working here.

"Sure, good music and nice girls, even though I can't afford, nor am allowed to be with them. But they are fun and kind. I don't work here every night though, even if it's fairly well paid: 60 shillings a night, which is good. But it takes time away from my studies. Actually, I ought to be studying now. If I don't get top grades, I'm screwed."

"Why? Can't you study further if you don't get good grades?"

"No. University is expensive. I can't afford it, nor can my parents. So without a scholarship, I have to stay here or do something else. But I don't want that."

I told him that university studies are free in Sweden, but on the other hand we have high taxes. He thought that sounded great and asked if he could move to Sweden. Then he asked me if it rains a lot in Sweden.

"Of course, and it snows too; snow is better."

"But can you grow anything in the snow?"

I had to admit that it was not possible. Which he didn't think was so good.

But then it's time to sleep and I say goodbye to my friend, throw my backpack on my shoulders and wave bye to the lady I danced with. She waves back cheerfully – no hard feelings. Malindi is a fairly quiet town as I leave the bar. There is always a special atmosphere in a small African town at night when most of the activity has died down. Malindi is blessed with the occasional street light and bats fly under them so I have to duck several times on my way to the beach where I intend to sleep again. Bats are not the only animals I encounter. Street dogs roam in small packs and can frighten anyone. A goat stands alone under a lamp post, quietly meditating and watching me – as it seems. Prayers are mumbled, despite the late hour, from a small mosque I pass. At the bus station, several of the small stalls selling simple food are still open; it smells nice and I hear laughter and guitar music from an open window in a house opposite. People laugh around the smoky food stalls while a child cries inconsolably on the back of a woman selling chicken skewers with tiny pieces of meat. A couple of buses are full and roll past me, illuminated, as I leave the bus station. It gets darker, but there is some light from some vendors who still don't want to give up. Three dogs run past me. From a transistor I hear a beautiful song in Swahili with eager guitar loops. I pass a young man selling tea in a large brass pot, or is it coffee? He serves the drink in small porcelain cups, so maybe it is coffee. I'm not having any anyway. Some taxis stand at an intersection and whistle at me if want a ride somewhere. I wave no thanks. The same to a couple of young, lightly dressed ladies in a doorway when they shout temptations. In another doorway, four men are sitting in quiet conversation. It is usually men who sit seemingly idle, while women at all times are standing or walking and always seem to have a purpose. Soon all the light has disappeared as I leave the city and only the starry sky shows the way to Malindi's southern beach. I find my way as I have walked here several times before. Suddenly, a guy appears in the dark and nearly scares the hell out of me; he asks if I want to buy a one-way ticket to the moon. "No, I'd rather have a return," I laugh. "Boy, you don't know what you're missing!" No, probably not, I think, and move on to the dunes among the coconut palms where I have slept earlier. And I do so again this night, alone and deep to the everlasting rolling of the waves. But I wake up early the next morning as the sun reaches me over the Indian Ocean.

At 07.30 I took a bus to Lamu.

The bus was full of passengers and we were several 'mzungus' going to Lamu for Christmas and New Year. It soon started to rain and the dirt road turned into a slippery muddy mess and it was slow going. To get to Lamu you have to cross the Tana River. We did this on a primitive but practically functioning ferry. The bus pulled up onto the ferry which was just big enough for the bus. All passengers got out and we pulled ourselves across with two thick ropes that ran through loops on both sides of the ferry. It worked well and efficiently. Then we continued and the weather improved the closer we got to Lamu. We stopped next to a quay where small boats were waiting to take us to Lamu. I boarded a barely seaworthy little boat that a couple of boys screamingly - why I did not understand - handled. It wasn't far to Lamu so it went well.

At Lamu's pier, we were all overwhelmed by people who wanted us to stay with them, whether it was a hotel or not. I knew where I wanted to stay and ended up at the best: New Shamuty, 3 shillings a night. For that price I got to sleep on the roof under a palm leafed sunshade, free tea and they also promised to wash my clothes. They even washed my sleeping bag. Fantastic, I thought. The hotel was a walled, whitewashed - like the whole village - three-story house. There was an open courtyard where the shower and laundry were located. Five young Kenyans looked after everything with great generosity and enthusiasm. I immediately felt at home.

The first evening I went to the movies with some other guests at the hotel. We took some time to find our way through the maze of narrow alleys. Finally we were out of the city where the cinema was - and perhaps still is - an old palace that they had turned into a movie theatre. For a shilling you could sit on mats of palm leaves and watch Laurel and Hardy under the open sky. I've always loved them but I don't think they've ever been as funny as they were that night! Which may have had something to do with the marijuana we smoked.

I wasn't the only European at the primitive theatre; it turned out that pretty much every Westerner on Lamu was there that night. Which was great as I met the entire 'mzungu' colony. Some had teamed up and rented houses for about 10 US$ a month and stayed for months. I planned to stay a fortnight so the hotel would be good enough for me. After the movie I joined a group to a house on the outskirts of the town and there we smoked more weed, drank tea and listened to music well into the small hours. A fine evening.

It was good to be back in a Muslim atmosphere. It was peaceful, quiet and the generosity and hospitality was almost limitless. I could once again wake up to 'Allahu Akbar' and mind my day as I wanted without anyone caring about me. Nice.

Me on the streets of Lamu.

Lamu town is said to have been founded in the 14th century by Omani traders, and is Kenya's oldest still inhabited town. Between the 16th and 18th centuries, it was an important harbour for the Indian Ocean trade in ivory, gold and slaves. It also became a centre of Swahili culture, both in terms of literature and art, which can still be seen in the beautifully carved doors of many of the city's houses. The town was also in rivalry with Pate Island just north of Lamu, which, together with the Mazrui clan from Mombasa, attacked Lamu in 1812. But Lamu prevailed and then asked the Omani dynasty in Zanzibar for protection, which, however, resulted in the end of Lamu's independence.

Today the town is on UNESCO World Heritage List as the best preserved Swahili settlement in the world. And the city is, and was in 1971 perhaps even more, a maze of narrow alleys and whitewashed simple houses with often beautifully carved wooden doors. No vehicles at all. I don't even remember seeing a bicycle. Donkeys seemed to be the main means of transportation. In the narrow alleys nothing else was possible, and cycling outside the city in the sand dunes did not seem very smart. The entire island consists of coconut trees and sand dunes as soon as you leave the city or the beaches. Today there are several modern tourist hotels, both in the city and along the beaches, mainly towards Shela beach, but then all hotels were simple and cheap and, in my case, magnificent. Only Peponi Hotel would then have been considered a tourist hotel and was, as it is today, out at Shela beach.

Most of the tourists on the island in December 1971 were like me: Long-haired backpackers from all over the world. We liked it here. We were left alone and it may not have been as busy as Goa in India, but at least in East Africa it had the same reputation, without the heavy drugs of Goa. Here marijuana reigned. In the 1970s, there were places like these in the world to which traveling hippies made pilgrimages: Amsterdam, San Francisco, Goa, Essaouira in Morocco, Zihuatanejo in Mexico, Baños in Ecuador, Chichicastenango in Guatemala and Pokhara in Nepal. I'm sure there were others, but these I visited as a long-haired hobo with my red backpack. They were all wonderful, though after a while there was too much drugs and smoking for my refined taste.

However, Lamu 1971 was just right and still relatively peaceful from a package tourist perspective. I bought a sarong, or kikoy as we called them in Kenya. It was important to blend in. Most men were dressed in jalabiya. No one wore long pants, too hot, and shorts are rarely part of a Muslim environment.

Christmas Eve was unlike any I had experienced before; warmer, no gifts or Santa. But James, a nice Brit who also stayed at Shamuty, and I prepared a good lunch of boiled potatoes, fried garlic and lamb with vegetables. Everyone staying at the hotel got to use their kitchen so there was a lot of communal cooking, which was nice. After lunch we took a long walk through the city and out to Shela beach where we swam in the warm and turquoise coloured sea. We met other Westerners, including Alfred and his girlfriend Melanie. He actually did look a lot like Santa Claus, big with long white hair and beard, and just as friendly. Melanie was very cute and I found it hard not to stare.

I had noticed that there were more female globetrotters here on Lamu than I had previously encountered during the trip. Interesting and suddenly after almost half a year I could flirt a bit. Doing it with Melanie was perhaps not the smartest thing to do, but she didn't seem to mind, on the contrary I felt.

Christmas Day began, after a simple banana pancake breakfast at the hotel, with a visit to the church at nine o'clock. There was a small Lutheran congregation on the island and I found its church. I was not alone; half of the guests were 'mzungos.' Everything was in Swahili, but I recognized the songs and it gave me some Christmas feeling. Afterwards I relaxed in the shade on the hotel roof with Tolstoy. Now I was in the final stages of the novel and deeply mourned the fate of Anna Karenina.

In the evening, James and I were invited to a Christmas party at the home of some people we had met on the beach, although we didn't really know who they were or their names. And it took a while to find the house, which was a bit out of town. We only got there when it was dark and everyone had already started eating. We didn't recognize anyone in the dark; apparently there was no electricity. The table was set by an open fire between two large houses among sand dunes and coconut trees. The food was plentiful and good with everything the island had to offer: fish, potatoes, pineapples, papaya, coconuts, lots of vegetables, chicken and bread. It turned out to be a good Christmas Day dinner, even if some Swedish herring was missing! I had a hard time blending in, though. Everyone seemed to be already engaged with one another. I didn't see Alfred and Melanie either, so after a while I gave up and parked myself next to a couple of guys playing great blues guitar by the fire.

Soon I was lying in the sand in only a tank top and kikoy, staring up at the palm trees and the starry sky at the second latitude south of the equator. I didn't feel sorry for myself at all, even if a bit lonely. But I was content and they played well.

Eventually I felt it was time to leave and slipped away unnoticed. I walked alone across the palm groves towards an initially quiet, still and beautiful Lamu. But the closer I got to the town, I heard intense drumming. Down by the waterfront, a group of Kenyans had gathered, playing drums and dancing. They had formed a ring which they ran into one at a time and danced solo. I sat on the wall by the quay and admired both the music and the dancing. My thoughts drifted home, wondering how they celebrated Christmas on Harpundsvägen. I knew of course, so really nothing to wonder about, but I could have longed for it, but I didn't. It was hard to beat this Christmas night.

When I went back to the hotel around two, the city was completely empty and beautiful in the faint light of the starry sky. I had my recorder in my shoulder bag and now took it out. I imagined that the acoustics should be phenomenal in the alleys. At first I started to play a bit cautiously because of the time. Soon, however, I forgot about that and blew all I could some Swedish traditional tunes. And no one complained, no one hung out of a window and told me to shut up. So I trotted around and played what little I knew, including Silent Night, which I thought was appropriate. Back at the hotel I fell fast asleep when I finally crawled into bed on the roof.

The next morning, I met some people who had rented a small boat and I joined them to a remote beach on the other side of Manda Island. There we could surf, snorkel and swim without disturbing anyone. But I was a fool: I was lying in the water and snorkelling without a t-shirt, so I burned myself something terrible. I didn't realize it at the time, but the next day when I woke up, I did. The following days I suffered all the hellish torments in the shade with coconut oil all over my body. I have hated that smell ever since. It was a shame that I couldn't go to the beach, as I have become quite good at body surfing. But to do that on Lamu there was a long walk out to the open sea. And now I was afraid of the sun. Not only was I burnt, but my whole face had exploded with acne. I looked bizarre and didn't want to show myself to anyone. I squeezed my pimples the best I could and tried to rest my back, but it didn't make me look or feel any better. Maybe I should follow James' advice to avoid meeting others; he had walked around the whole island on Boxing Day. It took him eight hours and he said it was a lovely walk: "You should do it Erik!"

But I never did. The cheap leather sandals I had purchased in Mombasa were now broken, so I bought a new pair of plastic ones. Then I sat on one of the many benches on the houses and just enjoyed the city life. Almost all houses in Lamu city were equipped with a brick ledge along the entire facade that served as a bench where you sat and socialized. Extremely pleasant! And there were no mosquitoes here. There was too much wind and no still water or grass to breed in. However, the flies were numerous and energetic. Thankfully no tse-tse flies, but I got to use my fly whisk from Ethiopia.

Alfred, Melanie and Henry came up to the hotel roof one day and tried to get me interested in sharing a big house. "If there are ten of us, it will only cost a few dollars per person and month!" It sounded interesting so I followed them out of town and looked at the house. A giant house among the palm dunes south of the city. Two floors and with a large kitchen. There was even some furniture. Beds or mattresses we would have to find ourselves. Water was only available from a well in the yard, but there was electricity in the house. I was still hesitant. Not sure if I really wanted to stay here that long. Besides, I really liked the hotel. So I declined. But we visited Basil who lived on his own in a house nearby. Not as big, but he had running water inside and a shower. We stayed late into the night and cooked a good stew together.

Most days looked the same; I enjoyed myself. Lying in my bed on the roof reading or wandering around the narrow streets of the town, eating a kebab, small sweet bananas, drinking pineapple juice and tea. Maybe go to the nearest beach and swim - with a t-shirt on.

At sundown several of us often gathered and cooked dinner at someone's house. Several evenings we went to Basil's house and cooked a lovely stew. He even had spoons for all of us, a change from the usual hands or chapatis. It was always pleasant and I specifically couldn't get enough of Melanie. I couldn't quite figure her out. She was obviously flirting with me, even though she was with Alfred and did so even when he was present. I was very fond of him and resented her flirting a bit, although I was flattered and certainly had a crush on her; she was very lovely and charming. Tricky, I thought.

Which it also was losing weight. I read in my diary that during the Lamu period I seriously tried to lose weight. I didn't understand how I could have gained weight. I thought I had hardly eaten anything since Stockholm, but apparently what little I had eaten was the wrong stuff. A lot of white bread in Ethiopia that had settled on my stomach. I had gained almost 10 kilos since I left. Weighed 80 kg instead of the match weight 70 (nowadays 80 is my match weight). So I tried to walk and swim every day and the food consisted mostly of vegetables, fruit and kebab sticks, so I probably lost a few kilos.

Several 'mzungus' became ill with stomach cramps and fever. Most likely the local water that did not agree with them. Many had come here more or less directly from Europe or the United States, so their bodies probably reacted unfavourably to new bacteria. It had happened to me in Egypt. Stan, for example, who also lived at New Shamuty, had flown here directly from Los Angeles and would fly back after the New Year. That sounded a bit crazy to me. But at least he managed to avoid stomach cramps. And he had money.

One evening he bought a couple of chickens and got two Indian guys from Nairobi, who were also staying at the hotel, to make a fantastic curry. They beheaded the chickens in the shower and we were standing on the roof looking down into the courtyard when the headless chickens came running out of the shower. Quite sickening. But the curry was wonderful! And there were many of us around the food, James and Stan, the Indians, as well as Alfred and Melanie and Basil, who all joined in. Nice evening on the roof of the hotel.

Then I finished *Anna Karenina*. What a novel! I still think it is one of the best books I have read, even in Swedish. I rejoiced with Levin and Kitty, suffered with Anna Karenina, how misunderstandings drive her to suicide, and marvelled at Tolstoy's incomparable knowledge of human nature. Is it possible to write better about love?

New Year's Eve was a quiet affair. No one on the island seemed to notice it. I had now also suffered from stomach cramps. When I went out early to the beach beyond Peponi's hotel to swim, I suddenly vomited. Turned around and went to bed in the shade on the roof of Shamuty. Fell asleep and woke up a few hours later feeling incredibly well. I was grateful, went down to the quay where I sat at the New Star restaurant overlooking the harbour and enjoyed myself. But I only dared to drink tea. Two guys in worn-out green coats with red stripes were sleeping over a couple of tables. They had probably been serving since early morning. The New Star was a popular breakfast spot. But I always broke my fast at the hotel every morning.

At night a large group of us ended up on the roof of Basil's house. Everyone slept over to see the moonrise, high as the palm trees from all the weed smoking. We lay on the roof and discussed whether we believed that someone actually had been up there, walking around and soiling the moon. None of us believed this insane allegation in the state we were in.

When I got home the next morning I went to bed and managed to sleep some, although it was difficult as it was too hot once the sun rose, even though I was in the shade on the roof. And the sun rose every day without a hint of clouds.

One night I decided to sleep out in the sand on the island. I took my sleeping bag and hiked out to Shela beach. There I first sat in the moonlight, enjoying the silence and the sound of the waves and the whispering of palms; a silence I broke with some blowing on my recorder. I then found a soft little pit up among the dunes, where I was protected from the wind and crawled into my sleeping bag to fall asleep. But soon I woke up with a howl. Large red ants with gigantic fangs had invaded my sleeping bag and bitten into my poor physique. It hurt terribly. Once up and out of the sleeping bag, I jumped around like a screaming lunatic trying to brush off the horrible insects. But it wasn't easy. With their large fangs, they were firmly embedded in my skin and I had to tear them off one by one, which hurt as hell. And it took its time in the dark as there were probably more than 30 evil ants wedged in to my body. Nightmarish and defeated I staggered back to the town and the hotel.

142

I had inquired about returning to Mombasa on a dhow. A few days before New Year, some people from New Shamuty had managed to join a dhow to Mombasa, which sounded wonderful and exciting. I also wanted to. On the fourth, a dhow would depart and I managed to buy a place on it. It made me really happy. And I had started to get a little tired of Lamu. Sure, it was beautiful and everyone was nice, the food good, the grass free and the water and waves fantastic. But even this became an everyday, and it was not to experience everyday I started traveling.

Alfred and Melanie had now come across a house that they would rent for a month, to start with. Apparently Mike and Debbie had lived in that house when they were here earlier. Now they had flown to Israel, I knew. Anyway, Alfred and Melanie threw a housewarming party. There weren't many of us so I ended up sitting with Alfred and Melanie all evening. They were really pleasant. It was impossible not to like Alfred, big and fluffy and ready to laugh with kind eyes in a red face with a potato nose, framed by a big white hair and beard. A beautiful human being. Melanie was still cute and charming, a little too charming perhaps. Anyway, we ate well: tuna salad with freshly baked bread; they had even got hold of some wine. And grass. As usual.

The next afternoon, Melanie shows up alone. I'm reading *Player Piano* when she appears at the roof and asks if I want to go swimming at the Shela beach with her. Of course I do.

"But where is Alfred?" I ask.

"He is at home and not feeling well. Throwing up with stomach pains, like so many others."

So we march out through the city and past Peponis to Shela beach. I can't hide my joy at being alone with her, while feeling a little awkward without Alfred. And when she takes my hand and gives me a kiss, I say so.

"Come on, Erik. He knows I like you and doesn't mind if we're together."

"Ok," I mutter, not entirely convinced but happy just the same.

When we find a secluded spot, Melanie naturally strips naked and runs into the water. I hadn't expected that, standing there like a fool with my swimming trunks in my hand. But, of course, I follow her example and run naked into the waves. And she laughs when she sees that I can't hide my joy at seeing her naked.

Soon we are swimming side by side and when we can stand on the bottom again, she pulls me to her, wraps her legs around me and takes me inside her. I am as surprised as I am happy. Afterwards we walk up the dunes above the beach and make slow love on a kikoy once more. By then I have forgotten my misgivings and accept that Alfred may be sanctioning this. Melanie is a wonderful girl and it is impossible for me to resist her. Afterwards we take another bath to get rid of all the sand and almost make love again.

As we walk back to the town, I again feel a little awkward and wonder to myself if I would dare to see Alfred again. Melanie notices this and laughs at me. But I never saw Alfred again. Nor Melanie.

I was alone on the roof now. Both Stan and James left after New Year's. Ali, one of the guys who ran the hotel smoked marijuana constantly, morning, noon and night, and was generous with the product. He would always come up and smoke with us. Stan in particular was good at smoking a lot which is why Ali enjoyed it but now that it was just me on the roof he didn't show up that often. I usually settled for a joint or two in the evenings, while they would smoke all the time. This is also a part of Lamu colony that I grew tired of. Marijuana hardly makes you more energetic. But some days I had tried to smoke all day. For breakfast and lunch and afternoon tea and dinner and the evening snack. I did this for three days to see what the results would be: nought, was my comment in the diary. After that, the evening smoke was enough.

Sam was my favourite of the people working at the hotel. Now that I was alone, he would come up and join me for a nice chat. He was always happy. I don't think I've ever met a person who seems to be so happy and content all the time. He didn't smoke much weed, but instead chain-smoked some smelly local cigarettes: Sportsman. But he was nevertheless a nice guy.

On January 4, I turned 20, and at 8:30 AM I left Lamu on the Jamhuri, a dhow. We were nine 'mzungus,' including Rick, with whom I had attended the Urhuru celebrations in Nairobi. There were seven crew members and it would take about 24 hours to sail to Mombasa. Although I wanted to leave, I felt a bit sad to leave Lamu; would I ever return? I didn't think so, and I never did, despite living several years in

Kenya. Flaubert calls it "mélancolies de voyage" in a letter home from Egypt: leaving a place you have enjoyed and knowing you will never return. The melancholy of travel that I mostly without thinking got used to.

On the dhow between Lamu and Mombasa.

The Jamhuri rolled comfortably in the waves. All that could be heard was the modest wind in the sail, the swell of the waves and the creaking and squeaking of the boat. There were no nails on the boat, it was all wood and rope. The toilet was a revelation. A little square box had been built over the port stern where you stepped out and crouched behind its little railing and did your business which disappeared straight into the sea below.

Besides us passengers, the boat was loaded with dried fish that smelled quite bad. But it tasted good. For lunch and dinner they offered boiled rice and some of the dried cargo. Most of us passengers, including Erik, had brought some of our own food. Mostly fruit and bread and drinks. In other words, no one starved. A memorable 20th birthday!

We sailed all the time near the coast of Kenya. Malindi we passed in the early evening, which was very clear with its shiny hotels and city lights. Sleeping was not that easy. We crawled into our sleeping bags or the blankets we had with us and did the best we could on the bales of dried fish. I had a freshly washed sleeping bag (and now ant-free) so put the rain poncho over the fish and then the sleeping bag. But it was not comfortable. Woke up often to change position.

At half past five we were all awake when the sun woke us up. We were all damp and cold, but the rising sun changed that immediately. However, it was calm; we just lay and rocked. No wind. The sail hung limply. And almost total silence. A magical monotony between sky and sea, as Joseph Conrad describes it somewhere. The sea was like a mirror and we did not move any. Without an engine there was of course nothing to do but wait for wind. And eventually we got some, but just a small breeze; it was very slow sailing.

The closer we got to Mombasa, the more crowded the coast was with tourist hotels and several boats with bathing and fishing tourists came out towards Jamhuri and photographed the beautiful dhow. We also saw dolphins and schools of flying fish soaring by at breakneck speed. Since we hardly moved, we asked the captain if we could jump in for a swim, which he said was fine and hung a rope ladder from the boat. But just as we were about to dive in, we saw a big shark that appeared right next to us. No one went swimming after that.

At three pm we finally docked at the marina in old Mombasa. And at six I took a night bus to Nairobi together with Rick.

Nairobi

Back in Nairobi again. Much has been written about the city. Karen Blixen has given both a romantic and realistic picture of Nairobi in *The African Farm*. Probably the best book by a Westerner about Kenya, although there are many to choose from. Negley Farson calls the city the Paris of Africa in his fine travel book *Behind God's Back*, from 1940. Here he describes the continental atmosphere of all the cafés and bars and how Westminster's edicts most often are ignored. The city was, from a European perspective, for long a home to shadowy figures who could make a comfortable life for themselves here, far from European justice. You can also sense this in Blixen's book and Elspeth Huxley's *My African Childhood*. Of course, this is not the case today, nor was it in 1971.

If you want to get a picture of a more contemporary Nairobi, Binyavanga Wainaina's *One Day I Will Write About This Place* is a good choice, and perhaps Mukoma wa Ngugi's *Nairobi Heat*, or all his father's books set in Nairobi, especially *The Wizard of the Crow*. None of this had I read when I again woke up one morning in my sleeping bag on the ground in the hostel's garden.

During the three months I spent bumming around East Africa, Nairobi became a bit of a hub for me, along with Moshi. I was also in Mombasa a few times but always tried to shorten the stay. So not in Nairobi. I enjoyed the city and did the same when I lived there in the late 70s, but not so much in the 2000s.

In the 1970s, the New Stanley Hotel on the corner of Kimathi and Kenyatta Streets and its Thorn Tree café was at the heart of the city's daily social activities, at least for those with a little money. When I was in town, I often found myself sitting in the café, meeting friends and making new acquaintances. The acacia tree that grew up through the roof in the middle of the café served as a bulletin board. There you posted requests for rides or friends.

Six years later, when I was living in Nairobi, or more precisely in Limuru, north of the city a little further out than the hostel, by the Tigoni Tea Estate, the hotel bar upstairs at the New Stanley was the meeting place, alongside the Norfolk Hotel of course. I was then living with an

English family who had lived in Rhodesia and Kenya since World War II. They belonged to a unique and exciting British colonial class that moved between safaris and country clubs, and subscribed to *Blackwood's Magazine*. Many of them were wonderful people, particularly the family I stayed with, and loved Kenya, even if "it was a bit too black," as one elderly lady put it when we visited her large villa in the Karen suburb. Most were proud of the British Empire, now a little dejected that it had been reduced to a Commonwealth, and as Wilfred Thesiger (whom I once met in the bar at the New Stanley) puts it in his memoir of his years in Kenya, almost paraphrasing Marlow in *Heart of Darkness*: "I am convinced that no empire in world history has been its equal in humanity and benign dedication to the welfare of its subjects." And while this may be true, it is certainly impossible to turn a blind eye to the exploitation, political injustice and fundamental racism of pre-Uhuru British Kenya. Somewhat surprisingly, Hannah Arendt seems to agree with Thesiger in her *The Origins of Totalitarianism*. But there are degrees, or rather circles, even in hell, Dante taught us.

East of Tom Mboya Street was the more Kenyan Nairobi. This is where you found the cheap restaurants. When I ate in town, it was always here, affordable even for me and always good. The atmosphere here was completely different from the other side of Tom Mboya. Back then, in the early 70s, it was safe to move around here as a European, you were never worried. I was back late one evening in 2004 when I arrived by bus from Dar es Salaam, terrified until I found a taxi to my hotel.

But Nairobi was a great city in 1971 and walking around the central areas, around Mama Ngina Street was pleasant. The post office on Kenyatta Avenue was a regular destination. When I arrived from Serengeti, beginning of December, there were several letters waiting for me, including from some classmates from high school and friends from Högdalen. And, of course, a couple from my mother; my father had also written a page. I see in the diary that I valued their letters the most and reread them several times.

It was still the hostel that was the centre and home for me every time I was in Nairobi. I got there quickly with bus no. 2 from the Globe roundabout. I always slept outside in the garden and used the facilities the hostel offered. However, I preferred to shower at the YMCA down

148

in Uhuru Park. You could sneak in and pretend you lived there and get a nice hot shower, which I often did when I was downtown.

At the hostel you also met many types of travellers. I remember a funny guy from Alaska who was almost impossible to understand. His dialect was strange and he talked faster than a Spaniard. One day four Swedes came by and camped in the garden. They had driven down through the Sahara and across northern Congo to East Africa. It was exciting to hear their account as I intended to partly take the same route, but in the other direction. During a few days, an obnoxious American also lived there, who constantly pestered everyone about how fantastic the United States was; big and beautiful, clean and tidy, very unlike this miserable Kenya. Painful to listen to and I wondered why he was traveling. Everyone soon avoided his America-conceited nonsense.

The evenings were always pleasant. During the days people disappeared in different directions, mostly of course down to Nairobi. But in the evenings we gathered in the large common room and its table or, weather permitting, out in the courtyard around a fire - or at Arthur's. There was persistent marijuana smoking every evening so you didn't have to puff on your own joint, but one could just sit and breathe. Often someone had a tape recorder with music or a guitar. Information was exchanged about travel destinations and where you could live cheaply and well, eat well, get a lift and what you should avoid. Often there were even political discussions in which I enthusiastically participated.

One December evening I sat at the small desk in the house and wrote in my diary. The large table was full of people from all over the world talking about travel and politics and faecal crises. Nadia from Australia had bought a cassette recorder to take to India on her way home. She claimed she would get paid well for it in India. Now she was playing Bob Dylan. A couple of German guys were playing chess in a corner. Some young local boys, who often came to visit, stood just inside the door and looked at us curiously. Three Japanese kept to themselves, planning in front of an Africa map. The air was thick with marijuana.

On another evening described in my diary, a mountaineer was sitting next to me at the table, working on his equipment. He was going to climb Mount Kenya the next day, he told me. He was Italian, so here I have to mention Felice Benuzzi's book *No Picnic on Mount Kenya*. In it, Benuzzi narrates how he and two other Italian prisoners of war escaped from the British prison camp next to Mount Kenya in 1943, only to climb it and then return to the camp afterwards. Worth reading!

Peter, from the Netherlands, who was sitting at the same table, told us how he hiked up Mt Kenya last week:

"I slept the night before at Naro Moru Lodge and after a delicious hotel breakfast I quickly got a lift to the road up the mountain and the national park. I walked on and soon came to the park boundary in the bamboo forest. There they stopped me. Under no circumstances was I allowed to continue alone. 'The forest is full of elephants and buffalo and walking alone is dangerous. There must be at least two of you if one gets hurt.' So I had to turn back. Disappointed and angry. But on the way down I met a car with two German guys going up. I managed to persuade them to give me a lift up and say that I was with them, that we were to hike together. That's how I entered the park. Just after the gate they dropped me off and I walked further up through the forest to some simple huts where I could sleep. I had brought some food and water and had a simple little meal. There were no mattresses but bunk beds where I climbed up into one and down into my sleeping bag. I hardly slept though; it was a bitter cold. My sleeping bag was absolutely not made for that kind of temperature."

"I know what you mean; I almost froze to death at night on Kilimanjaro," I added.

"So I woke up early and ate some biscuits and bananas. Then I started out. I had decided to walk as far as I could until noon and then turn back. I have no equipment or knowledge for technical climbing, which is needed to reach the summit of the mountain. With the sun in my eyes, I continued my hike. First it was through moss-covered forests on a wide path that looked excavated. And suddenly I smell cows, cattle. Strange. And then I hear a grunting of a kind. I shade my eyes and see a lone buffalo bull standing on the path about 10 meters in front of me. I know that they are considered the most dangerous animals in Africa. My heart probably missed a few beats and now I understand why I shouldn't be alone. What should I do now? I don't dare to move, but I see that there are roots hanging from the edge of the excavated path next to me. Quick as a flash I grab a couple of them and swing myself up above the path. The buffalo got scared and threw himself over and ran down the other side of the path. There we lay staring at each other. But what should I

150

do now? Turn down, or continue up? If I went down, might I not meet him again? Up, maybe there is a whole herd of buffalo? Where I'm hiding, I don't see or hear any other animals, so I decide that up is probably the best option. Plucked up my courage and climbed further up through the landscape, which now became grasslands with lots of lobelia plants before the steep parts with snow. At 12 I reached the first snow. I ate some chocolate, an apple and drank some water, looked at all the rock hyrax sitting in the sun on the boulders around me. Then I went down, which was quick and without any buffalo encounter. When I crossed the border, the guards, who were not the same as the day before, were surprised and wondered why I was alone. I blamed altitude sickness and they were even nice enough to drive me down to Naru Moru Lodge; I was definitely not allowed to walk alone through the forest down to the A2, they said. The next day I took the bus to Nairobi. I guess I was a bit stupid to hike up the mountain by myself."

"I was just as stupid," I said. "Went up Kilimanjaro alone, although I had company for a few days on the way up, but down I went alone."

"Insane!" we both laughed at each other.

The climate in Nairobi, which means 'cold' in Maa, the Maasai language, was, and still is, wonderful. Warm sunny days and cool nights. And I wore both socks and a cotton hat when I slept outside. No mosquitoes or flies to bother me. The best with sleeping outside was waking up. I usually awoke just before the sun reached me through the trees. There was a sudden stillness, as if nature was holding its breath and the birds were waiting for the sun, paused and when it finally arrived, they started singing again. I always remained a while in my sleeping bag with only my head sticking out, enjoying the early mornings. Then the pigeons began 'poabing' intensely. A sound I always associate with East Africa, even though they 'poa' just as intensely in Sweden. The smell of dew in the grass and leaves and flowers, the sound of some people starting to cook breakfast in the kitchen, others getting out of their sleeping bags or their tents, the occasional car passing by.

When I finally crawled out it was cold and I quickly got dressed. Rolled up my sleeping bag and poncho, and put everything in the house before I often went down to Arthur's for breakfast. There I frequently met someone who joined me during the day. There was a small forest if you continued up the road towards Limuru where a group of colobus monkeys lived. You could easily see them because of their long black and white fur and tail, sitting or jumping around high up in the canopy. The forest was also full of stunningly beautiful birds, including several shimmering sunbirds sucking nectar from flowers. A small excursion I made many times after breakfast.

I often took the bus down to Nairobi. Money from home, 1000 SEK, was again on its way and I needed to get visas for the rest of the trip. There were a few countries I was planning to pass through, and it always took at least a day to get a visa. First Zambia, then Congo, Central African Republic, Cameroon and Nigeria. I had to get these visas before moving on and it was expensive. But they are beautiful. Especially the CAR and Cameroon visas, which I bought at the French embassy, with three nice stamps adorning pages 20 and 21 of my 1969 passport. My diary says that I paid about 30 shillings per visa. But I had now managed to increase my travel funds in a rather cunning, if also deceitful way.

After reporting the theft of my traveller's checks to the police, I went to the bank and reported the same, with a certificate from the police. Then it took a few days for the bank to issue new ones. But I hadn't been robbed. Instead, it was all a manoeuvre to increase my travel funds on the black market, and to have enough money to satisfy border guards. Half of what I 'lost' I kept, remembering the events in Moyale and Namanga. Half I sold on the black market unsigned and made 500 shillings in one go, while the bank gave me new checks. Neat, but hardly legal.

It was to Hank, as he called himself, that I sold my 'stolen' checks; an Indian Kenyan, who showed up almost daily at the hostel or Arthur's to change money. Previously, I had once changed with Kenyan Asians downtown, but after a story Bill told, it was Hank who got my unsigned traveller's checks, although his rate was a little less than downtown. But safe and reliable.

Bill told me how he almost lost 100 US, when he had just arrived in Nairobi and was about to change on the black market without really having any idea where:

"At the Thorn Tree I ask around, like, and a couple of guys promise to help me. We enter a business building on Kaunda Street – I now know it was - and up half a flight of stairs above the elevator foyer, like. There some more guys show up and one of them says he wants to see my money, like. Then I want to see his as well, I say. Which I get, whereupon I show my 100US$, like. Then some more guys come running up the stairs, like, yelling and screaming and wondering if we're doing something fishy. When I sort of freeze in surprise, the guy with the money snatches mine out of my hand and runs down the stairs. The others close around me, like, but I had a small umbrella with me that I swing, like, and hit some of them in the head, like, so I get past them. I jump down the stairs instead of running and then out on Kaunda where I see him running. I scream: catch the thief! as loud as I can, like, and then I see that he realizes that the game is lost, like. He slows down and starts to take my money out of his back pocket, like, when an older guy somehow trips him and then sits on him. I catch up with them and then the guy already has my dollars out, which I immediately take. They ask me if we should call the police, like, but I say it's not necessary. Completely bushed, I then go to the New Stanley and order a double whiskey. After that I of course enter a bank and change my dollars. But once here I've of course used Hank."

In Nairobi, I also visited the city library where I could sit in peace and quiet and read. Outside on the street they sold second-hand literature, including East African literature in English. One day I bought a bunch of African novels from these sidewalk book venders. I then sent them home in a book package, together with some of the books I had read and wanted to save. But not the American Robert Ruark's *Uhuru*, and *Something of Value*, two at the time popular novels depicting the Mau Mau uprising in Kenya from a Western perspective. When I read them, I thought they were thrilling, but they have been rightly criticized by Kenyan writers and if one is interested in the events before Kenya's independence, it is better to read James Ngugi's (as the author was called then) fantastic novel *Weep Not, Child* from 1964.

I also visited the University of Nairobi. It was beautiful, next to, or rather opposite, the famous Norfolk hotel. However, its bookshop was not very impressive. And it was no better when I was back in 2002 to lecture on what makes an oral statement into orature (oral literature). The teachers and professors I met then told me that when they teach a novel, such as Ngugi's best novel *The River Between*, they may only have a couple of copies to share among the students. Each student has to finish it in a few days and then lend it to the next student and so on. It is difficult to have seminars on a text under such conditions.

In 2002 I gave a lecture on oral literature in Africa to teachers and professors at the university. But even more fun was the lecture I got to give at the Gikuyu campus north of the city. Professor Chesira invited me to lecture to his Masters students. We sat in a half-finished large building, in one corner where there were walls that shielded us from the cold wind. Chesira had said that his students were probably more interested in why I, a Swedish literary scholar, had become interested in African literature. So that's what I told them about: the first year I hitch-hiked around Africa in 1971; that I then came to live in Kenya for two years in the late 70s; that I entered the post-graduate program at the Department of Literature at Stockholm University and with simple arithmetic added up my interests: Africa + literature = African literature and that I came to defend my dissertation on the Ghanaian writer Ayi Kwei Armah, but now did research within a large world literature project and wrote, among other things, about literariness in the East African orature. It was a great afternoon. They, only young men in white shirts, were curious, inquisitive and unafraid to ask questions: the most rewarding and enjoyable lecture I have given!

I read in my diary that one evening at the hostel I made Swedish blood pudding for dinner. Apparently I had bought this in Nairobi, and together with garlic sausage and cabbage it became a remarkably good dinner. I offered generously, but no one wanted the blood pudding. But where on earth had I found the blood pudding?

It was also time to get a new cholera shot. I had taken the first dose in Stockholm, but now it was time for a refill six months later. With my yellow vaccination booklet, I walked into the City Council one day, where I was told that I could get a new injection. Which I did without any problems for 5 shillings. Now I was protected for another six months.

Some days I stayed at the hostel. If I cooked my own breakfast, I spoke with other travellers, some who had stayed here for months. I also got to know Josef a bit. He showed up every morning and cleaned up after we all had breakfast. And then he came in the evenings to collect the fee for the accommodation. The nicest guy in the world.

154

Other mornings I sat at Arthur's, reading, writing letters or my diary and sipping tea or coffee. Quite often little boys would come in and stare curiously. Sometimes they bought a cookie for 10 cents each. I could then be seized with some sadness at the state of the world, but was usually interrupted by happiness, whereupon I bought them cakes for a few shillings. Of course I was tight-fisted, but I could afford a few cakes.

When it rained, the hostel was not a pretty sight. One night it started pouring down around two. Everyone sleeping outside rushed inside and lay down on the floor and some on the tables. The breakfast scene the next day was a messy affair. Muddy water outside and the same inside. And everywhere mattresses and wet blankets and sleeping bags to dry.

Another day, Anthony, a Brit I'd spent some time with, and I decided to visit Nairobi National Park. We took two early buses to the park gate on Langata Road. First we convinced the guards that we worked in the country and got in cheaply on citizen's rate. Then we sat down and waited for someone who might want to pick us up. The park is not big, but there are almost all the animals of the savannah except elephants. It is fenced towards the city but then it is open towards the savannah south of Nairobi.

Soon a car stopped and picked us up. It turned out to be two Swedes from Stockholm who had decided to drive around the park in the morning before flying home in the evening. We saw both lions and rhinoceros that morning and I gave them my parents' phone number. They promised to call the next day. And so they did; they told mom and dad that I looked fine and that I had "become a bit chubby," as my mother put it in the next letter.

After a quick samosa lunch at a simple eatery by the park gate, we got a ride in the afternoon with an Indian father and his son in a jeep. The son was practicing driving. That was the purpose of their tour in the park. A little strange but it went well and we stopped by a small natural pool where there were both hippo and crocodile. So a successful day, both Anthony I thought, whereupon we ended it with a luxurious dinner at New Stanley. And a lovely visit to their clean and nice toilet. I had once again developed some faecal problems. Either I couldn't shit at all or it just ran out of me. Going to a clean toilet with a chair where I could sit for a while was a blessing. The restaurant visit was not only about eating well, but also about shitting well.

That I had gained weight was not something I was blind to either, even if surprised to read about it in a letter from mom. When I showered at the YMCA and saw myself naked in the mirrors, it was not a pretty sight. As if that wasn't enough, one day my jeans split in the buttocks and had to be thrown away. Even if they could be repaired - and there were plenty of skilled and willing tailors in Nairobi - they were simply too small now. I ended up buying a new and slightly more generous pair. Later, after Lamu, I had actually lost a few kilos.

One morning when I was going down to the city, I hitchhiked at the bus stop close to the hostel. And suddenly a car stopped and I was going to run after it but then suddenly and incomprehensibly one of my legs gave way. I fell flat on the asphalt and banged up one knee and one hand. However, I went downtown and got off at Uhuru Park and went to the YMCA. There I was able to wash the wounds with hot water as best I could. After doing my errands, mail, bank and visa, it was bus number 2 again up to the hostel. There I was helped to properly wash my wounds. Asphalt gravel in especially the right palm that required tweezers to remove. But it came to plague me for several days; fingers and parts of the hand swelled up so I could hardly write. At least it wasn't infected.

I also visited the Swedish Embassy a lot when I was in Nairobi, of course, although they rarely had up-to-date newspapers. The one in Dar was better equipped with the daily press. I wondered why?

I went to the movies a few nights. It was cheap and a way to kill a couple of evenings while waiting for visa and money from home. I saw *Diamonds Are Forever*, which had its world premiere in Nairobi. Apparently this was not unusual. They wanted to see how it was received in a sufficiently 'civilized' city before screening it in the US and Europe. And going to the movies in Kenya was different. It all started with the flag being displayed on the screen and the national anthem being played and everyone standing up. Then there were commercials. Then local Kenyan news, mainly about what President Kenyatta had been up to. Then commercials again. Then a children's cartoon. Then more commercials. Then trailers about upcoming attractions. And finally, after an hour or so, the main attraction that we had paid for began.

Another popular activity in Nairobi was the Ambassador Hotel's weekend lunch buffets. You could eat as much as you wanted. I don't remember how much it cost and haven't written it in my notes. But it can't have been expensive since we could afford it. You just had to wear cleaner and nicer clothes. Often we sent some people down from the hostel to eat and smuggle food in plastic bags from the buffet. It worked nicely.

I read in my notes, though, that I preferred to eat at a Kenyan or Indian restaurant across Tom Mboya Street: a huge plate of meat and potatoes and a small plate of vegetables, a chapati and all for 2.50 shillings. Then I often sat at the Thorn Tree with a coffee and socialized and looked at beautiful girls. And here you met everyone: Clint, an Irishman who had been on one of the trains in Sudan. He was now working as a hairdresser at the Hilton hotel in town. Wilma, who had been on the dhow and was now flying to London. Shirley, British, who had worked at the Sheraton in Stockholm and was now looking for a hotel job here in Nairobi. Rick, Joe and everyone else, including Kathy and Patrik on their way to South Africa..

Another day, as I sat there sipping on a cup of coffee, I heard someone happily shout: "Erik!". It was Debbie and Mike. It was a fond reunion; we had not seen each other for a couple of months. They had just arrived from Lamu after a month or so in a house there. I was then on my way to Lamu and happy to hear all the good things they had to say about the island. In two days, they were flying to Israel to work on a kibbutz for six months before returning home. When we parted, I promised to get in touch when I made it to the US. Which I did.

One morning in January, a couple of journalists from *The Daily Nation* turned up at the hostel to interview some of us. There had been a lot in the press about horrible hippies living in the hostel, smoking marijuana and corrupting the fine Kenyan youth. Anthony and I hitched a ride with them down town while they questioned us and took pictures, but we didn't want to give them our names. I never saw an article but knew that much was written about the hostel, and there were rumours that authorities wanted to close it.

Not only were there nasty rumours about all the creepy hippies up at the hostel, there were also thefts. Ellen had £5 stolen, May several clay pots she was going to fly home with and an American couple their backpacks. All in one night. The police arrived. They questioned everyone and announced that on Saturday, January 15, the hostel would be closed for good.

The next morning a camera had disappeared and the police showed again. This time they were really angry, not with us Westerners but with the staff. Josef and another guy who helped him at the hostel were beaten and taken down to Nairobi. We felt this was deeply unfair. Of course, any of us travellers could just as well be the camera thief. But if they were to arrest any of us, it could be complicated with embassies involved, so easier to get the local guys.

The next day, however, Josef returned. He was slightly bruised but no longer a suspect, but the other guy was. "He was the one who stole the camera. I know that," Josef said. "Dumb ass, now he's going to jail and they're not pretty. They almost killed him when they questioned us."

The atmosphere in the hostel was now at its lowest. Many long-time guests had already left and Josef didn't know what to do next. Arthur was also worried about his future. Hank was going to Arusha and not coming back: he was, rumours had it, involved in a diamond smuggling deal, I wrote in my diary. Hitchhikers were also moving on. Chuck and Karin, who I met on the dhow, left for Uganda. I missed them as soon as they left. I felt a bit stranded, but had to stay as the money from home had not yet arrived. My hope was that they would arrive on Friday before the hostel closed.

Which they did. I even managed to buy Tanzanian shillings from Hank before he left us for good. That day I was downtown, visited the bank, read some newspapers at the embassy, showered hot at the YMCA so I would be clean and nice when I left tomorrow. However, I had a big fat pimple right at the end of my spine, where the arse starts. Now I suspect it was a big fat haemorrhoid instead. When I showered, I tried to clean it as best as I could but it kept bursting and my underwear were soaked all the time. It also hurt to sit and would torment me for some time.

At the hostel they started throwing out furniture Friday afternoon and the evening became very low-spirited. Admittedly, they would tomorrow open a new hostel further up the road, towards Limuru, but it could not replace this one. Especially as there would not be a campsite, but just a big house without a plot. And like many hostels, closed several hours during the day. 'Our' home had never cared about that. Here you were welcome all hours of the day.

158

I spent the evening with Ben, a Scotsman I first met in Khartoum, and a few others at Arthur's. Arthur would try to lure guests down from the new hostel, or see if he could open a place nearby. He was worried but obviously had ideas. The next morning I had breakfast with him again and then an emotional farewell.

On January 12th it was six months since I had left Högdalen and three days later, on January 15th, I started my journey home after more than three months in East Africa. Now it was the Congo River and the Sahara that tempted me. "The name Sahara sounded in my ear indescribably fascinating, indescribably romantic, indescribably exciting," as Eva Dickson wrote when she decided, in Nairobi, in 1932, after a bet, to drive alone (together with Hassan Ali, her 'boy') in a Chevrolet to Stockholm, which she wrote about in *En Eva i Sahara* (An Eva in Sahara).

Likasi

I was again in Moshi and stayed a couple of nights with Charles and Jack. But on January 18th (my brother's 19th birthday!) Charles' sister and her husband, who had been visiting, although staying in a hotel in Moshi, were going to Dar and I could join them in their car. I got off at Chalinze, where the A7 turns off towards Zambia. They had a Peugeot, so my rump problems did not bother me much. It would get worse. But it took time. Many Zambian-registered trucks passed by with lone drivers who just shook their heads when I energetically waved my thumb. I guessed that they were forbidden to pick up passengers. Unusual, because everywhere since Asmara trucks had always been full of people in and on the vehicles, which meant a little extra income for the drivers. Quite a few Chinese trucks also passed me by; they did not pick me up either. This was not so surprising.

It took almost two hours before a Land Rover stopped, which is not long on most roads in Africa, but here the traffic was busy, so it felt long. The guy in the jeep worked in Mikumi National Park and when we got there, we entered the park and took a little tour at his expense before it closed. The rainy season was over and everything was intensely green and lush. We saw mostly impala and elephants, which seemed to dominate this part of the park. There were of course other animals as well before it got dark and we had to leave the park and drive to the small town of Mikumi. There he treated us to dinner: grilled chicken and a Tusker before heading home. Yet another kind soul whose name I can't remember. I was able to stay in a sort of simple hotel next to the restaurant for 17 shillings, including mosquito a net, for which I was grateful. However, my pimple/haemorrhoid bled all night. I slept with toilet paper in my briefs, so the sheets were fine, but it worried me; should I see a doctor? Of course I didn't want to, and didn't, instead I decided to wait it out. I felt pretty miserable. And now alone again. But also this night I finally fell asleep.

It took more than five hours the next morning before I got a ride to Iringa. With a truck whose seats were rock hard, tormenting my bleeding arse throughout the journey. Tough. I sometimes forgot about it as the Rubehoberg chain was beautiful after the rains with a wild exuberant

160

greenery. Not as many animals as in Mikumi or up in northern Tanzania, but magnificent views of mountains and river valleys reminiscent of northern Ethiopia. In my diary I wrote that it was the most beautiful landscape I had ever seen. I remember it that way too. And it pleased me that it was slow going. Often there were long and slow hills that all the trucks struggled up in the lowest gears. The roads were also fantastic. The asphalt was without treacherous potholes and with two lanes up the hills so that the faster traffic could get past the heavy trucks, which still dominated the traffic. Italians had built the road, I was told.

"They are good people. While the Americans are lazy but have lots of money to spend," the driver said. "But we don't like the Chinese. Sure, they are hardworking and build the railroad quickly. But they keep to themselves, don't spend any money and don't employ a single person. They even bring their own cooks with them. I guess they think African food is poisonous. But governments in Africa like the Chinese. They make no demands for democracy, as the West and the World Bank do. The Chinese just want to do business; that's what Africa's rulers like, who are almost always ex-officers with no democratic notions."

"But not in Tanzania, right?"

"No, Nyerere is a civilian, he was a teacher. But the Chinese like him anyway. Although they don't seem to be able to laugh! Sad, dull people," the insightful driver continued.

Outside Iringa, I stayed in a small guest house next to a Chinese camp that puzzled me. It was surrounded by a high fence with barbed wire and guards at the gate. Why? It looked like a prison camp. I sneaked around the camp trying to make contact with someone but they just stared and grinned at me through the fence when I tried to speak to them. Odd. Were they worried that some Chinese would escape, or that some hippie or Tanzanian would get in to fraternize? Apparently they had been given strict instructions not to socialise with Westerners or Africans. Strange and appalling, I thought.

At the guest house, I met several Somali truck drivers who also resented the Chinese. They knew some about Sweden and our prime minister. They praised both. This came to pass in those days, as mentioned, when politics in Sweden was fundamentally about solidarity. Also in Sweden: "A sacred universal public sector," as the Swedish poet Bodil Malmsten once wrote beautifully about our welfare. A welfare we now have dismantled in favour of venture capitalists, whom we always have to choose between; it's called freedom. What is wrong with the freedom of not having to choose? And now it has become apparent that it was the freedom of the venture financiers that mattered most. The rest of us are all supposed to be customers, also school pupils and hospital patients, and if you have no purchasing power, you are uninteresting. Correction is demanded from the poor and the meek: everyone should be their own boss, according to the neoliberal doctrine. Disgusting!

Well, well. The night at the guesthouse was, if not disgusting so miserable. I shared a room with a snoring Tanzanian and a rat scratching the wall next to my pillow. It was also sticky, humidly hot and millions of mosquitoes constantly wanted to get at my blood. Woke up, because I had apparently fallen asleep at last, all wet and itchy all over from all the mosquito bites. And bleeding in my ass. Changed the paper in my underpants before getting dressed and leaving.

I got a ride on a truck loaded with gasoline drums on its way to the copper mines in Zambia. The driver saw that I was tired, so he let me climb into the bed behind the seats and rest a bit. Soft and comfortable. I lay down reading *Seven Years in Tibet*, by Heinrich Harrer, which I had gotten hold of somewhere. Outstanding reading. He, the driver, not Harrer, also shared the food he had and when we stopped for the night outside Mbeya, I could spread my sleeping bag on the flatbed of the truck.

I didn't sleep much though. The gasoline barrels were far from comfortable to lie on and the boil on my ass was bothering me terribly. So, when the sun rose, I was grateful that it was time to move on. Soon we were at the border and in Zambia. However, customs had a lot of strange forms for me to fill out, which took a while. When they asked me about my return trip, I showed them my traveller's checks instead, both valid and invalid, which impressed them. I was welcome into Zambia.

But not welcome to continue with the truck. Just after the border we were stopped by a police check. A particularly unpleasant officer said that no passengers in trucks or lorries are allowed. When I asked why, he just shouted at me: "When I tell you to get out you get out, and no whys!" Nothing to do, even though the driver gently expressed his regrets without annoying the uniform.

I was joined by a Canadian, Dale, and an American girl, Jane, who had suffered the same fate. We walked far away from the border town to get a ride without any cops seeing us. But it took time. And soon it started to rain. We sat under our rain ponchos, or in their case plastic bags, and waited by the road. I was apparently playing on my recorder, so I wrote later.

Dale and Jane in the rain.

After a couple of hours, a Tanzanian truck that already had three passengers in its cabin stopped. But they crowded together so we, grateful and wet, could also squeeze in. We drove to Mpika, where we arrived after sundown. Now the country was completely different. Deserted, dry and completely without life as it seemed. In East Africa there were villages and settlements everywhere, and if not, it was full of antelopes, zebras and other game. Not so here, but from time to time there were still young children selling mangoes along the road. I did not see any houses or villages or mango trees so did not understand where they or their fruits came from. But of course we stopped and bought the world's most delicious fruit.

At night we spread out in and on the car. The driver, Ali and his helpers in the cabin; Ali in the bed, one guy on the floor and the other in one of the seat. The other seat an Mzee, an old man who never moved or said anything, slept. We, Westerners climbed onto the flatbed to sleep and it became a pleasant night. We lay and talked well into the small hours. A wonderful way to fall asleep when you don't have a reading lamp, and I forgot for a moment the pain and leak in my toilet paper stuffed underpants.

The next morning I could sneak around the truck and change the paper in peace; life was hard sometimes! But when we moved on, Jane and I were offered to crawl up into the bed behind the seats in the driver's cabin. I didn't mind this at all, as she was a sweet girl from Wisconsin.

Also on this day we were stopped at a police checkpoint. The officers went through our international passports, screamy and grumpy. They tried to find something wrong with our visas, but soon turned their attention elsewhere. The assistant rider, or mechanic or whatever he was, I think his name was Amid, apparently did not have a passport with him, so the police wanted to take him away. Ali managed to solve it with the predictable banknotes. Everyone was happy and we could move on. Zambia was obviously a bit different, or at least the attitude of the police towards their fellow humans, especially foreigners, whom they seemingly could not stand.

Zambia is named after the Zambezi River, I understand. Previously it was Northern Rhodesia, after the colonial crook Cecil Rhodes, and a British crown colony. The country does not have much more water than the river. One of its curses is that it is without a coastline: no harbour. When the white regime in Rhodesia declared independence in 1965, transport routes to the ports of South Africa were cut off. The railway to Dar es Salaam was embarked upon by the Chinese, and under construction now in 1972. President Kaunda, who had been in power since independence and of course graced the walls of every restaurant and official building, declared the country a one-party state that year and became increasingly despotic. However, he resigned voluntarily in 1991, something that was not so common in Africa in the second half of the 20th century.

Another curse of the country was and is its dependence on basically only one single natural resource: copper, although of course the country made a lot of money from the metal, or at least the already wealthy ones did. This means that the country's prosperity depends largely on the international price of copper. I was on my way to the copper belt now,

164

which is the economic artery of the country. It was home to 43,000 Europeans at independence and the copper mines were owned by international companies. In 1969, Kaunda nationalized the entire industry, but it is now partly privatized again. At the same time, much of the country is uncultivated, so Zambia suffers from the highest level of urbanization in Africa.

As with many countries in Africa, the population is young; the median age in 2017 (according to Wikipedia) was 16.8. It is also a very Christian country, initiated by David Livingstone when he explored and cleared the way for missionary work along the Zambezi River in 1851.

We continued south. Now the young Amid was outside on the flatbed as punishment. Evidently the engine had broken down outside Iringa in Tanzania, Ali told us, and it was Amid's fault. It took three weeks to fix. Ali had to go to Dar to get spare parts and Amid stayed with the truck to guard it. He was given a box of food and permission to sell some gasoline to get by for the three weeks. Apparently Amid sold 600 shillings worth and lived happily for three weeks, as best he could outside Iringa. Ali himself had spent 100 shillings in the same period in Dar. So he was pissed, which is why he occasionally punished the boy by putting him outside on the truck, preferably when it was raining. And now he sat there again. It didn't rain, but unlike in Ethiopia and the hills of Tanzania, where it was slow going, here Ali drove fast.

After an interesting gas stop in a Chinese camp, where, despite being inside the camp, it was impossible to make contact with any Chinese, we arrived late at Kapri Mposhi. There we slept again on the flatbed and the three of us again had a laughing good time before falling asleep. In the morning we found a modest restaurant where we managed some breakfast. Food on the road in Zambia had been a problem. Mostly white bread, washed down with brown water and the occasional mango. There were simply no villages or restaurants to stop at. But here we could get some toast and eggs.

When we got back to the truck, it had disappeared with all our luggage! We just stared at each other. "Surely he can't have run off with everything?" Jane said worriedly. Neither of us really believed that. Ali had been very kind so far. We sat down on a fallen log and waited. After half an hour we saw the truck driving towards us and we waved with relief and joy. But I had decided to skip the Victoria Falls, which I had been thinking about visiting. It was too expensive in Zambia. So I took my backpack off the truck and said goodbye to Ali, Dale and Jane and everyone else in the truck in Kapiri Mposhi. They were going to Lusaka and Dale and Jane to South Africa. I missed her immediately. I probably had a little crush on her. But now I turned north, so every step from now on was a step closer to Högdalen; it gave me some comfort, even though I was alone again. Which I felt. Jane was charming and I would have liked very much to continue traveling with her.

But soon I was picked up by a Toyota truck. I had to stand at the back between the flatbed and the cab, squeezed between chicken cages and the cab. Dangerous and windy, but good to stand for whatever it was that plagued my arse. It went well and soon we were on our way into Ndola. Before the city, two cantankerous policemen forced me off the car. They wanted to see my passport, my plane ticket, which I didn't have, and they got even more annoyed. My traveller's checks, however, calmed them down a bit. Instead they began going through my rucksack, throwing out large parts of my clothes on the ground. After a while they were evidently satisfied, even though I didn't offer them any money, and they left me alone, muttering. Why were the police here in Zambia so unpleasant, especially compared to all the others I had encountered in Africa? Neither then, nor now do I have an answer. Its colonial history is not so different from Tanzania's, so... Strange.

Ndola has gone down in world history: just outside Ndola, Dag Hammarskjöld, then Secretary-General of the United Nations, died in a plane crash on September 18, 1961. He was on his way to mediate between Congolese government forces and Tshombe's breakaway faction in Katanga province, which I was now entering. Since then, there has been speculation about the cause of the crash, and as recently as 2019, a Belgian mercenary was identified as having shot down the plane. But the question marks surrounding the 'accident' still outnumber the exclamation marks.

As I walked along the road, a guy in a car stopped and asked me if he could show me Ndola, of course he could. It turned out to be the most modern city I had seen in Africa, next to Nairobi. Clean sidewalks with street lights lining the streets, which in turn were surrounded by large,

166

modern houses. Chanda, as he was called, worked in the city's hospital, which he wanted to show me, obviously proud of it. Something I understood. Big and clean and, from what I could understand, well equipped. Then we ended it all with afternoon tea at some friends of his, in a garden with a pool and almost invisible staff serving tea and scones. There was a sense of affluence here, thanks to the copper, I presumed.

They asked me what I was doing; I told them and then asked them the same. Chanda worked in finance and administration at the hospital, while those we visited worked in the mining industry, or at least he did. The woman didn't say much, but was richly adorned. Then Chanda drove me out of town so I could continue hitchhiking. Which I immediately did with an Irishman to Kitwe-Nkana, in a car with seat belts! I think it was the first time I used one since Europe. In Nchanga he showed me the biggest copper mine in the world, or so he said - today I know there are several bigger ones. But it was an insanely large pit in the landscape. To my eyes it was unreal that people could dig such a large and deep whole - and so ugly! The trucks going up and down the winding roads along the walls of the mine looked like dinky toy cars.

It was clear that for most people here, copper represented their livelihood, and a prosperous one it seemed to be; I saw many Mercedes and Range Rovers. The houses were fancy, often behind walls with guards by the gates.

When we got to Chililabombwe, Dolan, as the Irishman was called, was going to visit several friends and I had to tag along. At one stop he exchanged a box of mangoes for oranges with an English family. We ended up with a Norwegian couple where he thought I could spend the night. And so I did. Not only that, I was allowed to immerse my filthy body in a tub of hot water. A wonderfully welcome bath. And I could clean the wound in my arse properly. It started to look better - I thought, because obviously I couldn't see it, but it felt better and the paper in my underwear was no longer as bloody and wet.

After a good dinner, where I ate unashamedly voraciously, we spent the evening in Scandinavian conversation in front of a small fire in the living room. They lived in a smaller house than most I'd seen since Ndola, but the two of them were alone so didn't need more. They still had a guest room, which I was to occupy. Both Harald and Marit worked

167

for an English-American mining company.

"But the Zambian state owns 51% of all the mining industry," Harald said. "President Kaunda pushed this through, after first having nationalized it all. And it's good for the country, but it means a lot of paperwork for people like us. Or rather for Marit who works in the office here. I'm an engineer, so I spend more time outside and at the drawing board."

"And we like it," said Marit. "We've been here for almost two years now, with one year left on the contract, so in a year's time we'll probably move back to Oslo again. But we are not sure we want to, so we'll see what happens, if we can extend our stay."

The next morning they served a delicious breakfast and I said goodbye, thanked them warmly and set off on the road to Lubumbashi and the Congo.

There I collapsed.

It was as if someone had stuck a knife in my stomach. And I dropped on the side of the road in agony. It wasn't long before people gathered around me and asked if they could help me.

"Doctor?"

"No need," I whispered. "Help me to my friends instead." With the help of some strong arms, I was able to stand up and suggested that it would be best if I could get to Harald and Marit's house again. They didn't live too far away so I could show them the way. A guy took my backpack while I hung between two strong shoulders and pointed where to go. It was slow going and it hurt all the time, but eventually we arrived at the house. I thanked the kind people who had helped me and knocked at the door.

Harald and Marit were of course at work, but their maid was at home and recognized me so I was allowed to crawl back into the same bed. She also called Marit who immediately came home. She was worried, but I reassured her that it was probably just a bit of food poisoning, or perhaps more likely the brown water I had been drinking along the roads in Zambia that made me sick.

"Anyway, you must stay here now until you get well. I'll make you some tea, and then I'll give you some medication for the stomach and aspirin." I refused neither one nor the other. After half a cup of tea and Marit's pills, I fell asleep and slept until they woke me up for dinner, which I managed to get some down.

168

I came to stay with them two more days. Mostly in bed. When I could, I finished Heinrich Harrer's fine book - a book I saved. Harald and Marit were infinitely kind and I felt safe in their home, even though I was weak and miserable. At the same time, I thanked the gods that I collapsed on the roadside in Chililabombwe, where a kind Norwegian couple lived. Thanks to their care, I was back on my feet again after two days.

"Are you sure you want to continue already?" Marit worried when I wanted to leave on the third morning. "You can stay as long as you want."

"Yes, I'm feeling great again. Thanks to your care and good food," I said, packing my things. "It was probably just a little food or water poisoning, which has now passed. But I couldn't have done it without you. So thank you very much," I hugged them as I left their house after another good and healthy breakfast. Today I wonder if they remember the hippie from Stockholm that they took care of a few days in 1972. I certainly remember them with warm gratitude.

Back on the road, I immediately got a lift with a jeep to the border with Congo, or Zaire as it was called then. No problems out of Zambia or into Congo. Since Moyale, I was always worried every time I crossed a border, even though I now had both a visa and a beautiful pack of useless traveller's checks!

I took a bus to Lubumbashi and then I got a ride to Likasi, from where I would take the train. It was just as modern and stylish this side of the border, all because of the copper. And just as green. As soon as the asphalt ended, the vegetation was rampant and wanted to take over. It was as if you could see how it fought against asphalt and cement. Of course, it will eventually prevail!

Here, between Lubumbashi and Likasi, the Congolese philosopher V. Y. Mudimbe walked one night in 1960, as the Belgian Congo, as he writes in *The Idea of Africa*, "got rid of its adjective." He reflected on his country's history and the fact that he could name both the colonial and traditional imprints he saw around him. He begins by stating that Africa is a colonial creation. When we say it was discovered in the 15th century, it is of course from a European the perspective: A European invention, as he writes in another important book. No people on the continent knew they were Africans, and no one called themselves that until the

20th century. Nor did they know that they belonged to a particular country. Nationalism is one of Europe's most successful and unfortunate exports since the 19th century. It can be interesting to contemplate about what Africa would have looked like without colonialism, without imperialism, if it had been allowed to develop independently in equal partnership with the rest of the world. We would probably have avoided the ugly face of racism, which chiefly is an invention of the West to justify the way it treated Africans, American Indians and other indigenous peoples who stood in its way. How else could people who called themselves good Christians treat other people the way they did?

Now it was French I had to speak. I had studied French as a third language in high school; since then I had only exposed myself to French a couple of times hitchhiking to the campsite in the Bois de Boulogne forest in Paris. But I had a miniature Swedish-French dictionary with me. I came to use it often, as from now on few people I met spoke English and certainly no one Swedish.

In Likasi, I first changed to the local currency, the zaire, which I recall was then worth about one Swedish krona. (Today they have Congolese francs since 1997.) After a visit to the bank, I asked around for the cheapest hotel in town. Found it. But it turned out to cost 25 zaire a night. Given that I had been living on just about this per day so far, I didn't want to pay that much for a bed. Instead, I went to a mission, as I had heard that you could often stay with missionaries in the Congo, especially if they were Western, as they rarely get European visitors.

I found a Methodist mission. Here the pastor was Congolese, but welcomed me nevertheless. He promised to let me stay with them until I took the train to Port-Francqui, from where there would be a riverboat to Kinshasa. But it wasn't Port-Francqui any longer, it had just changed its name to Ilebo. It was President Mobutu who had begun his 'Zaireination' of the country. Everything reminiscent of the Belgian era was renamed, including the country and all the towns and provinces. The Katanga province that I was now in was called Shaba, which it still is, while Zaire is once again called Congo (Kinshasa).

It was of course understandable that they wanted to erase traces of the Belgian period. At the Berlin Conference of 1884, the European colonial powers divided up Africa. Before that, there was little European presence on the continent except on the coasts. And there was a relatively short colonial rule in Africa, only 80 years: 1880 - 1960. Unlike in the Americas, where indigenous communities were virtually wiped out, African communities survived; they were apparently more resilient. But, as we know, societies did not fare well in Africa either; more than 10 millions Africans were slaved across the Atlantic to the Americas: The Middle Passage. Those that remained were often subjugated to racism, and worst of all in the Congo, which was given to King Leopold II of Belgium. He ruled the Congo Free State, as he called it, in an unusually brutal way, reducing the Congolese population by a third in slavery and murder, but making him insanely rich. (This is best disclosed in Adam Hochschild's fine book *The Ghost of King Leopold*, as well as in Per Erik Tell's book about the 522 Swedes in Leopold's service: *Detta fredliga uppdrag* [This Peaceful Mission].) Things didn't improve much when the country gained independence in 1960. Two political factions were immediately formed, ending with Mobutu Sese Seko Kuku Ngebendu Wa Za Banga seizing power in 1965 and holding on to it as cruelly and arbitrarily kleptocratic as Leopold, until 1997, when he fled to Morocco. Now, in 1972, he was portrayed everywhere on walls and banknotes in a silly leopard hat (looked like a night cap), but I didn't meet anyone who paid him the same tribute as Nasser in Egypt or Nyerere in Tanzania.

At the mission I was given my own room with a soft bed and a rattan reading chair. I suspected, I see in the diary, that Hosi Armando, as the pastor was called, had thrown some of his eleven children out of the room and given it to me. Made me a little uncomfortable, but the bed was comfortable and Hosi insisted.

I wanted to be as little trouble as possible, so I went downtown for dinner the first night. I found an excellent place. For one zaire, I got a big skewer, French fries and a salad. I would repeat that menu every night I was in Likasi. For one Swedish krona!

I had breakfast with the Armando family. And every morning it was a bit tricky, even though Hosi knew some school English. Some of the children were always present and when they dared to look at me or even talk to me, they laughed hysterically. I felt very clumsy with the little French I knew. I never saw any women at breakfast, and that was really the only time I spent with the family and Hosi.

On the first day, however, he wanted to show me around the mission, which was large and extensive. We started in a school class for young men studying for the priesthood. Hosi was waiting outside and the teacher welcomed me. When he introduced me as a Swedish globetrotter, the whole class surprisingly applauded. The teacher spoke English and translated their questions and my answers. They wondered how I financed my traveling, if I was going to write a book, how I found Africa, and so on. It was quite a nice question and answer session. Then Hosi and I moved on to another class. There sat the wives of the men I had just met, who also applauded me. However, they were studying other things, like sewing and cooking. But also they were curious about me. Now we had to rely on French and Hosi's little English. But we all laughed at and with each other. Hosi then showed me around the whole area and also the children's classes.

It was a huge and beautiful area. Several brick buildings around a large sports field. Not much grass on the field but several beautiful flower beds with magnificent flowers decorated the otherwise hard red soil that dominated the entire mission station. And above it all, the church dominated on a hill.

I found it a little awkward that every time Hosi introduced me, he compared me to Jesus. Awkward, even if I of course looked more like him than anyone else at the mission, especially compared to the picture of Jesus that graced most classrooms: a long-haired, blond, pious-looking young man not much like the historical Jewish Jesus. The next morning at breakfast, Hosi thanked me for coming to visit; he said that Jesus had sent me as I looked so much like him in my long sun-bleached hair. I didn't really know how to respond to this.

I liked him and the town of Likasi. It was, like Lubumbashi and the cities in Zambia's copper region I had seen, a relatively modern city. At the same time very green. It was also apparent that I was no longer in a former English colony. The women were much more visible – why the difference I don't know. But here, unlike in East Africa, women often came rushing by in beautiful colourful dresses on mopeds loaded with goods of various kinds. They simply seemed more independent than in East Africa.

The days in Likasi looked pretty much the same; I woke up every morning around seven. I stayed in bed reading until things calmed down

172

in the kitchen. At eight Hosi knocked on my door if I wasn't up already, and announced that breakfast was served. Usually porridge and a couple of eggs and coffee. And always good. Then we parted for the day; he was of course fully occupied and I felt quite grateful that I was left on my own. Did my morning toilet and then read some more in bed or in the armchair. If I sat on the porch of the house, I was always joined by curious and playful children. After a while, they got bored when we couldn't communicate and went back to their games. Games that all involved dancing and singing. Even if they were jumping hurdles or ropes, or playing ball, they were singing and dancing at the same time. I can't remember doing that at that age. And that was of course silly of me.

Around ten I went downtown. Did some shopping, some errands, explored the alleys and outskirts of this unbelievably verdant city. Then I always went to a café where I could have some lunch, sit and read or write in my diary. I returned there every day and already on the second day I was recognized, welcomed and everyone greeted me. Not so strange that they recognized me, as I was the only long-haired young man in town. All the other Europeans, and there were lots of them, were well groomed. In the café, it was good to sit and feel accepted, as if I belonged; I was a regular! It always made me happy when I managed that; it was important when I was traveling alone, so I always made an effort to return to the same cafés and restaurants if I stayed in a town or village – if they were nice establishments, that is. Here they were.

I needed some more local currency so went to one of the banks. There they refused to exchange traveller's checks. I had to talk to the manager who said it was the same throughout Congo, "but try Air Zaire, they can probably help you." A bit worried I found my way to their office; what would happen if I couldn't exchange money in this country? There I met an accommodating young Italian lady who spoke good English, which of course made things easier. She helped me but did not know the rate so asked me what it was. I suggested 10 zaire for one Sterling pound, as I had Barclay's checks in pounds. She accepted that and I bought 200 zaire. I don't know which of us won on that transaction, but it was probably her.

After lunch and a bit of wandering, I ended up in my room again, where I continued reading until it darkened, when I returned to the same restaurant and ate the same good barbecue skewers with fries. I also allowed myself a Simba beer; I lived for free at Hosi! It was just as good to sit and hang out at this restaurant as the coffee shop during the days. I was welcomed and recognized here too and since I soon realized that they spoke Swahili in Likasi, I could at least greet and say some words to the proprietor and other guests. I was now rid of the bleeding boil in my butt, which also made me feel much better. Completely gone now. But it had pained me for twelve days since Nairobi!

By nine I was back at the mission. I spoke a little with Hosi and perhaps some of the teachers with whom he might be socializing at home on the veranda. But it was short as my French was not yet sufficient for constructive conversation. But I could say "bon nuit" after a while and retire to my room.

One day I followed Hosi to church and a mass. As usual, it was solemn, as I often find in churches during mass, but not as boring as I always find it in Sweden. Here it was fast and cheerful. No one sat quietly, children were running back and forth. Hosi, who preached in Swahili in his everyday clothes, was obviously funny as everyone laughed in the pews at his Christian proclamations. He was a strange character. Outside the home, as here in the church, he was amiable, friendly and funny, but at home in the family milieu he was stern and dominating, often disciplining his many children. His wife, or wives - I never found out if he had more than one wife, but I hoped he did, notwithstanding being Christian, given the number of children - I saw very little of any woman in the house, didn't even know who was a wife or a maid. Nor did I understand if all eleven children were his, but I see in my diary that I wrote thus. At the breakfast table, if it wasn't just Hosi and me, he was constantly scolding the children or teenagers; it seemed I was the only one he smiled at in the home environment.

At my last breakfast, Hosi was not there. He had left for Lubumbashi, and without saying goodbye to me, even though he knew I would be taking the train that evening, Thursday, January 27. I thought this was a bit odd; I had certainly wanted to take a proper and warm adieu with many thanks for his generous hospitality. There was no one else in the family to thank as I had not met anyone else, except for some of the children.

I had asked around how long it would take with the train to Port

Francqui/Ilebo and always got different answers, ranging from one day to a week. Three days was the most common answer so I stocked up for three days and hoped that it would be possible to buy some food along the way, at least fruit. I bought ten buns, a jar of jam, margarine in a Blue Band can, two cans of sardines, a jar of Danish ham, bananas and also Nutella, I see in my notes. The train ticket was 8.50 zaire, third class. Cheapest.

Around eight pm I said goodbye to those I saw and walked through a relatively deserted Likasi. Outside banks and the larger office buildings, including Air Zaïre, there were guards with batons. Most had built a small fire to warm themselves in the chilly night, dressed in large uniform coats and hats. Street dogs had joined them and were sleeping next to the warmth of the fire. The lightning and thunder had not yet started, as it did almost every night, usually without rain. At a quarter to ten I got on the train.

Ilebo

When the train, at 22.00 punctually, rolled out of the station, there were only three of us in my carriage. I had eight shiny wooden benches with backrests to myself! But two opposite each other were enough, of course. It was nevertheless on the floor I slept. I spread my rain poncho under the seats where I was sitting. Then I put the sleeping bag on the poncho so that the zipper ended up on one side. The shoulder bag was as usual used as pillow, with all my most valuable things and then the Kassala blanket over myself. And I slept well.

The next morning we were still only three in the carriage. Would the entire trip be this empty? I didn't believe that, but certainly wouldn't mind it. I took a walk through the train and discovered that the coach between the one I was in and the locomotive had a small canteen where some food and drink was on sale. I could add coffee to my own breakfast, not bad at all. Several of the carriages were as full of people, luggage and animals as the trains in Sudan. I wondered if they placed me in the almost empty one on purpose, or if I was just lucky. Anyway, I was satisfied and also noticed that the windows could be opened, that it was clean and shiny in the carriage and that the toilet could be used without having to hold your breath, and equipped with a sink and tap, from which there also came some water.

The train stopped at every small town and people got on and off. We travelled slowly. Even if the stops usually lasted a few minutes, I never dared to get off. Soon, of course, also my car began to fill up. Even when it was crowded, no one wanted to sit next to the lone European; in the 1st class I had seen a few pale faces, but in the 2nd and here in the 3rd class I was the only white person. I had four seats to myself the whole first day. Very often, however, I was joined by young men who wanted to chat and have my address, as they all wanted to come to Sweden and work. I never give any of them any address. But I had many stumbling conversations in my still faltering French. And was it not somewhat paradoxical that while I was looking for, or at least appreciating, simplicity and silence when travelling, these boys wanted nothing more than to go to modern technological Europe. If we who travelled in Africa were looking for some kind of origin to revive ourselves, they

176

wanted our modernism to (out)live.

It was of course nice to meet people, but it became a bit much when I also wanted to sit and read or write or just daydream to the wild nature we went through. One guy in particular annoyed me, I see in my diary. He had a wooden leg - which of course was not why I was annoyed, but he was drunk and pushy. Something he unfortunately managed as he knew some English that he wanted to practice. He was on me already the first night and then from time to time the next day. And the drunker he became, the dumber he became and finally I had to kindly but firmly and tangibly tell him to fuck off. But he came back several times and wanted to buy me a beer. "No thank you!"

Another guy almost jumped out of his pants when he saw me and plopped down next to me and wanted me to come home and visit him in Kamina, where he lived. I kindly declined. But he was nice, funny and also knew some English. He told me that it takes four days to get to Ilebo. Now I didn't know what to believe, but nothing doing. I didn't really mind that it was slow. I was in no hurry and liked the train ride

When left alone I sat daydreaming and enjoying the country we went through. The sun was shining in a humid jungle haze and often, for me, exotic birds flew up frightened by the train. I could only admire them. Banana trees dominated everywhere where people lived, even small pineapple fields I saw. We also passed a lot of swamps where people in small canoes moved around.

I had time to reflect on my friends in Stockholm. I read through some of the latest letters I had received. The one from my classmate Kattis was surprising, my brother's was thin but warm, Stoffe's was fun, as was Niklas', my best friends. Mom's letter contained a little too much admonition - today I can understand them - but those letters were also the most important. I thought about this as I stared out into the dense rainforest, where trees and vegetation desperately fought intertwined, winding and in absolute silence to reach the very top of the canopy and its life-giving sunlight. In Lagos I was looking forward to a whole bunch of letters! I had asked everyone to write to Poste Restante, Lagos, Nigeria.

Throughout the journey, little boys walked through the wagons selling pencils, chewing gum, batteries, paper and some food and drinks from the small canteen. I wouldn't starve even if it took longer and I ran out of my own provisions. It was also possible to buy some edibles at the short stops where women with various foods in baskets or pots on their heads always flocked to the train windows. Peanuts, a corn cob and a pineapple, I bought the first day.

The second night we were stuck for several hours because an engine had overturned in front of us and blocked the track, I was told. I fell asleep before we moved again, so don't know how long it took. When I went to bed, there was a bit of a commotion as they apparently hadn't seen it before, that someone, or at least no white person, sleeping on the floor. They laughed, pointed and commented, but soon I saw more people doing the same, so...

When I woke up, we were in Mwadi Kayambe, which according to my map was about halfway.

It was now Saturday and I had slept well for two nights. A much better train ride than I had feared. It didn't compare to the ones in Sudan - or I guess it could, but then Congo's won. But I was seldom left alone. For a while there were seven guys sitting around me discussing my odyssey. They mixed Swahili with French; the latter is the official language of the country, while there are said to be about 200 ethnic groups with their own languages in Congo. I didn't understand everything, but it was clear that they thought it was hilarious of me to be traveling alone in Africa.

When I was left alone, I daydreamed again, read Dan Andersson and *Lord of the Flies* that I had got hold of in Ndola. I also reflected in my diary about how ignorant I was. That I had now been to Rome, Athens and Egypt without knowing hardly an iota about the high cultural history of these places. Nor did I know anything about the history of Congo, other than some vague information about the Congo crisis, Lumumba and the death of Dag Hammarskjöld. I promised myself to read up when I got home. Something I believe I have done.

I also sat with my Michelin map number 155, checking every village or town we passed through or stopped at to see where we were. One must do that when traveling; that's why a map is so great. Today, traveling only with GPS or Google map is not much fun!

Around six that evening, all hell broke loose. We stopped in Tshimbulu and it seemed all its residents were getting on this train. My carriage was suddenly packed with people, luggage and animals. There were now at least three of us sitting on each wooden bench. A little boy peed himself

178

next to me and it leaked on me. His mother apologized (I think) and put him on a sack she was carrying and wiped him off and put new pants on him. All the time singing to the boy and smiling at me. I smiled back. To the right of me sat a very old man with a big pink lady's hat on his head. I tried to make contact with him, a little curious as to why he was wearing this spectacular headgear. But he just stared out the window and never met my gaze.

A very beautiful woman sat opposite me. I guessed that she was in her mid-twenties, had traditional marks on her cheeks, dark brown beautiful eyes and her hair was of course black in braids. She was wearing a green, long dress with flowers and a pair of plastic sandals on her feet. She smiled but apparently didn't know any French so we just smiled at each other. She fell asleep soon after I helped her up with her luggage on the shelf above. When she woke up, she offered me peanuts, smiled and said "gentleman" to me several times. That made me happy. When she got off at Luluaborg, I helped her with her luggage again, she curtsied and took my hand and repeated "gentleman" and "merci." A meeting I remember even without reading about it in my diary. I wonder if she remembers it?

The night was a bit adventurous. In Luluaborg, almost everyone left together with the beautiful woman. It was then nine in the evening and new passengers got on, though not as many. I soon crawled down on the floor to sleep, after having eaten something - I don't know what. At about midnight I awoke to find that the carriage was full of life. From my floor view I saw feet and legs everywhere. The carriage was packed again. But I wanted to sleep so I turned over and fell asleep. Around four o'clock I woke again to turn over and now it was quiet and almost empty. Strange, I thought, but glad if it would stay that way the next day. But when I woke up at seven, it was again packed with passengers. What was going on?

It wasn't easy to get up in the crowd, but I managed to rise between all the feet and legs, and when I stood up it became dead silent. They had not expected that a young man from Högdalen had been sleeping on the floor. No one said anything. When I pointed to the spot where I had been sitting for two days, two women who were sitting there immediately jumped up and offered me the spot. It took quite a while for everyone to get their fill of my pale appearance before they began to return to their seats and conversations. Soon they offered fruit and biscuits and we tried to communicate but neither their French nor mine was impressive enough for a more substantial conversation. But we had a good time. And as usual, the children never got enough of my exterior. The looks were always friendly and happy; I never felt anything but welcomed.

It was now raining hard and the scenery was dominated by rainforest. In Mweka, where almost everyone got off - four seats again - I could buy more food and realized that we would probably reach Ilebo this afternoon. Which we did at three pm. It took 63 hours from Likasi to Ilebo. And it was a very pleasant train ride. Not much food, but I needed to lose a few kilos, so it suited me. I had met lots of people, slept well, seen fantastic country, read and daydreamed.

Traveling by train is the best!

In Ilebo, all passengers were ushered into a large enclosure in the pouring rain. We had to present our documents. I was the only obvious foreigner and thought I should take advantage of this to get out of the pouring rain as quickly as possible, which didn't seem to bother anyone else. So I made myself very visible to the inspectors who soon called me over before anyone else. As usual, I was a bit worried about what they would do, but they couldn't have been nicer. They looked in my backpack, at my passport and yellow vaccination booklet, then they welcomed me to Ilebo. Of course, I realized, even then, that this way of pushing forward, gaining an advantage because of my Scandinavian origin, my paler skin, was not so attractive. On the other hand, I think the advantage I gained actually had more to do with the fact that I was a guest in the country, than the fact that I was white; the kindness I met was chiefly because I was a stranger; I was visiting Africa, meeting helpful and generous people everywhere. If we turn it around and see a lone African, a Congolese, in a similar checkpoint with lots of Swedes at a railway station in Sweden, it would most likely look different: Africa is kinder!

The port, where the railroad also ended, was large and modern, but the city, which climbed up a long hill, was the first in a long time that was not paved, but consisted only of trampled earth. Still, it was beautiful, with wide streets and avenues everywhere. I found a large, white, almost Victorian hotel. They wanted 30 zaire for one night. Impossible! I left the hotel and asked around to see if there were any missionaries in town. At a school I learned that there was a large mission 2½ kilometres outside the town. I marched there, happy that it had stopped raining. And soon I was sitting on a veranda with a pilsner in my hand.

Two Belgian priests welcomed me and gave me a bed in a separate house with a large room that otherwise obviously served as a storage room. Along with a bed and a small table with a chair, there were lots of chairs stacked in a corner, barrels with various gadgets, tools, sacks, a large pile of clothes and other things unknown to me. There was a single light bulb hanging from the ceiling and I had been given a candle holder with a couple of candles. A spacious room I liked with a window and outside a small veranda with a shady roof, in front of a large meadow with tall acacia trees before disappearing down to the river.

I was a bit unlucky as there was no boat to Kinshasa this week, and I would have to wait nine days for the next boat. But Maarten and Herman, as the priests were called, promised that I could stay with them all the time. I asked if I could do something, work in the meantime. "Sure. You can help with the construction of the new school building. It's mostly bricklaying and carrying stone," said Maarten, who I understood was the head of the mission. Both of them only knew a few words of English so I would improve my French considerably these days. I was grateful to be able to do some work; it had been a while since I had worked with my hands and it would give me something to do while waiting for the next river boat.

At half past seven Maarten woke me up the next day and I had a quick breakfast at their house and then followed him down to the harbour. He had a few errands to tend to and I was supposed to buy my boat ticket. I really had to hold on in the jeep as he drove like a maniac on the gravel roads. But we arrived safely. Inside the ticket office Mobutu of course looked down at us with a serious face, which, however, was undermined by the ridiculous night cap in leopard fur he was wearing. I also recognized several people from the train and we cheerfully greeted one another. But we soon became upset when we were informed that all 2nd and 3rd class tickets were sold out for the next riverboat. Now only 1st class tickets were available, for 29 zaire. Nobody wanted to pay that.

They however let us sign our names on a waiting list for 2nd class, which would cost 7 zaire. I could afford that. We were also informed that the next boat would indeed leave on February the 8th and now it was the last day of January. Maarten then drove back and dropped me off at the school building.

The people already working there were a bit surprised even if they had been informed. At first they apparently thought I was going to boss them around, but when they realized that I knew nothing about building houses, I got to mix cement all morning and everyone was happy and satisfied. We were seven Congolese workers and me in the heat to finish the school building. When there was break time in the school, we were surrounded by school children who amusedly glared at the Swede who skilfully mixed the cement.

At noon I was picked up for lunch in the big house. I joined Maarten, Herman and three other Belgians for a fantastic lunch: first vegetable soup, then a steak with fries and an onion and tomato salad, and finally chocolate pudding. My God, I thought, if it was going to be like this every day, I was in for a treat every day. And the same for the evening meal?

But in the evening, Maarten and Herman went downtown to play cards with some friends. They gave me a couple of sandwiches and a big bottle of Skol. Locked myself in my room, read a bit, played the recorder and fell tiredly asleep with calluses on my hands.

The next day I got to change job. Now I was to help André repaint the exterior of the church. I didn't mind even though it involved hanging high up on a ladder with a bucket and brush. But it was quieter and André was funny and I got to speak a lot of French as he was extremely talkative.

The days then looked pretty much the same. After a good and quick breakfast in the dining room, I painted the church until lunch, which was just as rich and delicious every day. Then a few hours on the ladder again before André and I parted at three and I went to my little house.

André on the ladder.

There I now had company. Every afternoon when I came home, one or two toads would hop around on the floor of my room. Where they came from I never understood. But with a broom I could gently brush them out through the door. The next day they were back; although I never really understood if it was the same toads that joined me, or if there were new ones every day. They looked the same: brown-flecked with light, thicker bellies, large as a big fist. I was also joined by spiders, geckos, mice and cockroaches. The spiders were big and colourful, but they sat in their webs in the corners and didn't bother me; I kept an eye on them though. I hated the cockroaches and killed every one I saw. I liked the fireflies better: at twilight the lawn outside my house was covered with fireflies. They flashed brightly as they flew over the grass. A beautiful spectacle when the sun had just set.

I could shower in a small shed nearby where a bucket with a funnel with holes in it had been hung up. It wasn't easy to get clean as a bucket of water wasn't really enough to wash both body and my long hair. The most dramatic thing, however, was the giant spider that sat above the shower; the body was the size of Sonny Liston's thumb, with fuzzy five-centimetre-long legs. I stared anxiously at it every time I showered, not taking my eyes off it for a second, to make sure it didn't suddenly drop on me. It looked poisonous and deadly, even though it was beautiful with a brilliant yellow and black body, which however and unfortunately reminded me of a boring football team just north of Stockholm.

When it rained, we couldn't paint the church so I had to spend the day as best I could. One day, when it held up, I went down to the river next to the mission. There was a small jetty for canoes, where the local trade was conducted. It was exciting and I was left alone - now everyone knew who I was - and could stop for a while and admire the women who incomprehensibly and elegantly made their way up the steep slope above the river with almost meter-high goods on their heads.

The men, of course, were not carrying anything, not anywhere in Africa, as far as I could see! Butterflies: unbelievably large swallow-tailed giant butterflies swarmed and flew unpredictably in their folded flight and looked almost dangerous. Mostly, of course, they were beautiful in their incredible colours. When the French writer André Gide travelled

184

to the Congo in 1925, he captured every beautiful and unknown butterfly he could find. When you read about it today in his *Travels in the Congo*, it seems a bit strange and I certainly had no intention of catching butterflies. What would I do with them? Nor could I store them. But Gide wasn't traveling alone, he had more than 60 carriers with him, so probably plenty of room to store all the butterflies he wanted. Nor did Grahame Greene travel alone on his 1935 trip to West Africa. In *Journey Without Maps*, he concludes that a minimum of 25 porters must accompany one during a walk in West Africa. Of course, the famous authors travelled grander than yours truly, but on the other hand, there were now better roads and means of transportation.

I could also take long walks around the mission into the town on those days when the rain stopped and found Ilebo to be a town full of life and commerce. This was of course due to the large port and the fact that the railroad from Lubumbashi stopped here. Many Belgians also seemed to have stayed on after independence.

One Sunday evening there was a big dinner set for eight at my host's house. The guests were to arrive at eight, but the priests and I met on their veranda beforehand and had a couple of pilsners each. There were lovely smells coming from the kitchen: promising and Maarten said that Gordon had worked hard tonight. We were to dine in the large dining room, where we had lunch and dinner if there were guests. Breakfast was usually a quick affair at a table next to the kitchen. But this dining room was now set with the best china and two large candelabras with lighted candles. Then two young Belgian couples that I had met earlier, and a young man on his own showed up, all speaking English. First we were served a good onion soup and then something they called 'moambe,' apparently the country's national dish. Chicken in a coconut sauce that was heavenly delicious. Good French wine with this and then a sweet white wine for the cake that finished it all.

The conversation was initially mostly in Flemish, so I focused on the food. But soon they started asking me what I thought about Africa, Congo and especially about Africans. They said that, like Albert Schweitzer had claimed many years earlier, the African is a brother, but a little brother who must be led, otherwise he falls into laziness and dishonesty, which, they said, characterized the Congolese in particular. I disagreed with them, but as my experience of Africa was undoubtedly limited, they overlooked my judgment.

As the clock approached midnight, everyone was soused and they began singing obscene songs; I understood this even though they were in Flemish; they laughed their heads off. Suddenly Maarten said that it was my turn to sing something in Swedish. I tried to get out of it, but unsuccessfully. The only thing I could come up with at the moment was a lullaby. I sang it and when I then translated and explained that it was a lullaby, they took it as a hint that it was time to go to bed. "No, no!" I assured them and soon I was excused and the party continued. At half past two I rolled into bed, bushed with blurry eyes, which, whoever, was nothing compared to the two priests who could barely stand up when we all retired.

They were a bit unusual for men of the church. Were they even priests? I wonder today. But everyone addressed them as Fathers, so probably. Maarten, a big jovial fellow, who laughed and was always heard and seen. Herman was a bit more reserved. Instead of a car, he had a little moped he rode around on with a silly little helmet on his head and a chin strap that was a little too tight so he looked squashed in the face in it. Both were noticeably appreciated by everyone in Ilebo and funny in their own ways and certainly kind and generous to me. When every other night they went down to some friends in town to play cards, I always got some food and a couple of beers from them, as there was no dinner those days.

In my diary, I see no record of any religious activity in the church. During the nine days I was there, there ought to have been mass at least once. If there had been, I would definitely have attended and written about it. I find that strange today. Maybe it was because we were painting the church? Nor was religion ever discussed at dinners or lunches. The only time my diary mentions anything like that is when Herman one day asked me if I was a Protestant.

"I was confirmed in the Swedish church," I replied. "But I am certainly not religious."

"It's okay," he said.

How lucky for me!

André, who I painted with, was a small, stocky guy, maybe 25 years old and full of funny stories. We worked well together and when I wanted to work harder, he didn't mind. Our working hours were 8.00 -

11.30, lunch, then 12.30 - 15.00, which suited me perfectly as it gave me some time for myself, to read or wander around and get a bit lost somewhere. One afternoon André wanted to borrow money from me, so I lent him 10 zaire. Which he still owes me. So it goes.

We always had lunch together with the same three young Belgians. Bachelors who had arranged the lunch in this way and the priests had some company, which they badly craved, apparently. The food was always insanely good. In my diary I wrote about how fantastic it was also culinary to travel this way. Not that I always ate well, but one day there might be hardly anything at all to eat and the next day good and plentiful; after three days without cooked food on the train, mostly fruit, biscuits and preserves, I ended up in Ilebo, with Gordon's incomparably good cooking. One day we even had monkey for lunch. A bit hairy but quite tasty and a first for me. Otherwise it was mostly bloody steaks with chips and salad, sometimes fish, after an always delicious soup, which was the best.

Soon, however, I would be on a river boat with, I was sure, simpler meals. I did manage, with Maarten's help, to get a 2nd class ticket to Kinshasa for 7 zaire. 3rd class cost 1.50. Here at the mission I was living nine days with free room and board, so I felt I could afford 2nd class. I was a bit worried about what 3rd class would look like on the river boats.

I make a big deal in my diary about sewing a button on a shirt one day here in Ilebo. Apparently the first time my mother has not done it for me. A bit touching, I think today, many buttons later. I also counted the frogs I had to brush out of my room; before I left there were 23, or was it the same?

Some days there was no work after lunch. I never understood why. I had time to wash my clothes and it gave me more time to wander around, including in the African neighbourhoods. Here everyone had their own little house with a plot of land where they grew some vegetables. Neat and tidy. But it wasn't thanks to the men's, at least it didn't look like it. They mostly sat in the shade under a big tree and listened to a loud transistor all day. The women worked all the time, often with a baby on their backs. Incomprehensible! One guy I saw several times, not surprisingly as he stood out almost as much as I did, was the village albino. There was only one in Ilebo, according to Maarten. I found him hideously ugly, I read in my diary, and so wrote Joseph Conrad in his

Congo diary about an albino he met on July 4, 1890. But perhaps we were the only ones who thought so.

If I took long walks, I always got sweaty and sticky as the days were hot and humid, while the nights were mercifully cooler. After work, I would sometimes just sit on a chair outside my house, stretch out and take in several litres of soothing evening air. Often, I would watch a nearly transparent gecko lizard magically approach its prey at ultra speed, step by step, one leg at a time, without actually moving it seemed, next to the lone light bulb in the porch roof. And then suddenly, an equally invisible quick attack. Once in particular - I think it was the same lizard all along - it caught a large dragonfly that I could see as it slowly disappeared down the gecko's throat. What incredible digestion it must have, I thought.

From my little porch I almost every evening saw the sun set over the field where young kids were playing soccer. The crickets sang almost deafeningly along with an undertone of the frogs' bass line. It was probably the best moment every day. Sometimes, of course, disturbed by the children, but they were kind, if at times a little too curious. They sometimes hung outside my window in the evenings, even after I had gone to bed. I tried to chase them away in French, English and Swedish, but it was only when, after a couple of evenings, I just waved at them as they ran off in fear and shouted 'moja' that they disappeared.

Ilebo is one of those places in Africa that I remember fondly and would love to return to! But when I left Ilebo, I was quite convinced that I would never see it again. Very sad to travel with that realization, as Flaubert wrote. Of course, there were many places during the trip that I knew I would never see again, but not all of them had been as pleasant as Ilebo - although André still owes me 10 zaire.

I counted my money and found that I had 2500 SEK left. Today, two and a half thousand sounds unbelievably little, but apparently it lasted almost six months, thanks largely to the fact that I was often able to live for free at mission stations in West Africa.

We finished painting the church before I left, Tuesday, February 8. After a last of Gordon's fantastic three-course lunches, I said goodbye to him and thanked him for all the lovely food, hugged Herman and then Maarten drove me down to the harbour. There it was full calamity as everyone apparently wanted to get on the boat at the same time. The police used batons to disperse and managed some kind of order. I kept my distance after thanking Maarten for everything and promising to send some postcards. When the policemen saw me, they waved me forward and let me embark in peace; they even bowed! Here in Congo, women had curtsied and men had bowed me because I was a guest in the country! Or perhaps only because I was white?

I don't know.

Kinshasa

The first night on the boat was awful. The cabin I slept in was right next to the bar and dance floor in 2nd class. Outside my door were two large speakers playing loud Congolese dance music until three in the morning. It was also stuffy, humid and hot as we could not have the door open because of the music. I shared a cabin with two other and the fourth bed was empty where we could all put our luggage. I ought to have enjoyed the songs as it was most likely soukous music. A wonderfully swinging and monotonous dance music from the Congo, I love today. But then I hated it, almost crying before it quieted.

When I woke, I felt so miserable that homesickness again overwhelmed me. I started meditating about how to get home as quickly as possible. Sadly I realized that it was not so easy where I was: on a riverboat almost smack in the middle of Africa - so I continued down the Kasai River.

But I opened my maps and started to calculate how long it would take if I rushed it, and came to the conclusion that just over two weeks would suffice. How I reached that conclusion I do not understand, but it surprisingly put me in a better mood and already after a meagre breakfast I felt better and looked forward to the river trip.

My cabin was in 2nd class but during the day I could be on 1st class. Often I would stand and lean over the railing of the first class boat from its second floor and look down on the third class deck, which was full of people, animals and goods, where things were happening all the time. The three-storey boat of the first class was lashed together with two second-class boats, which had two floors, where I slept next to the bar, and a third-class barge which consisted only of a large open deck in front of the first-class boat. Our vessel thus consisted of four iron-chained river barges of varying standards.

During night we mostly lay still, the first night at Dibaya-Lubue. It was apparently treacherous to travel at night on parts of the river. When we did, the boat navigated by means of two large searchlights on the bridge of the third deck which scanned the two river banks, found a white-painted rock or tree, and then steered towards that mark. The

190

other searchlight then began scanning the other river bank for the next white marking. I was able to visit the bridge for a while and see how it was done. Fascinating.

On the second day I met a group of young Congolese men who sat and drank beer all the time, at least every time I met them. One, an engineer on the boat, had studied English, which made communication easier, although my French had improved considerably. They also stood out in their stylish clothes: Tight flared jeans, pointed boots and sparkling colourful shirts. Obviously, they belonged to the big city, and I later learnt that the Congolese, in both Kinshasa and Brazzaville, as well as in Paris, are famous for their extravagant dress, no matter how poor they are. The king of the, so called, Sapeur-movement was the musician Papa Wemba - I am listening to his music as I write this.

These young men were not so elegant, but in this environment, they certainly stood out. The captain came by while we were socializing, althhough he didn't look much like a captain; wore jeans, though not flared, and a short-sleeved light blue shirt. His peaked cap was what set him apart. He stopped by me, took my hand: "Ca va?" "Ca va bien!" "Bon." And marched off without giving the others a glance. But they thought this was all right. I was an obvious stranger, lone paleface on the boat. And, as so often on this voyage, that brought some advantages. The captain's mess boy even gave me some extra food on the first day: chicken and rice. Now I felt better.

And the second night I slept well. I stuffed folded toilet paper in my ears and went to bed at ten and woke up at six am, reinvigorated, surprised and happy. Before crawling into bed, I had been standing at the bar outside the cabin, listening to the music and watching everyone dance. At one point I am chatting to one of the Sapeur-guys I've met before; a woman comes up and whispers something in his ear while grabbing my balls with one hand. I jump in surprise. But everyone just laughs and we end up dancing a few tunes together. The lighting was so dim that I never knew who I was dancing with and we couldn't talk as the loud music didn't allow it.

The next day I spent most of my time on the second floor of the 1st class boat, with a view of the 3rd class and the entire river in front of us. I had been looking forward to the riverboat in the Congo but the scenery was surprisingly dull; we were just traveling through an uneventful and endlessly green wall of monotonous vegetation. And no hippos or crocodiles as I had hoped. Sometimes the river was kilometre-wide with small islands, sometimes narrower and we carefully navigated between smaller or larger islands. Maybe it would be more adventurous up the Congo River? Now we travelled down the Kasai.

Instead, it was the people that were captivating. Down in 3rd class, I discovered a very beautiful woman, and she me, so we started flirting a bit. That embellished my time a bit. But of course I didn't think anything would come out of it, still a little exciting.

It was also exciting when we approached and docked at a village. Then all the villagers seemed to flock to the boat to sell goods, mostly food and especially fish. There were often small fights over the most attractive fish. And on day two, the 3rd class deck was packed with goods, people and animals. How they managed to find a place to sleep I never understood.

It became really dramatic if we did not dock but just sailed past a village and people paddled out in their narrow dugout canoes to meet us. They first needed to catch up and then to attach their canoes to our boat at speed. We didn't slow down. Many succeeded, but it was sad to see those who did not. We generated waves with our size and speed, making it risky for the slim canoes to approach us. Quite often they overturned and all their goods sank to the bottom. They were able to save the canoe and themselves, but this week's earnings vanished. Those who managed to dock alongside us were subjected to fierce commotion. People threw rags, scarves and blankets at the various fish in the canoes in order to reserve them. Then followed a heated argument about whose rag it was and the fisherman tried to mediate while trying to get the best price. Soon things calmed down and everyone seemed satisfied. Mostly fish were sold, ugly catfish-like creatures, often alive, but also smoked and salted fish. A very popular product was a lump of dough wrapped in palm leaves; if these were offered for sale, everyone went bananas and a fight almost broke out. I later tasted them, chewy and bitter, and decided that it was not for me. But everyone else on the boat disagreed, obviously. Was it manioc? I wonder today. Live and dead animals were also on offer: of course fowls, parrots, pigs, goats, ducks, but also monkeys and I saw a small crocodile. It was particularly sad to see a cage with

192

ten dead monkeys.

It was equally sad that I couldn't find a proper toilet. The toilet in 2nd class was awful and in 3rd class I could not find one – how did they do it? In 1st class there seemed to be a toilet only in the private cabins. I mentioned it to Joe, the engineer with the English and he allowed me to use his cabin for number two. Considerate of him.

On the second afternoon, when we docked at Bandundu, where the Kwango River flows into Kasai, we could go ashore. It was a fairly large village. Great wide avenues lined with single-storey mud or wooden houses with braided palm roofs. I was joined by one of the guys in my cabin and we found some fresh bread and a bar where we each drank a beer for 1 zaire, or one Swedish krona; the cheapest lager I've ever had.

When we got back to the boat, I just put the bread in the cabin and returned to Bandundu. I figured the Sapeur gang was probably sitting in some bar. And they were, and already a bit tipsy. Immediately I was given a large beer mug and no matter how much I drank it was always full of beer. Don't know how it happened, but they were generous. I could also see that women were represented here. Previously in Africa, all taverns had been male-dominated, along with the young ladies who served. But here were groups of young and old women having as much fun as we were.

I must have looked out of place with the cool, snobby guys I was sitting with, in my work boots and short pants and already quite dirty long hair. After a couple of beers, I didn't care and I can't have looked that bad because one woman suddenly wanted to get me up on the dance floor, something she however failed to do.

When we later returned to the boat, we had brought some beer and sat on the deck with a cassette player full of music and continued the party. I also got a plate of white rice and dried fish from Joe; dry but it went down fine with some beer. Soon the woman I had been flirting with came by and I spoke to her, encouraged by the lager. She came over and surprised me by sitting in my lap, but there was no dialog as she did not know French and I did not know her Bantu language.

"Do you love her?" Joe asked me.

"Sure," I laughed.

Joe reasoned with her a bit and then said: "It's ok. You can use my cabin." I didn't understand what he meant at first but suddenly she kissed me and I got it.

He followed us down to his cabin and left us there. It was not large. A bed along one wall, a table and chair and a small bookcase. The wall was adorned with a mirror and a painting of a sunset over a palm beach. A ceiling light was burning relentlessly and I turned on the bedside lamp instead. How do we do this, I thought. She seemed even more shy than I was, but probably wasn't. "Moi Erik," I said, pointing to myself, trying to break the awkward silence. She replied that her name is Biloa - I think she said. We couldn't talk more and it all seemed comical, but we started to undress and soon she was in just a pair of red panties and I in my underwear. But she was pretty, smiled and soon took off her panties too and crawled up onto the bed. I did the same.

Afterwards – and it was a quick affair – she surprised me again. She wanted to be paid. It had simply not occurred to me, but when she said it, it was obvious given who we were and where we were. However, I managed to bargain down from five to three zaire. Not one of my prouder memories, I admit, but I was so into haggling over everything it came naturally. And she didn't mind. But I was certainly not a gentleman in that encounter!

When we got up on deck again, Joe and all the other guys were smiling and he asked me if it had been okay. "Yes," I replied a little awkwardly. And Biloa quietly disappeared to hers.

The next day we smiled shyly at each other, but she proudly showed me her son, a sweet boy, I guessed was five years old. I got to spend part of that day with the captain who was interested in Sweden, while bragging about Congo, yet talking trash about Mobutu and preferred to flirt with the women on the boat.

In the evening we docked near Kinshasa, but without entering the city. As we lay still, a little boy fell into the water. He could obviously not swim, but everyone just stood and watched him splash around in the water. Finally the captain threw him a buoy and one of the sapeurs leapt in and got him out of the river.

Early the next morning we docked in Kinshasa. The captain accompanied me ashore so I quickly got off and avoided all the commotion when everyone wanted ashore at the same time. He also helped me to buy a boat ticket on the Congo-river to Lisala for 6.50 zaire. It was now Saturday and it would leave on Monday.

In the harbour I soon met a Japanese who told me that everything was impossibly expensive in Kinshasa. "I have left my packing at my embassy and slept in a park nearby. It's been great." I thought this sounded like a good idea, especially if I had company. The Swedish embassy was in the same neighbourhood as the Japanese and he showed the way. We both went up to the embassy, which was open even on an early Saturday. They were friendly, understanding and I was told I could leave my backpack with them until Monday. We also both got to use their clean toilet, which we appreciated.

Then I met the Embassy Secretary, Gunnar, who said that it was not at all okay that I slept outside in a park. "You can stay with me until Monday!" Of course I could not refuse this generous offer, so I said goodbye to the Japanese, who was a little disappointed as he had been looking forward to company in the park.

Instead, after a couple of hours and a hot shower, I ended up by a swimming pool with a gin and tonic in my hand. Mysterious is the fate of the hitchhiker. From a stuffy dark cabin on the riverboat to a beautiful villa with a pool and a GT. Nor did I mind that I once again didn't have to pay for my bed. Gunnar lived in a semi-detached house with a shared plot and pool. In the other one lived Lennart and Berit and their four-year-old son, who was sickly, and afraid of me. He immediately started crying when he saw me and ran to his mother's arms. In small villages, including the old quarters of Mombasa, I had sometimes found that children became frightened of my appearance. I always thought it was because I was a European and a long-haired blonde: a terrible revelation. But here I was scaring a little Swedish boy. I must have looked hideous in my long hair and thin striped beard.

Lennart also worked at the embassy. They invited me to luncheon when Gunnar had to return to work after driving me home. After lunch I lay by the pool all afternoon and read Swedish newspapers.

Later that day at Gunnar's I met Pierre from Paris; he spoke some Swedish as he had studied agriculture in Sweden. He was a conscientious objector and did community service for 14 months on a development project here in the Congo. He asked if he could invite me to dinner and later to a nightclub that night. I answered that he could.

I borrowed some nicer clothes from Gunnar, which perhaps did not fit me so well. But it had to do. We first went to Pierre's home and met another Frenchman who joined us. Then we visited a neighbour who offered whisky and cashew nuts in a fantastic house with a view over the whole city. The three of us then went to the Okapi hotel where we had a lovely French and long dinner with good red wine. The hotel had one of the city's most popular clubs, I was told, and we glided down into it as the clock approached midnight. Strengthened by the good wine, I immediately asked a Congolese beauty for a dance. She didn't know any of my languages, which didn't matter, as it was impossible to converse in the thunderous dance music. This time I liked it. But a couple of dances with her was all for me. Instead, I ended up in front of a strange umbrella drink Pierre had ordered and watched the dancing. The whole club was decked out in gold and mirrors. The people seemed to be the same. And in leopard print; apparently Mobutu's fashion had rubbed off, at least on the Congolese who were there.

Then it occurred to me again that I could have been sleeping in a park right now, if I hadn't met Gunnar. As mentioned, the fate of the hitch-hiker is unfathomable!

When we got home around two o'clock, Gunnar also showed up. He had, as he put it, "been blown by a chick." So we had another whisky while he was feeling sorry for himself for a while. Pierre also slept over.

For breakfast I had a sandwich with Kalle's caviar, a very Swedish traditional bread spread!

After a quiet morning by the pool, I was invited to lunch with the Swedish Ambassador to Congo. He sent a car to pick me up and it became a very unusual afternoon. The ambassador was nice, as was his Belgian wife. They lived in a large villa in a beautiful green garden surrounded by fences and guards at the gate. We ate on porcelain decorated with three crowns (national symbol of Sweden) and he told me that he had had a meeting with Mobutu in the morning, even though it was Sunday. Then there was a lot of talk about travel, mine and theirs. They had lived in Nepal, which they loved. They also talked about the former Swedish prime minister, Tage Erlander and Dag Hammarskjöld, how they were as people and how much they admired them both. A captivating lunch for a hippie from Högdalen in jeans and workers' shoes.

In the evening I was left alone at Gunnar's and helped myself to the fridge and pantry. Nice to have a quiet evening too.

The next day I followed Lennart to the embassy where I left my backpack. Then downtown for bank visits, some food shopping for the river trip. I also found a bookstore with some English literature. I bought a couple of books by André Gide; a writer I was curious about and a little surprised to find in English here. Later I realized that it might have something to do with the fact that he made an extensive trip to the Congo and written about it. I also met the Japanese outside the embassy who told me that they had changed the departure date. "The boat leaves tomorrow!" We went down to the port and got it confirmed.

It felt a bit embarrassing to go up to the embassy and tell them about the delay and ask if I could stay one more night with Gunnar: "Hell yes! Of course." Lennart then drove me home and we had lunch together. Their son was still sick, so Lennart wanted to go home and see how he was doing.

In the afternoon I was at the pool again with a bunch of Swedish daily papers. These embassy folks were so incredibly nice that it was even hard to thank them properly. Particularly Lennart I felt I had a fine contact with and hoped that I could meet again - something I never did. Gunnar was a more typical bachelor. Talked a lot about girls, had a stock of *Playboy* magazines and obviously partied a lot. And he hated that the embassy staff (of course not the ambassador) drove a Renault 4 with an umbrella gear stick. Other embassies had more stately vehicles: "You had to be ashamed on behalf of Sweden's cheapness." But he had an interesting library with lots of Marx and Mao and Strindberg. I read the first fantastic chapter from Strindberg's *Röda rummet* (*The Red Room*). As usual, Strindberg''s language dazzled me.

I was left alone in his house again this evening and made a big omelette with browned cabbage and bratwurst. With that I drank beer and then whisky. Had a great time listening to Swedish news and reading some more Strindberg before falling asleep in a soft and cool bed.

Before I went to bed, I squeezed the last of the tube of toothpaste I had brought with me from Stockholm. It had lasted a long time! This was mainly because I could go several days without brushing my teeth. And sometimes I used toothpaste only in the mornings so I didn't have to buy a new one. But now I had to. I had not yet started using a wooden brush. But I had tried. Broke off a twig, chewed one end and then brushed. Not bad at all, but now I had a toothbrush, so I didn't need a stick - it also had to do with my breath. For many in Africa, the stick seemed to work like I sometimes use a toothpick or a long blade of grass: something to pass the time with, and chew on during long boring moments. And it's certainly nicer than chewing gum as too many people do: revolting!

On Tuesday, Lennart drove me down to the harbour after a generous lunch. This time the boat would really leave the capital. I said goodbye and thanked them and marvelled at their generosity. During the days in Kinshasa I had lived in luxury and it had not cost me a penny. Now it would be different again. And that, of course, is the way to travel. It has to do with the rhythm of journeying: arrival, meeting, rest, departure: renewal, repetition and continuity. Now I was breaking up from a very pleasant stay and would meet a new riverboat, new people, while at the same time there would be a partial repetition of the previous boat.

Businga

This time I was not the only Westerner on the riverboat. There were some Americans in 1st class that I would spend some time with, as well as the Japanese, who travelled 3rd class and slept on deck. This vessel was larger, consisted of six harnessed barges where the engines, like the one on Kasai were on the 1st and one of the 2nd class boats, the rear barges of the whole vessel. This riverboat was also more modern. On 1st class there was a saloon where I came to stay a lot. As on the Kasai River I now quartered in a 2nd class cabin, no. 14. It was similar to the one on the previous boat. This time I shared it with a family who distributed themselves a bit strangely in the beds - which were deep as hammocks. The four children slept in one bed, the mother in another, the luggage in the third and the father slept on a wooden bench outside the cabin, as did the Japanese, Riko.

On the first morning he and I were sitting on one of the benches outside the cabin when an obnoxious character came by and started shouting at us. He didn't like Chinese people, so he began screaming at Riko. He also disliked hippies, so attacked me as well. The remarkable thing was how the others around us reacted. They literally threw themselves at him, dragging him away and excusing his behaviour: so rude to us, guests in the country. He himself came back later and apologized and I was given an MPR (Mouvement Populaire de la Révolution, Mobutu's party) badge, which I put on my shoulder bag.

It was raining and windy on the first day so I ended up sitting in the lounge playing canasta with two of the Americans. It took a while for me to remember the game. I hadn't really played before, but my parents always played when my mother's relatives visited and my brother and I often sat around and watched, so I was not completely foreign to the game. But I lost because we didn't play in pairs. We also drank beer, which again cost one zaire each. I made a note in my diary that from mainly having been drinking tea since Alexandria, I had now switched to beer here in Congo. Mainly it had to do with the fact that everyone else drank beer, but also that it was astonishingly cheap.

Food was another matter. It was, if not a problem, certainly limited. I had brought some, but it wouldn't last me the whole trip. On 2nd class there was some for sale, but basically everyone had brought their own, while 1st class passengers had their food served in their cabins. Something I fortunately soon discovered. My lunch the first day consisted of a tin of sardine in tomato sauce that I had brought from Gunnar's rich pantry and for dinner I had a jam sandwich with peanuts and a green orange. But already on the second day I noticed that a Congolese family in 1st class, didn't eat it all their food. When they finished eating, they put the tray outside their cabin door with the remaining food. I stood leaning on the railing close by every day after lunch and dinner and could quickly empty their plates of the leftovers. Often it was a lot, and certainly tastier than the little food I had with me; mostly it was chicken fried in various ways, but also fish and tough steak of unknown origin, along with some rice or chips; everything slipped gratefully, quickly and voraciously down my stomach before anyone came by.

Now I was on the Congo River. But traveling up that river is no longer "like going back to the beginning of the world," as Marlow in *Heart of Darkness* claimed and of course it wasn't at the end of the 19th century either. On the second day, when I was mostly in the lounge playing canasta, we went past Bolobo, where a certain Frenchman, Captain George Antoine Klein, is buried. He died on board the riverboat Roi des Belges on September 21, 1890, and Joseph Conrad, who was then in the Congo, took command of the boat. Klein is probably one of those whom Conrad used as a model for Kurtz in his short novel. (In *Blackwood's Magazine*, where it first appeared in three issues, it was, however, called **The** *Heart of Darkness*. Why did he drop the definite article?) While the discussion of Kurtz's background is lively and never-ending, with the journalist Henry Morton Stanley among the candidates, in his first manuscript Conrad calls him Klein, and then changed it to Kurtz. What would I have done if I had known then and there that it was Kurtz we were passing by in Bolobo? Probably nothing, but I should in any case I have read the novel on board, but instead I was reading Gide - who had also been in Congo.

I believe I am excused if I bring up Conrad's novel, because it is difficult, almost impossible for a bookworm like myself not to mention *Heart of Darkness* when recounting a journey up the Congo River. Other travellers in Africa have certainly read and referred to Conrad's novel.

Paul Theroux reads it twelve times [?] during the journey he describes in *Dark Star Safari*, even though he is nowhere near the Congo River. The Swedish writer Sven Lindqvist uses it as the starting point for his journey in the Sahara, in his book *Utrota varenda jävel* (*Exterminate All the Brutes*), without getting anywhere near to the river. I had not read Conrad's novel in 1972, but later spent many hours reading it several times, lecturing and leading seminars on the book at Stockholm University.

Also on this boat I often stood by the railing of the 1st class, with a view of the whole river ahead and down over the 3rd class flatboat. No lady to flirt with here but the same exciting activity among people and animals as down the Kasai river.

Just as on the Kasai, people paddled out in their canoes to try to dock at the 3rd class barge and sell their goods. This time we were going up river, which meant higher swells, therefore even more risky to dock at speed. It was heartbreaking to see how many failed, as about a third of the canoes did. Most simply couldn't catch up with us, and if they did, it was a gamble if they would be able to dock to us on the move without overturning and losing their goods. Much ended up on the river bottom and they themselves often in the water. When they succeeded, the same intense commerce began as on the previous boat. Occasionally it ended with loud rows and minor fistfights: the goods, often fish, were pulled and tugged before they ended up with a victorious customer.

The further up the river and into the jungle we went, the more beautiful the scenery became. Still, as on the Kasai, the riverbank was often a monotonously dense wall of rainforest - hiding what, I wondered. Sometimes we navigated between islands, in a river that was then more like a lake in its width and size. Often islands of water hyacinths floated past us. At Bolobo it really was like a big lake with lots of islands and skerries. Some were covered in papyrus, others overgrown with jungle and sometimes there was a small village with palms and banana trees. Before we approached a village the river was always full of fishermen; two men stood in each dug-out canoe, casting and hauling in their nets. Quite beautiful, even if a bit risky it seemed to me, in the fierce river.

Unlike the boat on Kasai, we rarely stopped and travelled all night. One evening I got to be on the bridge and see how they navigated in the dark. It was just as fascinating on this river boat as the previous one. One officer searched one of the river banks with a large spotlight until he found a white-painted rock or tree. Immediately, the boat was steered towards the white mark and the second searchlight began scanning the other bank. When it spotted a new white mark, the boat headed for it, and so it continued all night. Here it was more professional; the captain seemed to always be present on the bridge. He also looked like a real captain in a white uniform and peaked cap.

In the late 19th century, Swedish missionary Edvard Vilhelm Sjöblom also travelled up the Congo River to establish the Swedish Babtist mission in the country. He stopped in Bolengi, just before Irebu, where the Ubangi River branches off to the north. He stayed here for four years, between 1893 and 1897, after which he wrote articles in the Swedish press, travelled to London and gave a furious speech on the atrocities he had seen in Leopold's Congo. This lecture had a huge impact throughout Europe; Adam Hochschild praises him in his book. Sjöblom returned to the Congo but died in 1903 of fever in Ikoko, east of Bolengi. His diary entries were published in 1907: *I palmernas skugga* (In the Shadow of the Palm Trees). In it he mentions how on one occasion he "saw a soldier pass with a basket containing 18 hands of men, women and children". Leopold's own militia, the 'Force publique,' cut off the right hand of those they punished to show that they had not wasted ammunition on anything but people; if three cartridges were spent, three hands had to be accounted for! The missionary Sjöblom could not keep quiet about this, even though there were other missionaries who turned a blind eye to the horrors. He often found himself in dispute with merchant agents and militias he encountered. In his diary he wrote long passages about the atrocities of the rubber gathering that made Leopold rich and decimated Congo's population by at least a third. A true Swedish missionary hero.

On the second day I had problems with nasty rashes on my back. It didn't look like I had been bitten, instead inexplicable red rashes and they stung, stabbing my skin, rather than itching, when I leaned against a wall or backrest. It made it impossible to lie on my back and I was plagued by it throughout the river journey. Onerous!

It was then good to be able to sit in the 1st class saloon, in a soft armchair, leaning slightly backwards, reading and writing in my diary or an aerogram to a friend in Stockholm. It was always pleasant to write. Nowadays I don't write letters, nor does anyone else: "gone is the voice of handwriting." A sad development!

The lounge had a small bar where you could order something to drink and something to eat. Two groups of sofas and three tables with chairs, of which we canasta players sometimes occupied one of them. There were more Westerners on the boat than I first had realized. Including two mixed couples, one with a Congolese woman and Belgian man, one where the woman was Belgian and the man from the Congo. They all stayed on first class and were nice. It was also Donald and Keith that I usually played canasta with; I got to shower in their cabin a couple of times, which I really appreciated.

I did not, however, the Congolese clown and his friend who attacked me and Riko the second day when we were sitting outside my cabin. The clown was apparently a TV celebrity in Congo and dressed as Mobutu. He insisted on giving Riko a bed: "Whites can never go 3rd class, only

Africans!" Riko's French was worse than mine so I was loudly addressed, got upset and said so, to this idiot number two. The first one disliked Riko because he was Asian, this one the opposite -? It was apparently the skin colour that made a difference. The atmosphere became toxic, but he insisted. They even turned off the music and the Mobutu-clown made a speech to the congregation that he couldn't understand why no one had offered Riko a second-class berth before. Everyone applauded when he said that he would now give Riko a bed in his cabin. Riko did not really appreciate all this, but could not do much else but thank him and was probably happy to get a bed for free. The clown was dismissive of me for the rest of the trip, something that did not bother me one bit. Of course, you should leave indignation at home when you travel: a good traveller accepts (almost) everything, but there are limits.

On Saturday we crossed the equator at Mbandaka. We docked there for a few hours and it was nice to go ashore for a while. The city surprised me by being completely paved and electrified. Not what I expected after three days through rainforest on the Congo. Nothing on Kasai had prepared me. Here it was more like Kinshasa. So I could buy some food and especially fresh bread. Sjöblom was also in Mbandaka at the end of the 19th century. On February 19, 1893, he writes in his diary that "drunkenness was rampant. Both men and women sat around large vessels filled with palm wine." But what else could they do under the oppression of Leopold's militia?

After Mbandaka, one of the other Americans offered me to sleep in his first-class cabin, as his male companion had left us in Mbandaka. But I kindly declined, as I was fairly convinced that he was mainly lusting after my body. He sulked and did not greet me for the rest of the trip. He had flown to Kinshasa to go on a riverboat with his friend who was now on his way to East Africa. He would fly home to Los Angeles directly from Kisangani. He was only here for the river trip. Another way to travel, I noted in my diary.

However, it was so hot and humid that I almost regretted it. It would have been nice to sleep in a real bed in an air-conditioned cabin; the temperature was always between 30 and 35 degrees, slightly cooler at night. I still slept pretty well every night with paper plugs in my ears despite the depth of the bed and the rashes on my back. The first-class

204

lounge was otherwise an oasis where I didn't feel sticky and hot. Even from there, I could enjoy the nature, which at times became something other than the green monotonous forest wall. Sometimes we sailed near islands that could be more barren with various palm trees and baobab where birds of prey sat and surveyed. Occasionally we encountered flashes of rain, which was also beautiful, especially from the comfort of the lounge. Sunsets were fast and spectacular in a different way than on a west coast: it flared up and went out before you knew it.

On Sunday we stayed a couple of hours in Mobeka and our boat was invaded by canoes with people selling chiefly fish. When we were about to leave, the canoes moored to us were ignored and almost half of them overturned and all their goods went to the bottom. A father and son who lost a whole canoe of smoked fish was particularly painful to see. He fell into tears at having lost everything he had hoped to sell.

At one point, a guy jumped into the river for a paddle he had dropped and when he tried to swim to catch up with us, he was unable to reach us. We saw him lying by his paddle and disappearing down the river while we continued upstream. There were no canoes nearby so I don't know what happened to him. Probably he swam ashore on an island or beach and waited for a boat to help him. But he looked very lonely and abandoned as he disappeared behind us.

It strikes me now as I write this that I don't have a single record that we encountered boats other than canoes on either of the two river trips I made. Strange I think today, and wonder if I was mistaken, blind, or simply didn't care.

At six in the morning on Monday, February 21, we arrived in Lisala and it was time for me to go ashore. The night before we partied a bit in the saloon and in Keith and Donald's cabin. Keith also had a recorder so we did a lot of blowing together, which we both thought was fun, what the others thought, however, is not clear from my diary entries. We also played canasta and according to my diary I won big with over 6000 points. I have never played canasta since then.

In Lisala, I met a group of hitchhikers coming from West Africa, heading for East Africa, and now boarding the riverboat to Kisangani. They told me about how difficult it was to find transportation in Congo; it had taken them over a week from Bangui. That I refused to believe. My map told me that it was only about 500 kilometres to Bangui. On the other hand, there were eight of them who had stayed together, so I was sure I'd fare better on my own. And so it turned out, as on the very first day I found a truck to Businga without having to pay a penny. I even had time to eat a good breakfast at a hotel in Lisala and mail the letters I had written on the boat before leaving.

I sat on the flatbed with other passengers and it was lovely. A fresh breeze in the otherwise hot and humid air. In addition, I could fully enjoy the view: a seemingly crazy vegetation without control, completely wild without visible traces of human presence. But then suddenly there were people waving us down and wanting to join us, or children cheering and waving. The people we saw were almost naked. At a small stream, three pygmies were pointed out to me. An older grey-haired man and two women who were washing clothes, I think. Sometimes the jungle was replaced by dull rows of rubber trees, a reminder of Leopold II's reign of terror, which I knew nothing about at the time, but just noted that it looked ugly.

When we arrived in Businga after eight hours, I ended up with Diego, who had been driving the truck. He was from Portugal but had lived in Congo for 24 years now and was married to a beautiful young Congolese woman and had four children. Marrying over the colour of your skin, so to speak, was not at all unusual in Congo, I had understood. It was and probably is not as horrible to 'go native' as it was and perhaps still is in the Commonwealth. I was to meet quite a few Belgians who were married to Congolese. Here, however, there was a Portuguese who once a week went to Lisala and met the boat from Kinshasa to pick up supplies and the beer he had bought from the capital. He had a spinning mill near the little restaurant I was having dinner at, which he also owned. He invited me to spend the night at the restaurant, though I wasn't sure where, but I soon found out.

As I am eating - beans and sausages - one of the women who served at the place comes and sits down next to me and says that we will sleep together tonight. I get the feeling that Diego has asked her to do this. But I'm not interested and she gets a bit upset, but leaves me alone after a while. When I want to go to bed, I still have no idea of where, but they show me a large, rather empty room to sleep in. No bed, but I put together some armchairs into a sofa and prepare for the night. Then the young woman appears again and insists:

"Vous et moi la!" pointing at my made bed.

"No!"

"Oui!"

"No!"

"Pourquoi?"

"Je vouloir dormir. Je suis fatigue"

But suddenly she takes off her clothes and is standing naked in front of me. I get really irritated, even though she is pretty, and collect her clothes and put them outside on the veranda and ask her to leave. However, my irritation is nothing compared to her anger as she stalks out screaming and finally leaves me alone.

The next morning I wake up at six and, after doing my morning toilet in the restaurant's simple bathroom, get some breakfast. I am served by the woman from last night who reluctantly and with dark eyes dumps an omelette and a cup of black coffee on the table in front of me. I can understand her; I have insulted her and again hardly behaved like a gentleman. Diego laughs at her and of course also at me for declining to share the night with her.

I was now rid of the rashes on my back without having understood what they were, but probably something on the riverboat bothered me; maybe I was allergic to the boat? Now I was instead plagued by mosquito bites on my elbows and kneecaps. Never understood why in these particular places, but it was annoying and made it difficult to sleep. In other words: constant torture.

It was nevertheless now time to find some transportation to Bangui. I walked around Businga almost all day, asking around, but not a single vehicle would leave the city that day. Incredible, and I began to understand why it had taken the people I met in Lisala so long to get from Bangui. So I returned to Diego and his restaurant. Fortunately, he was understanding and allowed me to stay another night. The young woman from yesterday was not as friendly. But at least I didn't have to face her advances that night. Instead, the Portuguese invited me to dinner with his children and wife. We ate lots and well. But he scolded his wife for forgetting to charge for two beers during the day; he called her all sorts of awful names and she started crying and soon the younger children as well. I felt rather uncomfortable having to witness this, but soon I was alone with him and he apologized. "But you have to keep them short, otherwise they forget who is in charge." I never understood whether he meant the women or the Congolese - maybe both.

Early the next morning Diego found a small Fiat that would take me to Karawa, but he said that from there it would be difficult, as there was hardly any traffic going north and no bus service in these areas.

The Fiat stalled several times on its own and we had to push it going again. Soon the guy driving gave up and we turned back towards Businga. Would I never get out of here? were my thoughts when we met a truck that I managed to get to Karawa with. It was an old worn-out Ford with no shock absorbers, so it was a four-hour painfully bumpy journey. I had only had one cup of coffee before the Fiat, so I was desperately hungry when we reached Karawa - and that was as far as I got that day.

I found a trucking company, or maybe it was just a loading dock; either way, there was nothing leaving that day. Unsuspectingly, I put my backpack leaning against a loading bridge and walked around to see if perhaps tomorrow... Then a big German Shepherd-like dog came over and lifted one leg to pee on my backpack. I was just in time to kick it before it performed its natural needs, but then of course it flew at me with a roar. I jumped quickly up on the loading bridge so the hound only managed to scratch my arm and stomach, tearing my t-shirt. I was lucky I was not bitten! The men at the grounds sprang on the dog with sticks and beat it to death before I could stop them. I understood the dog; I would also have been furious if someone had kicked me when I went to take a piss. My t-shirt was ripped over my stomach and there was some bleeding, also on my arm, so they bathed it with some red antiseptic liquid. I threw the shirt away and they were kind enough to take me to a nearby mission station.

It turned out to be a Lutheran mission. The people who ran it were Swedish-Americans who thought it was surprisingly pleasant to have a Swedish visitor. They gave me their nice guest room with 'en suite' bathroom. A wonderful hot shower was the first thing that happened to me. Then a good dinner with two ladies playing the Swedish Christian singer Arthur Erikson on a cassette player. Not really my kind of music, but it was agreeable and I ate a lot. They understood when I apologized, explaining that I hadn't eaten anything all day. They told me that there were 25 Americans from the Lutheran Missionary Society in the US living and working there.

"But what do you actually do?" I asked.

"We run a hospital, have two schools and of course a church where we preach the word of God."

"I get the feeling that there are more missionaries in Congo than in other African countries; is that true?" (Even Tintin met missionaries on his trip to the Congo!) George Washington Williams, an American officer and politician who travelled in the Congo, wrote a report to his American president in 1890. He found that the Christian missions were the only reason for some future hope for the country. He mentions that nowhere in Africa were Christian missionaries so quick to establish themselves: 27 of them at the time, including two Swedish ones.

"Perhaps. Our church has a long tradition of being in Congo, since the days of Albert Schweitzer. But it's not just about missionary work; we want to help these people, who are often poor and many are sick without a hospital nearby and the children have no school to go to. Now they do."

"And they all must convert to Christianity?" I asked. "What is wrong with the native divinities, the local religions?"

"Well, ideally everyone should be saved for their own good! Of course, we want as many people as possible to meet Christ and live in the Christian family. The local religions may not be so bad, but our church encourages us to do missionary work. We believe in one God for all!"

From the 16th century onwards, missionary activity was in the political service of European expansion, justifying the ravages of imperialism. This cannot be ignored, as well as their contribution to the destruction of domestic political structures in most countries. At the same time, according to Richard Dowden, missions and Christian churches have provided "more real development" to people in Africa than all governments, the World Bank and aid organizations combined. And it's hard not to like this good work; it's when they insist on everyone becoming Christians that it's harder to sympathize. At the same time, they are often more sympathetic than the white people who live in the cities of Africa; the latter often despise the African and feel sorry for themselves.

I now know that missionaries have had a great impact on the continent as they virtually monopolized primary schools throughout sub-Saharan Africa, for better or worse. Almost all first- and second-generation writers in Africa started their education in missionary schools. One can think what one likes about missionary work, but it was great that Chinua Achebe learned to read and write. He could have done so in a national school - if there had been any - but there wasn't one where he grew up. So instead of Igbo, Nigerian or African history, he had to learn the history of England and instead of *Sunjata* he had to read *Hamlet*. Achebe, happy to have learned to read, has nevertheless said, wise as he was, that he could not imagine any Igbos traveling halfway around the world to try to persuade anyone else to change their beliefs.

The next day my visa for Congo would expire; I had been in the country for a month. But I wouldn't reach the border tomorrow and was a bit worried.

After a great American breakfast, I got a ride into Karawa and went out of town and sat down to wait for a possible vehicle. At a nearby trucking company they said no one was going north that day, so I had low hopes. But in the middle of the day a truck arrived and I was able to squeeze into a closed flatbed. There were fifteen of us sitting in the dark jolting along to Gemena. That was as far as I got that day. I didn't have to pay for the lift here either, while everyone else had to. I was a guest in the country, the driver said, and so should not pay. Beautiful of him, I thought.

In Gemena I also found a mission station. A small one right next to the road. There I first met the lady of the house who gave me the open garage to sleep in for the night. I thanked her for that even though I had hoped for better, spoiled as I undoubtedly was by now. It would be difficult to sleep in the open garage, I thought, with all the flies. Here they were the most frantic since Ethiopia. They looked like tse tse flies with overlapping wings. Whether they were or not, I don't know - but I slept well. This was probably more due to the fact that when her husband, the priest came home, I was told to move into the guest room and a soft bed. There was a faltering dinner with them as their French was only slightly better than mine, but the food was fine.

The next morning I was up early, determined not to miss anything heading towards Bangui. Now I was in the Congo illegally too; my visa had expired. I said goodbye to my hosts and stepped out of the gate where the road was and sat by the side of the road as the sun rose. But it didn't help. At noon I gave up, went back to the mission where I left my backpack and into town to see if anyone was going to Bangui in the afternoon. At 2 pm, I was told, a truck would leave to Libenge and I was allowed to come along if I was there then. I promised, picked up my backpack at the mission and found a simple hotel where I could get a decent lunch. At two I was back at the truck and now had to pay 2.50 zaire to get to Libenge. Quite okay, even though it was the first time I paid for a ride since Ethiopia.

Before leaving Gemena we were stopped by a uniformed police officer who of course wanted to see my passport. I was really worried and prepared to bribe my way out of a tricky situation if he understood that my visa had expired. But he didn't, and after a while he waved us on.

We arrived in Libenge after dark, at eight o'clock. I asked around and found a Protestant mission here too. However, only the night watchman was home so I had to sleep on the veranda of one of the houses. But I was given access to a bathroom with running water so I could wash and brush my teeth, which I appreciated. Then I spread out on the veranda and started fighting the mosquitoes. But not just mosquitoes. In the dark, I suddenly feel something big crawling on one shoulder. I brush it away and realize that it is worryingly large. I find my flashlight and see a scorpion crawling away. With the light beam pinned to the insect, I find one of my shoes and strike it as hard as I can. I hit it perfectly and it became a very dead and flat scorpion. What if it had stung me? I think and wonder if there are more creatures who intend to visit my physique. Soon I get more pleasant company from a dog who wants to be patted and to lick me. I don't allow the latter, but he slept next to me all night. Felt safe.

I didn't get much sleep, but some, as I woke up with the sun and left after thanking the night watchman and the dog. I got a quick ride 19 km to a T-junction, where I anticipated more vehicles. Not so. But there was a little 'duka' nearby where I could buy small sweet bananas and some rolls with dead little ants in them. As the ants were dead, I did not care about them but spread my Blue Ribbon margarine on the bread and had something like a breakfast. Then I sat by the roadside, in the shade under a tree and wrote in my diary. This attracted some attention. Not only children sneaked around me, peering in wonder at the writings of the weird-looking long-haired figure in shorts. It was a fine way to pass the time while waiting, not really expecting much in the way of transportation. Traveling this way in Africa meant a lot of waiting. How long had I not waited for jeeps to start in Ethiopia, lifts in East Africa, trains in Likasi, river boats in Ilebo and trucks in Congo. But I was in no hurry, so...

But wonders still happens: a truck appeared and I was allowed to join it to Zongo and the border. And I did not have to pay: "Guests should never pay!" said the driver and the others in the truck agreed. I didn't argue with them this time either. In Zongo I was able to leave Congo without any problems. They did not care, or they did not notice that I had overstayed my welcome in the country.

Bangui – Casablanca

Garoua-Boulai

In Bangui, Central African Republic, getting my passport stamped was tricky at first. There was no border station that wanted to see my passport. I could have slipped into the country without a visa stamp, but I knew that would be stupid. Instead, I went down to the harbour and there at the port police they stamped me welcome into CAR, as the country was called for short. They also invited me to stay with them in a guest room that surprisingly was available with four wooden berths – I was even able to wash some clothes. An Ethiopian and a guy from Jamaica were already occupying two of the beds. The former was from Asmara and had lost his passport, which he was waiting for here at the police station. The Jamaican did not know what to do. He had tried to enter Nigeria from the north, but they hadn't let him in, so now he had walked around Lake Chad and was going to try it from the east. What he was doing this far east I never understood. He was a silent figure who hardly said a word and mostly lay in his bed, sleeping or staring into oblivion, probably in despair about his predicament.

I took a walk in the city that rose up from the Ubangi River that flows into the Congo. Bangui turned out to be quite large, which was not surprising as it is the capital of the nation. CAR has a sad history, also postcolonially. It was a French colony from the late 19th century until 1960, when most African countries gained independence. In 1965, however, Jean-Bédel Bokassa seized power in a military coup. The same year I was there he declared himself president for life and four year later he proclaimed himself emperor of the Central African Empire, as he renamed the country. In 1979, French troops entered and deposed Bokassa. Since then, the country has suffered one military coup after another. Today there is a semblance of democracy with the latest elections in 2020. However, parts of the country are controlled by different military factions, so it is still a troubled country.

In 1972 it was relatively quiet, as it can be for a tourist in a dictatorship. I quickly realized that Bangui, of course named after the Ubangi River, looked like many African cities I had been to, with a mixture of

214

new and old, African and European. It reminded me a lot of East African cities, with what seemed to be a fairly large European population.

One of them stopped in a Renault next to me on the sidewalk as I was promenading around in the city. He rolled down a window and wondered what I was doing and who I was. I answered cordially and then he asked if he could show me the city. I answered in the affirmative and got into the car. We went through the whole city, back and forth, up and down in his little Renault. We visited its Notre Dame church and saw Bokassa's palace, the fantastic marketplace where we strolled around. Jacques, as he was called, then bought us lunch down by the river and told me that he was from Lyon but had been living here now for seven years working for a French import company. After lunch he insisted on showing me his house. It was a small unassuming building in, what I understood to be the African part of the city. But nice and he had books on bookshelves along almost all the walls and also stacked over large parts of the floor; obviously a big reader. He offered me a beer and then said that we were going to take an after-lunch-nap. "No, merci," I said. But he undressed down to his underwear - which were minimal and in leopard print - and crawled into bed. I don't know how much he slept but I spent the time browsing through his bookshelves. Very fine literature and just the fact that he had furnished with books was beautiful and appealing. As Jorge Luis Borges writes somewhere, the book is mankind's most astonishing contrivance. All other tools are extensions of the human body, but not the book, which is "an extension of memory and imagination." In this light, it is peculiar that people today seem to shun books so much, at least in their homes. If you look at interior design TV, or magazines with the same focus, books are conspicuous by their absence. Sad and impoverished. A house without literature indicates trivial people and it is extraordinary that it seems to be trendy to be dull. Strange, even if you don't have to be a geek, like the writer of these lines, who even at this age buys new bookshelves to fill with fine literature.

When Jacques felt he had slept enough, he offered me coffee and asked me if I had never made love to a man.

"Nope," I replied. "Nor have I ever had any desire to do so."

"Too bad. It's really nice."

"Perhaps, but I prefer girls."

He understood, accepted, even if disappointed. This I realised when he in silence drove me into town and I was able to find my way down to the harbour police again. Here they were still kind and offered us food so we didn't have to go to a restaurant that night. All the time they were inquisitive and wanted to know everything about the three of us, what we were doing, where we came from, where we were going, etc. I have never met friendlier cops.

After a liver paste sandwich, courtesy of the constables, I found myself at a police checkpoint out of Bangui the next morning. Here all cars had to stop. Perfect for a hitchhiker. Now I had also changed map, from 155 to 153, which would guide me across the Sahara to Morocco. The police here were just as friendly. This despite the fact that Bokassa, or Papa Bok, as he was called, stared sternly at them from the compulsory portrait: vain with a medal-heavy uniform. After I showed my passport, they promised to arrange my first ride of the day. While I was waiting for the truck they had arranged, a caravan of Land Rovers passed by. A Swedish older couple was with them and we talked a bit. They were on their way to East Africa and had driven through the Sahara in their convoy. They expressed surprise that I was traveling alone, whereupon I felt a bit grand.

Then I rode on a truck to Bouar, thanks to the police. If I had been a little more informed, I could have stopped at Boali, a few miles after Bangui, and the Mbali River waterfalls close by. André Gide described them as wonderful when writing in his diary next to them on September 28, 1925.

Knowing nothing of this and not having read Gide I arrived at Bouar at midnight where there was no hotel and disturbing a mission was out of the question. When the driver realized my situation, he offered me to sleep in his house. He lived alone in a small wooden house with a corrugated iron roof well outside the city. The house had two rooms and a small kitchenette; I slept on the couch in the living room and slept well, even though I was badly bitten by mosquitoes.

In the morning he offered me a breakfast of maize porridge. I thanked him heartily, even though our conversation was a bit halting as his French was even worse than mine. But he understood that I wanted to find the way to Cameroon and told me about a bus a few blocks away

216

I could take. He showed me the way and I got on the bus. When I wanted to pay, I wasn't allowed. "Guests in this country don't have to pay!" How different it can be; in many countries it is often the other way around: tourists pay double. But now I had encountered this beautiful policy on several occasions in Francophone Africa.

At a roadside market in Bouar I managed to get some tea and a sandwich with some kind of sausage. Good. I also bought more bananas. And reflected in the diary that my banana diet in Africa will surely turn me into one. I probably ate between five and ten every day. But on the other hand, they were small and sweet and tasty and filling, so...

Then I found my way out of town and the first truck stopped and I was taken to Garoua-Boulai. I sat on the flatbed and could see that the countryside was no longer rainforest, here it was more reminiscent of southern Europe, but with Africa's terracotta red soil. As in East Africa, there were small villages and small farms everywhere. At the border with Cameroon they insisted that I pay for the lift, but the driver refused: tourists should not pay! Sympathetic, I thought again. Entering Cameroon was no problem, except that here too I had to fill in a lot of more or less incomprehensible forms. My concerns about borders since Moyale had now subsided. It was painless every time!

Now I was filthy again. When I left Bangui I was clean thanks to the harbour police's showers, but these dusty dirt and mud roads immediately and stubbornly soiled me. On most rides I sat outside on top of the truck beds and the dust swirled. But even inside a fully loaded Peugeot car, the dust whirled in through the open windows. I made sure I always wore the same clothes when I travelled and then in the evening changed into my cleanest dirty clothes, especially if I was in a mission and invited to dinner, which happened. It was horrible to put the filthy traveling clothes back on the next morning. After a few days, the T-shirt could almost stand on its own. I used my few underpants for at least three days. There was a lot of washing when the opportunity arose.

They used the same currency in Cameroon as in CAR, which was good (500 francs = £1) as I had money left over from CAR that I didn't have to worry about spending before entering Cameroon. Often the currencies of African countries were not even exchangeable in neighbouring countries, so you had to spend your cash before leaving a country. Here it was pegged to the French franc, so it would be exchangeable, but I planned to get rid of it all before Nigeria, where they probably used shillings like in East Africa.

In Garoua-Boulai I managed to find another mission. There I met Bob and Brody. A Canadian and an Australian who had just arrived and moved into the guesthouse offered by the mission. Here you had to pay 500F per night, i.e. one Sterling pound. But it was worth it: it was a beautiful one-story stone villa. When you entered, you immediately found yourself in a large living room with a leather sofa and deep armchairs, bookshelves, a fireplace and a dining table. The room was lit by several floor lamps in the corners and a large crystal lamp from the ceiling over the table. There were three generous bedrooms and two bathrooms and a spacious and well-equipped kitchen. The house was on a hill under large fig trees, overlooking a valley with a small stream. I stayed for two nights, as it was such a fabulously beautiful and comfy house. I was also able to wash myself and my clothes again.

Once we had settled in, the three of us went to a market in the small town and bought food for dinner and breakfast. We made a good meat and vegetable stew for dinner, fruit salad for dessert and coffee that was available in the house. Then we lit a fire in the fireplace and sat and talked for a long time about Bod Dylan, Africa and Stalin, inter alia, while it began to rain and thunder outside. A real thunderstorm was nearing. Suddenly there was a deafening bang and a flash of lightning at the same time. The house shook, all the lights died; we looked at each other with concern and got out of our deep leather armchairs, afraid that lightning had struck the house. We saw smoke from a large tree nearby, so we guessed that it had been hit by the lightning. We all had flashlights and soon found some candles, but were a bit shaken. After sitting up for a while and watching lightning dance across the black sky, above and between the trees, we disappeared to separate bedrooms and into clean sheets in made-up beds. And there were no mosquitoes to haunt me either. I slept like a baby, despite the rumbling back and forth across the sky.

The next day an Austrian and an English guy arrived and they shared one of the rooms as Bob and Brody moved into another. I was alone so I kept mine. The four of them were all going to East Africa so they questioned me about everything I could tell them, which was quite a lot.

218

I questioned them too, of course. They scared me quite a lot about Lagos: a terrible city! Then, as is not uncommon among globetrotters, we got talking about upset stomachs and diarrhoeas and terrible toilets. My story from southern Ethiopia and the toilet where I fell and ended up sitting on the urinated floor won that competition!

Also this day we went to the market and bought food together. The Austrian found some exciting sausages that he promised to make a good sausage stew with, and he did. I then spent the rest of the day on the veranda. After the night's rain, the damp grass smelled fantastic and all the flowers were happily reaching for the sun, the land was freshly washed! I thought that this was so beautiful that I decided to remember it for the rest of my life - but I didn't. Not even with the help of my diary today, 50 years later. Instead, on a bookshelf in the house I found William Faulkner's *As I Lay Dying* in a handsome Signet paperback, which I started reading immediately and decided to take with me. Powerful reading and the book is still found in my bookshelves here at home. I left Leon Uri's *Exodus* behind, which I had finished. It was pleasant to sit and read one afternoon in peace and quiet on a shaded veranda in Garoua-Boulai. The others went about their businesses or were out on exploratory walks. We never saw any priests, even though the church was fully visible on a hill behind our guesthouse. We paid a teenager who showed up in the afternoon and seemed to act as a factotum on the mission.

After dinner we became quieter this evening. The Austrian had a guitar with him and played beautiful classical pieces. I read and journaled, as did the others. A nice quiet evening in Cameroon; in 1925 André Gide stayed, according to his own account, a few wonderful days in Baboua, close by, so this was perhaps a blessed region.

The country is rather unique with two colonial languages as official, English and French, along with about 25 indigenous languages. And it is a member of both the Commonwealth and La Francophonie. This is of course because England and France have both colonized parts of the country, but the Germans were first. Though some Portuguese were before them. And before the Portuguese Arab slave traders and before that hunter-gatherer Pygmies about 50,000 years ago. These were displaced by Bantu people from what is now Nigeria sometime in 200 BC. In the late 19th century, Germany colonized the country, but after World War I, England and France divided it between themselves. Like much of Africa, also Cameroon gained independence in 1960. President Ahidjo ruled for 22 years and, despite the country's fractured colonial history and several different ethnic groups, managed to unify the country in an extraordinary way for the continent. He balanced old ethnic rivalries with representation in the National Assembly. In 1982 he handed over to Paul Biya, who is still running the country at the time of writing. Remarkably for Africa, idol portraits of president Ahidjo appeared only in official buildings, not in every shop or restaurant, as so often in other African countries. The country even has a multi-party system nowadays, but Biya is firmly in charge even though the English-speaking part of the country, since early 2010 struggles to free itself and Boko Haram has terrorized the north of the country.

When I woke up next day, however, everything was peaceful and after a quick breakfast I got a ride with a truck even before I managed to take off my backpack. It was on its way to Yaoundé, 600 km away, which pleased me. Maybe we would get there the same day, the driver hoped. But we didn't. We stopped in Bertoua. Before that, impertinent and arrogant gendarmes had stopped us and asked me if I was paying for the trip.

"No. No one has asked me," I replied.

Then they said that I had to.

"Never!" the driver insisted. Then the gendarmes attacked me. They grabbed my backpack and tore out parts of my luggage on the ground, looked several times at my passport without knowing what strange country Sweden was, but they saw my visa. Then their boss came out, drove them away and apologized for their rude behaviour and gave me a coca cola to comfort me. And we could to move on.

The driver was also really upset about how they had treated me and apologized for their behaviour. "Ca va bien. C'est rien," I said in my now improved French, as we rolled on. Now I noticed that it was greener again. Deep forest and less people. We arrived in Bertoua around 5 pm and I found a small restaurant that offered meat stew with rice. We stayed in town and I took a walk and discovered that the country apparently suffered from football fever. Everywhere, people were glued to radios and listening to the African Championships, where Cameroon was successful. I remember the Cameroonian Lions from the 1990 World Cup as one of the most exciting football teams I have ever seen, with Roger Milla as the big star. It was particularly sad when Gary Lineker scored an undeserved penalty on extra time in the quarter-final, and The Lions were ousted.

When I got back to the truck I could sleep in the driver's cabin, which I was grateful for. It had rained heavily during the night so the truck bed was wet. At three o'clock I was awakened and it was time to move on. When it got light, we stopped and slept for another hour, after which we found a simple restaurant that could offer some breakfast. I had an omelette, a cup of tea and bought peanuts and of course bananas. In Yaoundé, the driver organized a free taxi to take me out of town to the road towards Douala. There was apparently no limit to how helpful people were here!

Everyone who saw me at the roadside said that there would be no more cars that day, but instead they advised me to take a taxi to a mission outside the city. After a few hours I did so when it began to grow dark. It cost 100F (2 SEK); I could afford that. Once there, I met two Cameroonian priests who told me that they had no room for me, but they gave me 200F so I could take another taxi to a larger mission further out from Yaoundé. I now read in my diary that later that day I wondered if we Swedes would be as kind and generous if a lone fellow from Cameroon came hitchhiking through Sweden. Probably not, was my gloomy answer, and I have no reason to change that verdict today. Quite the contrary, as there are now brown-shirts, xenophobic and dangerous clowns in the parliament who call themselves friends of Sweden, when that is exactly what they are not!

It turned out to be an adventurous taxi ride. The road consisted of wet and slippery mud, and we skidded along as if it had been a freshly washed sleigh run. The Peugeot 504, which of course it was, had a low battery and the driver chose to drive without headlights. But he managed it brilliantly. Driving carefully with his eyes up to the sky, he followed the strip of light that the starry sky formed between the tall forest on both sides of the road. Fortunately, we didn't meet any other traffic. I did not have to pay for the trip either, so I earned 200F, very undeservedly.

At the next mission, I met a Cameroonian priest who offered me a sandwich and a beer and thanked me for allowing him to meet a Swedish citizen for the first time in his life. Not that remarkable, I thought but he insisted. Perhaps I would have thought the same if he showed up on Harpsundsvägen. I remember when there were rumours that a n... had been seen - I almost wrote the n-word, which we used then and Sven Lindqvist uses unreflectively in *Exterminate All the Brutes*, in 1992. Well, a black guy had been seen in Högdalen centre and we small guys threw ourselves on our bikes to see if we could spot him. May have been in the early 60s. A lot has happened since then. The world is more exciting today, also in Högdalen.

After a pleasant conversation, I am given a candle and a key to a small house where there should be a bed and a chair, which there is. But I am not alone in the room; I have disgusting company. I hear a familiar quiet scratching and rustling along the walls, and when I turn the candle to the wall I see that it is full of cockroaches, each the size of a thumb. I take off one of my shoes and start killing as many as I can. Soon I realize it's futile. The walls are covered with them! I just dirty the wall and there are far too many for my one shoe. How can I sleep in this cockroach inferno? The British explorer, Harry Johnston, has said that these repulsive insects do not hesitate to attack people at night. They sneak up to your mouth and suck saliva, eat at your toes and if you have a wound on your body, they will happily attack it. So, what do I do? And then I become suspicious of the bed. It looks clean, but when I lift the mattress, I see millions (it seems me) of the same nauseating bugs crawling under the mattress. I can't sleep here! But I have to. It's late and pitch-black outside. Finding another bed is out of the question. So, I spread my rain poncho over the bed so that it hangs down over the edges of the bed. Then I put the sleeping bag on top of it, then myself, and then the Kassala-blanket over me. I decide not to worry about cockroaches in bed: they can't climb up my poncho I convince myself, and I manage to fall asleep - something that still amazes me.

I woke up as the sun began to shine in through the only window, happy and surprised that I had survived and slept well. I checked for cockroaches, but the only ones I could see now are the ones I had crushed against the wall. Had I dreamt about all of them in the bed? No, the remains on the wall indicated the opposite. I brushed them off as

222

best I could before leaving the room. The priest from yesterday met me and offered me coffee and wished me good luck.

A Peugeot soon offered me a ride to Douala. The road was now partly paved, but full of treacherous potholes, so he had to drive carefully, which he did not do at all; we passengers bounced up and down in the car all the way. It went smoother on the parts that were not paved.

Now it was deep rainforest again and many of the simple houses were made of wood, but the mud ones looked better. I also noticed that many people had graves in front of their houses. Probably family graves and convenient to have also the dead close by. Even though 70% of the people in the country are Christians (20% Muslims and 10% animists), the circular view of life probably remained with many. In addition, people lived, and still do in rural areas, in extended families, so it may be logical that even the dead should remain in the shared family environment.

Now English was being spoken more and more. I had gotten used to French and had become fairly fluent, but of course I preferred English. Meanwhile, the driver suddenly wanted 500F from me. I was surprised and at first a little upset, but soon realized that it was of course perfectly fine - 2.50 SEK I could afford, although he could have told me before we set out.

Douala was the craziest city I have ever seen. The traffic was completely chaotic. The streets were only wide enough for one car, but they went both ways. It was also full of bicycles and mopeds and how it all worked I never understood. At one crossing a stray car was blocking all traffic. A couple of policemen stood a little further away and watched the spectacle with amusement. Some drove onto the sidewalk, others tried to hit the car to push it out of the way. In the end, some hardy men took the car and lifted it out of the way with relative ease. I nevertheless got out of the city somehow and soon sat by the side of a road again after a sausage sandwich and a coke. And some bananas. I was lucky to leave Douala quickly. Gide had to wait a week in a lousy guesthouse in Douala for his boat back to Europe in 1926 and found the whites he met here to be "ugly...stupid...vulgar." Glad I didn't have to meet them!

Everyone who saw me at the side of the road insisted I had to take a taxi, but soon a Mercedes truck stopped and I was driven to Loum. A town surrounded by large plantations of bananas, pineapples, rubber

and coffee. I had not seen anything like that since East Africa. I also saw
rice fields terraced along the mountains. Still, I went on; I had heard that
there would be lots of missions in Kumba, so after some more bananas
and peanuts, I took a taxi there for 300F. A packed 504 where we could
not move, but the driver drove like a car thief so we were soon there.

In Kumba, I surprisingly found that there was only one mission in
town. There I was refused accommodation for the first time by a mission. An English-speaking Catholic priest: "We've had trouble with your
kind before."

"My kind?" I asked, surprised and quite upset. But there was nothing
to do but wander off. I found a hotel in town that wanted 1500F for a
room. I didn't want to pay that so I said I would find something cheaper.
I got a couple of hundred meters when a guy caught up with me and
promised a cheaper price: 300F for a room (6 SEK). I could afford that.
The guys who managed the hotel also showed me to a restaurant where
I had a big dinner for 50F. It was a nice evening and I had come a long
way this day, almost 500 km.

Tomorrow I was hoping to get to Nigeria. But they told me that the
road is one-way between Kumba and Mamfé. One day you could drive
in one direction, the next in the other, and on Sundays it was free in both
directions as there is no commercial traffic on the road. Tomorrow was
Sunday. And I quietly wondered how dangerous it would be on the road,
but I wanted to go to Mamfé tomorrow because on Monday the traffic
went towards Kumba, where now I was.

The hotel had hardly any water but I was given a bucket of water to
wash myself, also managed to somehow and somewhat wash a pair of
underwear. As always, I changed clothes for the evening. Wonderful to
put on a fairly clean shirt and jeans in the evenings. The shorts I always
travelled in had ripped at the back, but no one noticed so I continued
traveling in them. I spent the evening with the guys who ran the hotel.
We sat in the small lobby and spoke of football, politics and girls in
English.

The next morning I marched out of town and it took almost two
hours. Exhausted in the heat, I sat down by the side of the road and
hoped for a lift, in spite of it being Sunday. Here again I was told that
no cars were coming. But I didn't want to give up. This was how it was
to hitchhike in Africa; you waited and waited. No car comes, but like a

miracle one suddenly shows up anyway and you stop it and ask if there is room. There seldom is, as all cars, no matter what kind, always are full (except in Zambia), but miraculously they always find room and you always get to go with them.

So I sat and waited, admiring the butterflies and birds in the intense vegetation, as well as the funeral processions that passed by on the road. It was Sunday and people were dressed up and singing monotonously and beautifully to various drums as they strode past me with a coffin and weeping families. Little boys ran playfully past with their miniature cars they had built from tin cans and steel cables. A European who lived next to the road also came by and promised that I could stay with him if I didn't get a ride. As it turned out I did not have to take him up on his offer, which pleased me: he was a fool. He told me not to worry about all the "black apes," but to stick to white people. How can such a prick live in Cameroon? I wondered. "The less intelligent a white man is, the more stupid he thinks blacks are," André Gide insightfully said of the racism he encountered.

After a few of hours by the road, a couple of young locals came by and took me to a small bar where they offered lukewarm lager on wooden benches. After another couple of hours when we mostly had talked football, we went to the brother of one of them where they offered dinner. Now it was dark and I wondered where I could sleep. I asked around and they promised that I could spend the night with them, which of course I accepted, much better and nicer than with the white fool. Abel, as was the name of the brother, had a large family. They lived in a simple wooden house by the road. Everyone was extremely friendly and his mother took my shorts and mended them with needle and thread. How on earth did she know, or discover that they were torn, I wonder now. Surely, I couldn't have asked her to mend them?

They served rice, meat with a hot sauce and plantains for dinner and we all sat on small stools around the food and ate with our hands. I remember really enjoying this, how pleasant they were. I opened up as best as I could and answered all their questions, told them about Sweden and my family and some of what I had experienced in Africa.

Then we went to a neighbour's house in the rain and drank palm wine and listened to football. Cameroon had previously won against Congo in the bronze match, and now it was the final between Congo-Brazzaville and Mali; it ended 3-2. There were about 15 of us, all male, in a room with a dirt floor and clay walls; we sat on small stools, with a kerosene lamp hanging from a hook in the ceiling, listening to a crackling transistor radio. Silence prevailed but everyone had opinions about the players and the game, but mainly why Cameroon had lost the semi to Congo-Brazzaville by 0-1. The radio report was, however, rather peculiar. The commentator, or if there were two of them, alternated between English and French. Every ten minutes they switched language. Nothing strange about it, apparently, but it didn't seem like my friends understood French very well, as they asked me about the French comments. This was useless, however, as I seldom managed to follow the French commentary.

In the middle of the game, some children came in with frogs that had rained down from the sky. I expressed some scepticism, but everyone assured me that it happened sometimes when it was raining and windy. And they were good to eat, especially for pregnant women. They didn't look very appetizing to me - but frog legs are supposed to be good, so... The Lord's second plague on Egypt in *Exodus* is about frogs. It doesn't say they rain, but they "flooded the land." If you read up a little, you realize that it can actually look like it's raining frogs, and also fish. Tornado winds suck them out of waterways and they fall down somewhere else. Not so common, but it is documented, and now also in Kumba, Cameroon, on Sunday, March the 5th, in 1972.

I shared a bed with Josef, Abel's younger brother, and slept well as the bed was wide and I was in my sleeping bag. In the morning I had some porridge and then thanked everyone as much as I was able. Truly a stay to be remembered with warm gratitude; it is such meetings, evenings that make traveling worth the inconveniences that also occur along the hitchhiker's galaxy. I photographed the whole family in front of their house before saying goodbye. The photo of the family is in my album. It's a bit dark, but in the centre the father is sitting with a proud posture in a traditional big shirt and a tilted hat. Behind him are his two wives and then six children and some cousins and Abel in white shorts a little to the side. He gave me the address so I later sent him a copy of the picture and thanked him again for a memorable evening. Hope it got there.

226

As I sit here reading my diary and writing about all these kind and generous people, it's almost as if I'm making it up; surely everyone I met couldn't have been that nice? It also strikes me that nobody robbed me during my months in Africa; nobody even tried to! In fact, the kindness I describe here was what I experienced 50 years ago. No lie or exaggeration. Harry Martinson, the Swedish poet and Nobel laureate, wrote somewhere in his travel prose that it is when you are at the bottom of society that you get to know the true, good and caring nature of mankind. Now, I was hardly at the bottom of society, even if I was stingy, but I certainly met kind people.

And it continued. The next day I got a lift in a 504 with three uniformed men who were incredibly friendly and one had studied in Leeds and was craving Mars-bars. Of course, no road controls bothered the uniformed car and we were off to Mamfé. Before that we stopped in a small village and drank Guinness. The restaurant was located above a valley with great views and the greenery overwhelmingly intense. In Mamfé I stayed over at a Presbyterian mission, where I again could wash myself and some clothes. I seemed to be washing clothes all the time, according to my diary, but the roads soiled me terribly. On top of that the humid heat. And I didn't carry a lot of clothes, but always a bar of washing soap. That night I slept almost nothing because of the heat and the mosquitoes. The guest room was as simple as Abel's, but there the night had been cooler.

I got stuck in Mamfé! There was simply no traffic to Nigeria once I got on the road. What traffic there was, I was told, was full taxis who already had left earlier in the morning. But I sat for a few hours and waited hopefully for nothing, as it turned out. Well, an old lady came by and took pity on me and gave me a pineapple and three oranges! Then I trodden back to the mission where a German already had taken the guest room and the bed, but I slept that night on the floor. And just like at the Sikh temple in Mombasa, it was a little cooler and fewer mosquito on the floor, so I slept better than the previous night. The hard floor was no problem. Before sundown that day, a young man from the mission came and took me out into the jungle to a couple of spectacular iron suspension bridges that the Germans had built in the early 1900s. They were like something out of an Indiana Jones movie, but very sturdy and solid so were still used extensively. We crossed one of them over a deep river ravine. A bit scary, but I am sure they are still there, today 50 years later. On both sides the jungle towered like a green impenetrable wall, I was glad I didn't have to traverse. It simply wouldn't have been possible.

The next day I made sure to rise in time and managed in a packed Peugeot 504 to get to the Nigerian border.

Lagos

Soon I was in Nigeria. Africa's most populous nation, seventh most populated country in the world according to Wikipedia; almost 200 million inhabitants and every sixth African is supposed to be Nigerian! There are said to be around 250 different peoples and languages in the country. English is the official language, while Hausa and Fula predominate in the Muslim north and Yoruba and Igbo in the mainly Christian south. The crises between the south and the north in recent decades have highlighted the absurdity of colonial boundaries. While people all over southern Sahara, the Sahel, have more in common with each other: how they are born, grow up, marry, and die, likewise peoples along the coast of West Africa have more in common with each other; Nigerians in the south do therefore share little traditions or customs with their compatriots in the north. The colonial powers drew borders according to their own imperial designs, without any consideration of the people in these areas; where the English and the French had port fortifications and the ability to raid north to kidnap people for American slavery, a nation was born.

Of course, Nigeria was not called that before the British formalized their rule over the area in 1900; the name originates from the Niger River, as does the country of Niger. The earliest known use of the name "Niger" for the river is in the African historian Leo Africanus' work *Della descrittione dell'Africa et delle cose notabili che iui sono*, published in 1550. The name is believed to come from the Berber language: 'ger-n-ger' meaning 'river of rivers', or from 'n'igherren,' 'river'.

Nigeria has a long and fascinating history, much older than the arrival of the first Europeans. In the north, from the 11th century onwards, the Hausa-nation ruled over large areas and the trade across the Sahara, only converting to Islam in the 14th century. The Yoruba people also have a proud history since the 12th century in the southwest, as evidenced by the bronze statues found in Ile-Ife. In the southeast, Igbo communities were more decentralized, which may have been due to its humid and warm climate, and its dense forests and swamps. In any case, this stopped Europeans from settling for a long time.

229

It was to this Igboland that I first arrived on March 8, 1972 after crossing a spectacular border bridge. At the passport control they were accommodating and exchanged 10 US$ to Nigerian pounds (today the Nigerian naira is the currency of the country); even if it was a poor exchange rate, I was grateful. But it took some time before I journeyed on. I was soon joined by two young local boys who were also heading west. We chatted and had fun for a while and swore over the fact that no cars came by that wanted to pick us up. Finally, however, we were able to squeeze into a full Peugeot taxi. Pretty soon, however, we were stopped by an army checkpoint.

Two soldiers with imposing guns ordered us all out of the car and then they confronted me: "What are you doing in Nigeria? Where are you from and where the hell are you going?" I answered their questions as politely as I could. But it didn't help. They threw everything in my backpack out on the ground and yelled at me to stay away. And I did. Scared shitless that they would seize me, although I didn't understand for what. They didn't care about the other passengers or the driver at all, who stood by quietly and watched. When one of the soldiers threw my underwear into a mud puddle, I became thoughtlessly angry and shouted at them to stop. But they didn't understand Swedish, at least they didn't care about my tirades. They just grinned at me. But eventually they were satisfied and left us alone. It was only my pack, they went through. They left the Nigerians alone. Afterwards in the car, I was told why: it was not so long ago that the Biafran war ended in January 1970; the soldiers were looking for weapons and ammunition. In my underwear!

We moved on and when they realized I was Swedish, they started talking about Carl von Rosen, who I remembered even then had flown relief missions in Biafra during the civil war. I now know that he also started a small air force on behalf of Biafra that was relatively successful, destroying Nigerian fighter planes and thus stopping air attacks on the Biafran military and civilian population.

My next ride was with a converted truck to Abakaliki. Its body had simply been converted into a passenger bus; I had never seen that before. It was also emblazoned with a thought-provoking message: *Don't Fear, God Is Thy Shelter*. Other truck-buses I saw were illustrated with, among other things: *Jesus Saves, Labor Before Pleasure, Baby Come Back I Feel*

230

Allright.

In Abakaliki, I got stuck and before dark found an Irish Catholic mission. The first thing they asked when I knocked on the door was if I was English. "No, I'm from Sweden." "In that case you're welcome!" I was shown to my own little guesthouse with clean sheets and mosquito nets, a ceiling fan, a bathroom and I could enjoy a hot shower and wash my hair before they called me for dinner. At dinner I joined two Irish priests and an Irish couple visiting from Dublin. As was often the case with white missionaries, the table was set in a fancy dining room. The large windows looked out onto a beautiful, dimly lit veranda. Inside the room, a crystal chandelier above the large table spread a hospitable light. The food was also exceptional, the conversation fun, as they constantly castigated the horrible English. And it was the first time that the meal did not begin with grace on a mission; even in Ilebo every meal had begun with grace. Here the fathers were nevertheless of the same stock as Maarten and Herman; beer and whiskey were freely offered and afterwards they played cards while I wrote in my diary. A memorable evening.

After a lovely breakfast, I bid them a fond farewell and went into town. I immediately found a truck bus (*JF Kennedy Bus*) to Onitsha. There I was dropped off at the market. A world-famous market, at least in Africa. One of Africa's most famous literary movements emerged here in the 50s and 60s. Onitsha-literature consisted of quickly produced romance and detective novels, as well as manuals on how to succeed with women and money. Quickly written, printed and distributed pamphlets by the authors themselves. The customers were the young literate men who craved edifying romance and do-it-yourself books on how to be successful. And they sold: *The Nigerian Bachelor's Handbook* reportedly sold 150 000 copies. In the novels, dangerous and voluptuous women often lured young successful men into fatal traps. One of the more celebrated books is *Mabel, the Sweet Honey* ("whose skin would make your blood flow in the wrong direction") by an author who called himself Speedy Eric.

Now after the Biafran war, the market was still large and dynamic, although certainly nothing compared to before the war, when it was said to be Africa's largest market. It still took some time to get through and everyone seemed to want to sell me something I didn't need. But not everyone, of course; markets in Africa are mainly the domain of women. They are not only in majority among the vendors but especially among the customers. The market was like the church on Sundays, or the village well, in our old Scandinavian villages, where people met and exchanged information, gossip and perhaps also goods. The latter sometimes seemed almost irrelevant here. I sometimes saw women selling six corn cubs or two heads of lettuce or fifteen potatoes. I wondered if it was because they had nothing more to sell and were poor, or if they were really there chiefly to meet their fellow sisters. The African market was, and probably still is, in many ways the fundamental force, the meeting place for all human communication in the community. And Onitsha was the most famous.

Once on the road to Benin City, I was surrounded by begging children who I tried in vain to get rid of. It was impossible to hitchhike, I was barely visible. Seven women dressed in white soon came by and managed to persuade the children to leave me alone. I realized that they belonged to one of the many evangelical churches in southern Nigeria. There are reportedly hundreds of different Christian sects, denominations or churches in the country, each with its own agenda and some with tentacles across the Atlantic to the Nigerian diaspora. Often the first thing I was asked was what church or faith I belonged to, which I soon realized was a serious and important question, as Festus had stated. I came to answer that I was a Lutheran. Simplest.

Anyway, a Volvo truck stopped and picked me up. I got a little childishly excited by reading Swedish signs in the car, but it was still not a good ride. First he drove around Onitsha for a couple of hours on various errands before finally turning onto the highway again. Then we were almost immediately stopped by an army patrol. The driver apparently didn't have the right documents which is why he didn't get any further and consequently neither did I. It was only for me to get out and start all over again.

There was a lot of traffic so I was hopeful. I was close by the bridge over the Niger River, Africa's third largest river. A river which, of course, several Western explorers have competed to be the first to find its source to, including the Scotsman Mungo Park who wrote a readable account of his West African adventures. He died in Bussa, Nigeria during what was meant to be his last journey, and so it became when he was killed in an attack by locals. It was not easy to find the source of the Niger as it mouths into the Guinean highlands and then runs north, but turns south at the Sahara and flows into the Gulf of Guinea just south of Onitsha.

As I stood reflecting on the river life beside me, completely ignorant of the most basic history or geography of the river, my luck turned and I was picked up by an initially empty truck-bus (*Love and Peace Bus*). It cost five shillings to Benin City and was a pleasant but creaking journey as the wooden passenger compartment whined and squeaked on the bumpy roads. At one point the car suddenly stopped and everyone - I was no longer the only passenger - jumped out and climbed a tree full of fruit I didn't recognize. They filled bags and were thrilled that they could nick these lovely fruits out in no-man's land. Many years later I realized that it was pomegranates we gluttonously devoured. I had not seen or heard of them then, but here discovered that they were delicious, but hard to eat, when they offered me as many as I could eat.

In Benin City, the driver promised to pick me up again at seven the next morning outside the Catholic mission in the city, I found with his help. There I met a couple of helpful Nigerian priests who gave me a guest room with a clean bed. There was no shower, nor did they offer any food. This was in the middle of the city so I easily found a modest restaurant where I could eat affordably.

Next morning I was up in good time to wait for the car from yester-day. Had a cheese sandwich and a cup of tea before seven and waited. But in vain. I instead had to march out of town. On the way, I was har-assed by two different police patrols who absolutely wanted to see my passport, check my luggage and preferably have some money before they let me continue. It was unpleasant, but at least I didn't have to pay for the inconvenience. When I finally found my way out and past police patrols, I got on a truck bus (*I Am For Peace No 2*) for 10 shillings to Lagos (they had the old British system of 20 shillings to 1 pound and 12 pence to 1 shilling: confusing). It was heavily loaded with Guinness and crawled slowly forward. At first I sat on the bed and got all black with road dust and soot. After a while I could climb into the driver's cabin, for which I was grateful. I didn't mind the slow pace either. Everywhere you saw car wrecks after collisions and accidents. Often bridges were only wide enough for one car and some places it looked like there had been a race from both sides to see who would be the first to reach the bridge. Whoever came second seems not to have had time to brake and ended up in the river. There were often wrecks in river ditches next to bridges. In Nigeria I was scared for the first time when I got a lift.

I was told that on April 2 this year the country would switch to driving on the right-hand side, whereas now it was left-hand traffic. I did not want to stay in the country for that. At first, it was apparently planned that commercial traffic would start driving on the right side one day and private cars the next day. But they had changed their minds and now it was April 2 that applied to all traffic. Wise. It was already dangerous, however, as there were motorists who already were practicing driving on the right side in order to get used to it. Thus, of course, there were even more accidents.

I wasn't the only one who thought Nigerian roads were dangerous: Wole Soyinka, Nigeria's only Nobel Prize winner for literature, set up his own traffic police, the Oyo Road Safety Corps, when he was a professor at the University of Ife, to improve road conditions. He also wrote a play, *The Road,* in which death on the road takes on mythological dimensions as Ogun, the Yoruba God of war and death, administers death on the roads.

I have written in my diary about a bend in the road, with a sign warning about it being sharp, urging drivers to slow down. Not everyone did, and certainly not the car I was in. We made it, however, and halfway through the curve I saw a sign saying: "we told you so!" Today I find it hard to believe that this is true; it sounds more like Soyinka's drama where signs lure drivers to their deaths.

In Lagos, the traffic was of course chaotic, slow and incomprehensible. I was lucky though: there was a Catholic mission in the suburb where I was dropped off. It was now Saturday and I only had four shillings left and no banks open until Monday, so I was hoping to sleep for free here. I knocked on the door and it turned out that there were nuns living there. I was nevertheless welcome and they arranged a mattress for me in their library, which suited me just fine, even though much of the literature was in Latin and Nigerian languages, but there were some in English too, of course. Fun to browse.

They also offered food and were curious. Two young English nuns also sat at the table, but they were quiet and, as I understood it, suspicious of me. The Nigerian ones, however, were very nice, especially one of them who had just returned from studies in England, and we had a great time together. But then I slept badly because of the heat and mosquitoes, so I was glad when it was six and I was awakened. I had been promised a lift into town and the YMCA by the Mother Superior who wanted to leave early to avoid the worst of the traffic. Before we parted, she showed me a nun's mission near the YMCA where I could eat. Noted.

It cost 11 shillings a night at the YMCA, about three dollars, which was acceptable. After finding a bed and making it mine, I headed downtown and the Poste Restante. Inside, Major General and Head of State Yakubu Gowon smiled down on everyone from the indispensable portrait. His smile didn't make up for the fact that, extremely disappointed, I only had two letters waiting for me. I had hoped for a whole bunch of them. One was from Klas and the other, of course, from my mother; I could depend on her. Klas told me that he and Axel had moved up to Drevdagen, in northwest Dalarna, Sweden. There they worked as teachers in a school closed down by the municipality; teaching eleven primary and middle school pupils for free. Nice of them and I wrote an appreciative aerogram.

I then found the Swedish Embassy where I had greetings to convey from Kinshasa, which I communicated and read some daily papers in my mother tongue. They also told me that I did not need a visa for the countries I was going to after Nigeria, which pleased me.

Back at the YMCA, I got to play a lot of ping pong, which was a long time ago, fun, and I didn't lose every game. Next door was a basketball court where high-quality basketball was played, which was exciting to watch. It also became a way to interact with other spectators, guests at the YMCA. But it was not easy to understand them. Their English, NPE, as it is called (Nigerian Pidgin English) was much more pidgin than the one I encountered in East Africa. It serves as something like the country's lingua franca and is influenced by all the major languages of the country and thus slightly different, mainly in vocabulary, in different parts of the country. Full of new words and phrases, even the whole sentence structure was sometimes syntactically changed. Later I have come to appreciate it in Nigerian literature, mainly in Ken Saro-Wiwa's *Sozaboy*, a novel he wrote in "rotten English". A bit of a challenge to read but worth every minute! I met the author at an ALA conference in

Accra, Ghana, the year before he was hanged by the military dictator Sani Abacha in 1995. A lovable man, Saro-Wiwa, that is, who spoke up for his people, the Ogoni, that had the misfortune to live in the oil-rich Niger Delta where Shell, along with the generals of Nigeria, were mining the black gold. Saro-Wiwa fought for his people and was hanged for it. His death resulted in international disgust and Nigeria was thrown out of the Commonwealth. That same year, Niyi Osundare, Nigerian poet who fled the country under Abacha and is now a professor in the US, wrote insightfully that "in Africa it is dangerous to think, and risky to argue." And already in 1983, Chinua Achebe wrote that it is the leadership that is *The Trouble with Nigeria*.

I had expected Nigeria to be similar to what I had seen in East Africa. But it wasn't. The main difference was all the people. There were many more of them. And here, even the men were dressed in colourful pyjama-like clothes; not nearly as many Western suits as in Nairobi. Sympathetic, I wrote in my diary. I thought it was more exotic together with the Muslims in galabeya. The women were, as often on the continent, more traditionally dressed than the men and here it was specifically their headgear that impressed: the so called 'gele,' a large colourful scarf wrapped spectacularly over the head.

After the first night in the YMCA, I found some beds on the roof of the house where I slept much better. Cooler and less mosquitoes thanks to the wind from the Gulf of Benin and here I also had company of rainbow-colored, rather large and beautiful lizards.

The next day it was finally a weekday and I could visit a bank and exchange some local currency. But I didn't do that, instead I had gotten wind of a guy who offered a much better rate for the 15 pounds sterling I wished to exchange. Then I found a well-stocked bookshop where I spent a lot of happy time, and some money. I came out with three thick books: *Moby Dick*, *Doctor Zhivago* and the entire *USA*-trilogy by Dos Passos in a Penguin volume. Now I would have something to read until I got home, I hoped. At the same time, I got rid of some books when I mailed a package of literature home. Books I wanted to save and still are found on my shelves, 50 years later. At the post office I also checked with the Poste Restante and now there were four new letters for me. I

236

was really happy about that and especially one from Tina who was thinking of coming down to North Africa to meet me. That would be fantastic. Her father worked for SAS and in those days family members could fly almost for free, so she thought she could afford it. On Tuesday I spent almost the entire day writing aerograms, 16 of them according to the diary.

If there were attractions in Lagos, I missed them. Not because I thought the city was as awful as I'd heard, but at the same time not something I'm looking forward to return to. I saw a couple of escalators for the first time in Africa in an air-conditioned mall. So there was money in the city, while the streets were full of beggars and watch peddlers. As a white tourist, I was approached all the time. A bit annoying, also the fact that I was constantly addressed as master, or rather 'massa'. Gave me some unpleasant associations. But I made the best of my stay. Washed all my clothes, ate ice cream and drank a lot of milk which I realized I longed for again.

After a quick and easy breakfast, Wednesday morning I got on an early bus to a large taxi and bus market. There I found myself in a complete chaos. Everyone seemed to be selling biscuits, loose cigarettes, pineapples, chocolate, plastic bags and everything else I didn't need. Others pulled the only blonde person they saw to get me into their car or bus. I found it hard to resist so the one who pulled and tugged the strongest won and soon I was in the passenger seat of a 504 on the way to Ibadan. He drove like an idiot and I was terrified the whole trip. But we were fast and soon I was in the country's largest city by area, with almost four million inhabitants at the time of writing, and the third largest city in Nigeria by population. It is famous for its university, which was founded in 1948 by the British and has long had a considerable international reputation, where writers such as Chinua Achebe, Wole Soyinka, J. P. Clark, Christopher Okigbo, Kole Omotoso, Abiola Irele, Femi Osofisan and many others have studied and later often taught.

The country is the literary giant of the continent. Only South Africa comes close to matching it. Alongside the writers I have just mentioned can be added today's shining stars such as Ben Okri, Chimamanda Ngozi Adichie, Helon Habila, Chriss Abani, Teju Cole and Niyi Osundare, as well as older ones such as Amos Tutuola, Flora Nwapa and Buchi Emecheta. There is now talk of a specific Nigerian literature, while since

Achebe's debut in 1958 with *Things Fall Apart*, it has always been about the literature of Africa, the continent's.

At the Gothenburg Book Fair in 2010, which focused on African literature, many African writers complained that organizers had lumped together all writing from the continent and not recognised the literature of the individual countries in Africa, as we do about the literature of Europe. Understandable criticism, even though they themselves were discussing from stages and podiums the particularities of African literature and rarely about the literatures of Senegal or Kenya or Nigeria. In such a discourse, it is important to realize that we are dealing with a "socio-historical situation among African writers which generates similar problems. It is not a metaphysical consensus that creates this common situation," as Kwame Anthony Appiah writes in his fine book *In My Father's House.*

From a Swedish perspective, it is probably still okay to talk about Africa's literature if one is aware of Appiah's distinction. I have certainly done so in lectures and in classrooms. Yet one can spend a lifetime reading literature from Nigeria alone and never regret it, and new talent is constantly emerging. The sad thing is that a majority of them are no longer in Nigeria and perhaps they write almost exclusively in English, which is rarely or never their mother tongue. According to Ngugi wa Thiongo from Kenya, this is then not African literature, which can only be written in African languages, he insists. Ever since a conference in Kampala, Uganda in 1962, the language issue has been a constant source of debate among writers and literary scholars in Africa. Both sides are understandable and should not really be incompatible. What is absolutely tragic for Nigeria, as well as several other countries in Africa, are the dictatorships that have forced writers and academics into exile and left the country poor in intellectual capital: an African brain drain from which the continent suffers.

Getting out of Ibadan was not easy. Taxis wanted astronomical sums to take me to the road to Oyo, the old medieval Yoruba capital. But I was lucky, a couple of students from the university picked me up and drove me to where I wanted to go, while intensely questioning me about what I was doing. One of them said he had a girlfriend in Malmö so they thought it was amusing that I came from Sweden in light of that, and I suppose it was. Then I took a truck to Ilorin, where it was raining and I got stuck in a bus and taxi station. There, everyone became eagerly involved in my situation and ran around looking for a car for me. An old woman gave me bananas, biscuits and a coke while I waited. And then I was in a truck again, on my way to Kaduna.

The driver claimed he would drive all night, which he almost did, but thankfully we stopped and ate at a bus station on the way - I hadn't eaten properly since the early breakfast in Lagos. Around three am we stopped again and slept until the sunup. I found a narrow bench under a roof nearby and managed to get a fair night's sleep. When the sun rose, they woke me up and it was an all-day drive to Kaduna, where we arrived at six that evening. During the trip we stopped and ate a couple of times, when several passengers also took the opportunity to spread their prayer mats towards Mecca. Then we rolled on through an increasingly dry countryside and a changing cultural landscape. People's clothes and buildings were different from southern Nigeria, and the mosques became more and more numerous.

I didn't want to remain in Kaduna, so I got out of town and was lucky enough to be picked up by two Lebanese in a Mercedes. After 24 hours on a bumpy truck, it was nice to sink into German soft leather seats and listen to Fairuz on the stereo. They were nice businessmen and were going to Zaria, as was I at the time. In Zaria we stopped at a Lebanese club where they were members. There they offered a dinner with food I had never eaten before. Discovered there and then how amazingly good Lebanese food is. I also got to sleep over at the club on a couch in a small room next to the office.

I was woken up early and kicked out of my couch by the people working at the club. My hosts from yesterday were long gone. However, I found my way to the road north where I got on a VW bus to Kano for five shillings. In Kano I had intended to stay as the city has an interesting history with a 15th century wall around the old town. For a long time, the city was the final stop of the caravan trade through the Sahara and therefore an important trading place for the Hausa people. The local monarchy still survives and at that time the throne was held by the Emir Ado Bayero. In 2000, Sharia law was introduced in Kano province which led to unrest and many non-Muslims left the region. Since 2012, Boko Haram Islamist terrorists have been bombing in Kano. So it's not a healthy place for a fellow from Stockholm today, but it was in 1972.

I nevertheless left (silly of me) and got a short ride out of the city. There I met a young man who had studied in the Soviet Union for five years. He offered me some food and beer and showed me the big market next door. Then we parted and I sat down by the side of the road. Nothing happened and after a couple of hours the 'Russian' came back and drove me to a small town, Dura, eleven kilometres from the border with Niger. There I got stuck again. But then he came back again and had found a truck going to Zinder in Niger. It cost 15 shillings, but it was worth it and I thanked the 'Russian' and left Nigeria.

Tamanrasset

In Niger it was raining, which cannot be that often in arid Sahel, which I now travelled into. The Sahel is the belt of sterile semi-desert in the southern Sahara that extends from the Atlantic Ocean to the Red Sea, the southern region of the Sahara Desert bordering tropical Africa: Sahel means border in Arabic.

It was dark. The border was crossed quickly. They were more interested in the driver and his load. Fifteen minutes driving after the border-check, the truck suddenly stopped and they threw bundles of packaging over us, while more passengers climbed onto the truck. Packing and passengers they obviously did not want the customs at the border to notice. It became crammed on the flatbed of the truck and two guys sat on me, but with some rough elbows I forced them to stand up. Everyone insisted that as the only white person, I should move forward into the driver's cabin, but I wanted to remain with my backpack; why I suddenly was afraid to leave it alone I don't know, but so I wrote in the diary later. It all became a bit comical as I began to sing in the silence of all other passengers and the pouring rain. The rain drenched us and I quietly sang to myself; what else could I do? And no one minded. I didn't know many songs or tunes, though; they included some traditional Swedish songs from school, *Yesterday* and *Desolation Road*. I didn't know all the verses of the latter, but enough to keep me busy. At 11 pm we arrived in Zinder soaking wet and my repertoire had run out.

But where would I sleep? There were hardly any missionaries here. I wandered around the dark city and found a small bench under a market roof where I spread out my poncho and sleeping bag and fell asleep, even though the bench was hard and narrow. An unpleasant and troubled night. The last three days had been intense with limited sleep and food, but now the Sahara was approaching, so I felt excited.

Just before sunrise people started to flock to the market, I awoke and managed to find something to eat among the many stalls. Then I walked out of Zinder and found the road to Tamanrasset - and to Stockholm. There I sat in the shade under a lonely tree. The sun shone relentlessly from a cloudless sky today and the intense heat was numbing both mind and body. A heat that was now dry, however, so okay. But I didn't see any cars. A nearby police patrol told me that a truck would leave for Agadez this afternoon. If no other vehicle came, I put my hopes to that truck.

The milieu had really changed. Not just the nature, but people and buildings as well. The houses, though simple and made of clay, were smooth, round, in beautiful shapes and often ornate. So were the people. Not dressed in colourful costumes as in southern Nigeria, but full coloured suits with leather jewellery. The women were often scarred in the face; I thought it was beautiful. Many men carried large swords in decorative leather belts and sat on equally decorated saddles on their horses. Camels, or dromedaries really, I had also begun to see again. It was hot and the air was dry. I was glad that I still had some ChapSticks left from Högdalen. Even if I stayed in the shade I was dry and thirsty and my lips cracked. Breathing was like a hair dryer straight into my mouth. But I liked sitting there. The heat slowed everything down. It was quiet and people left me alone. I could sit by the road in the shade and wait and write a little in my diary and no one cared about the Swede with the red backpack.

I had also managed to exchange some money; 50 francs was equal to one Swedish krona. And now it was French again. I surprised myself a bit by rather effortlessly conversing with the world around me, happy to practice my French again.

But there was still no traffic. I was in no hurry, although a letter from Tina ought to wait for me in Algiers. I enjoyed being left alone. While there were no cars, things happened around me all the time. Large herds of spectacular long-horned cattle came by, surrounded me. And suddenly a manicurist sat down next to me. Apparently this was his usual spot as he immediately got customers, both men and women, wanting nail maintenance. All the while vultures sat in the trees hoping for something to be run over by the absent vehicles.

After a couple of hours, the police officers called me over and offered me to share their lunch: rice, meat, carrots and cabbage in a delicious stew. Three of us sat around a small table in their shack, ate well and listened to The Beatles. They had a cassette player that played Beatles all the time. Lovely, I thought, even if I found it a bit unexpected. But why wouldn't a couple of policemen in Niger also like The Beatles?

At 14.35 I could finally climb onto the promised and fully packed truck. I squeezed myself down among all the other passengers. This caused a bit of a hullabaloo as I was the only European, and in shorts. Soon everyone got used to me and after 100 km we stopped in Sabonkafi, told my map, and changed tires as two had exploded in the heat. During the tire-change, I sat in the shade of a house wall with some fellow passengers who offered dates and suspiciously grey water. But saying no was out of the question. I was thirsty all the time. Some camels sat in the sun close by, ruminating curiously on us, surely just as thirsty. Opposite me against another house sat an older, handsome gentleman with a dark experienced face, framed by a large white beard: a Tuareg, one of the blue people. "They were the blue warriors of the desert, veiled and armed with daggers and long rifles, they walked with great strides without looking at anyone," as Le Clézio writes in his novel *Desert*.

They are called the Blue People because of the indigo-coloured clothes they wear, which are said to rub off on them. This handsome nobleman was dressed in a white burnous and the obligatory blue turban, with a large knife in an embroidered leather sheath at his waist. He kept to himself at all times, both while we were waiting for the tire change and during the ride on the flatbed. When others were curious about my pale person, he did not give me a glance. It made an impression on me, this lack of curiosity, which I interpreted as pride. I tried to make eye contact with him both now while we were waiting, and on the truck, but in vain. It was a different story for Eva Dickson when she drove home across the Sahara from Nairobi in 1932 and was offered 30 camels by a Tuareg chief to become his wife.

After about an hour, we moved on through a seemingly dead stone desert. We stopped a few times for prayers and some food, or for someone to disembark and disappear alone into the desert. At one stop I was offered dates and foufou we all dipped in a bowl of rather strong sauce. As I voraciously devoured the rather unfamiliar food, the old Tuareg at last smiled at me! And pleased I smiled back.

At one point we passed a caravan of over 50 camels. Impressive and exotically beautiful, I thought. Around midnight we stopped and slept for six hours, where, I don't know. It was cold by then so I fell asleep in my sleeping bag on the sand next to the truck. The others did the same, some also in sleeping bags, others wrapped themselves in blankets.

At 11 am the next day we arrived in Agadez. I had hitchhiked from

Lagos to Agadez in five days! I did not really understand why I had been in such a rush, but everyone I met in Agadez was impressed. And here I ran into other traveling Westerners again, and tourists. From now on I would not be the only hitchhiker anymore, I realized with some disappointment. It had been exciting and fun to travel alone, which I had done since I left Moshi the last time in January. When you are alone, you meet more people and experience more; traveling becomes more rewarding. At the same time, it was of course nice to have company. And I came to enjoy myself in North Africa.

I spent most of that day by a police patrol outside of Agadez with a Frenchman and an American. We had been told that a truck on its way to Tamanrasset would pass by later. While waiting we actually enjoyed some horse racing. Next to the road was a race track. It was now Sunday and race day; the police told us. It was spectacular when they stormed by at full gallop and the riders' big clothes fluttered in the wind. It looked as if the spectators were betting on the winners, but gambling isn't allowed according to the *Koran*, is it? I wondered.

Nothing else happened and the promised truck never materialized, so the three of us, Rick and Jean-Claude and I, found a small eatery of a sort on the outskirts of the very scattered Agadez town. Here we were almost picked up by two very beautiful and seductive young women who, although they didn't stick their fingers up their noses, clearly managed to convey what they were offering. We declined and settled for some food and a cold Skol lager each; they had a fridge! No Beatles from the transistor here but traditional Arabic music. Colossally beautiful. I have been in love with Arabic music ever since: its monotonous but ornate melodies, strings holding the sucking melody and the oud improvising, homophonic, today reminding me a bit of John Coltrane's late music. And it doesn't get any better that!

I had now started with *Doctor Zhivago*, which promised to be a good read, although in the heat of the desert it was hard to imagine the cold and snow of Siberia. I read a few pages before the three of us found a small park where we slept in the chilly night in our sleeping bags.

At half past six the next morning we managed to get on a truck that was going to Tamanrasset. 3000F it cost us each. 60 SEK, a bit steep, but we couldn't haggle and it was a journey of many miles across the Sahara, so... The three of us and seven Arabs sat on top of the fully

244

loaded truck and five more in the cab, all men. Admittedly it was hot in the sun on top, but there was at least a breeze and you had a view and could move around a bit, in other words better than a cramped driver's cabin. It was also slow, agonisingly so on the lowest gears in the sometimes loose sand. We did not drive on anything that looked like a road. Only wheel tracks from previous traffic showed the way. But that seemed to be enough. The journey was long and eventful.

Around noon we stopped in a 'wadi', a dried-up riverbed. I hoped they knew it hadn't rained up in the mountains, because then the river could come rushing in with tsunami force. At night you should definitely never camp in a wadi. Now we just stopped for lunch and a fire was built and tea made. And everyone ate the food they had brought with them. The sweet mint tea was what we were offered. Good but hardly filling. However, the three of us had bought some food in Agadez, including Heinz canned vegetables that I ate a can a day along with some dry bread. This would have to do. Then we climbed up on the truck again and went further out into the Sahara.

Lunchbreak in the Sahara.

At seven we camped at a small oasis. Everyone spread out and found their beddings. We had been joined by another truck so now we were a group. A fire was built and food was cooked, which the three of us were only allowed to look at. But then a flute came out. Not my recorder but bamboo flute of the drivers' who was exceptionally skilled and from then on played every night after dinner, accompanied by drums and hand clapping and singing. Lovely.

Now we were out in the sand desert, full of the large and beautiful sand dunes you always see in movies. Sleeping out in the Sahara in an oasis under its gigantic sky was something I had dreamed of at home with the maps in my room on Harpsundsvägen, and now I was there! The starry sky was spectacularly large; a myriad of stars shone in a 180-degree vault from horizon to horizon. The Milky Way really did look like a street, a wide, glowing avenue with lots of street lights cutting across the sky. I crawled into my sleeping bag, fully dressed as it was chilly, and burrowed down into the sand to a comfortable bed. It took a while before I rather euphorically fell asleep.

We awoke to screaming camels greeting the sun as it inevitably crept up over the horizon. Four Bedouins on their camels had arrived during the night. Now they were begging for tobacco and food. One of them wanted my pens when he saw me writing. I promised to give him one if he wrote something in my diary. And he did. I still have it next by me as I write this and I now know roughly what it says: "Westerners are friends of the devil but one day they will all love Allah." It was perhaps not very polite of him, and fortunately I did not understand it at the time. Instead, I thanked him and gave him the pen he wrote with. His Arab script is nevertheless beautiful.

We stayed in the oasis until late afternoon. They dismantled and then reassembled the entire engine of one of the trucks. I never understood why. The three of us took it easy in the shade of the few palms and other small trees that the oasis offered. There were some unknown birds singing in the bushes and under the palms; I think I saw a pied wagtail. At least that's what I wrote in my diary, and it's a bird I recognized even then. Large trembling dragonflies flew everywhere and were a bit scary. There was a small well that was visited by goats and camels. We wanted to walk around a bit but it was too hot. I couldn't even stand still for long in the hot sand without burning my feet through the soles of my leather shoes. And it is true that you can fry eggs in the sand every day in the Sahara, as the Swedish soldier, Thorsten Orre wrote in 1922 in his *Sketches from the Desert*, describing his time in the French army in northern

Algeria.

While the others ate, the three of us got to watch. A bit strange that they did not invite us, we had also paid for the trip. But we had to blame ourselves that we had not brought enough food. When we finally took off, it was four o'clock in the afternoon and nice to moving again. But it wasn't long before we got stuck. It was like driving in loose snow. One pair of wheels cut into loose sand so we almost tipped over. A good thing that we were two lorries now. Both had shovels and several sheet metal plates with holes that they placed under the wheels when they shovelled them relatively free. Then they had to drive up on to them to get a grip. With the help of the free truck and all of us pushing, the truck was after about an hour able to drive on. Soon the landscape was completely dead. Flat. We didn't even see any camels. This flat, dead stone desert is rarely seen in desert romances, where there are always beautiful sand dunes as far as the eye can see. But on this route through the Sahara, there was at least as much stone as sand.

The next stop was at eleven in the evening in Assamaka, just before the Algerian border. By then we had been freezing for quite a while on top of the truck and were grateful that we stopped. Everything, including the border, was closed so we couldn't enter Algeria but camped at Niger's border control. Several people did the same and it became a pleasant evening around several camp fires and good music. Rolling Stones from a cassette player were mixed with traditional Bedouin music. Not bad at all.

There was also a tap at the border checkpoint with clear running water, which tasted wonderful compared to the grey water we had been forced to drink so far. They had sewn goat skins hanging upside down along the trucks that were filled with water. The neck serves as a faucet and there I filled my water bottle with the grey and warmish water of the desert, full of sand and dirt. Then I put a chlorine tablet I had from Lagos, in my bottle. But now we could fill up with clear, clean water that was even cool. All the bottles and goatskins were filled. In addition, we probably all drank too much. Which meant that the next day we were almost manically thirsty. I have since then learned that you need to ration your drinking - even of water, at least in the desert.

Entering Algeria the next day in In Guezzam, took time. For us Westerners it was fairly quick, but for everyone else there were endless forms to be filled in and, we realized, money to change hands. At a small office of a sort we had time to buy some Algerian dinars, one to a Swedish krona.

Then it was off into the desert again: the dry ocean. It was flat and hot, and the mirages made it seems like we were "traveling through a vast archipelago where fresh water sparkles and beckons in the sun," as Sven Lindqvist once wrote from about the same place in the world. We had now been joined by another truck and were now three. In the cabin of the third truck was an elderly French couple on their way home after adventures in West Africa, but mostly we were Arabs and West Africans on their way to Europe.

The road was not marked any better here, we followed the wheel tracks of others heading north. I guessed that the drivers had made the journey before, so they found their way. To my Swedish eyes there were no natural landmarks. Instead some unnatural ones; lots of blown car tires lined our route all the time and tin cans were thrown everywhere. In some places some creative individuals had made small sculptures of tires and cans. We also passed car- and animal- carcasses. Otherwise it was all dead. Flat, desolate and hot. As I now sit on a rainy early summer day in Roslagen, Sweden and write this, it is striking how differently I now, compared to then and there, perceive the sun. In Roslagen the sun is a friend and in the Sahara it is an enemy. No desert romance could be cultivated on the truck bed.

Me at a water hole.

In the afternoon we stopped at a watering hole, a well that was full of camels and Bedouins. And flies. In the desert there are no flies, but of course around waterholes and in oases, where people and animals attract them. There was a dreadful noise from the camels as they screamed (or did they moo?) and fought to get to the water their riders pulled up out of the well in leather buckets. Elias Canetti writes in *The Voices of Marrakesh*, that he finds that camels remind him of tea-drinking elderly English ladies; I'm not sure I can agree with that. I doubt they sound as much drinking afternoon tea as this cacophony. First camels got water, then people; a desert justice illustrating the status of desert life, I presumed. There we rested and ate; now they shared some of their food when they saw the three of us sitting and staring hungrily at them. I had finished my last can the night before. Now we were offered some tea, dry bread, rice and tough dry goat meat which we shared very evenly. Delicious.

We arrived in Tamanrasset just before sunset. That we approached Tamanrasset had been noticeable for some time: nature was changing. We saw clouds for the first time in days around the Ahaggar Mountains, which rose slowly and the road now went steadily upwards. Tamanrasset is 1300 meters above sea level and is cooler than the surrounding Sahara. The Tuaregs long dominated the population and used the town's market during their wandering existence. A nomadic life that is now well circumscribed by the borders drawn by Europeans with a ruler at the end of the 19th century. Since 1960, the Tuareg have been in constant conflict with Mali and Niger in particular, and a couple of outright wars have been fought.

In Tamanrasset there grows fruits and dates and the town has been an important oasis and trading post for caravans from Niger and Mali for centuries. And probably still was to some extent, although my main impression was that it was something of a tourist oasis compared to the towns I had passed through since Lagos. It was a long time since I saw so many tourists and not just hitchhiking hippies. By the hotels there were trinket peddlers and I had not seen that since Malindi. Still, I liked Tamanrasset with the beautiful red Ahaggar Mountains rising around the city. The climate was also pleasant, not as infernally hot despite the sun shining from an equally blue sky.

Rick, Jean-Claude and I found a quaint little hotel that offered small individual straw or palm huts, a kind of hut that I later realized was the traditional housing of the Tuareg. Here the hotel had made them more permanent and there was a bed, a chair and a small table, no windows, no electricity but the doorway let in the only light. Here you did nothing but sleep. It cost three dinars a night and the same for the first meal. Extremely hungry, we found a restaurant where we could eat a three-course dinner: camel steak with couscous and vegetables, and a very sweet dessert. We ate as if we had never seen food before.

In the afternoon we visited a Turkish bathhouse, a hammam. It was my first acquaintance with that splendid establishment and lovely after sitting on a truck bed for several days and being ravaged by sun, sand and wind. I had expected the hammam to be warmer, like a sauna, but it was rather lukewarm. Still, it was wonderful to be pampered and washed and beaten, as I was. And I became clean. Also this cost three dinars; everything seemed to cost three dinars here!

In the evening, we went back to the same restaurant and this time the three-course menu included goat's brain. A little hesitant, we started cutting into the grey little bun, but it turned out to be quite tasty. The first time I ate brain.

Already the very next day I started planning to move on. I liked Tamanrasset though, even if it was a bit too touristy; I was simply unaccustomed, spoiled by being the only Westerner. The town was also beautiful, reminding me a bit of Kassala with the surrounding mountains, even if they there were only to the east. But now I had decided to move on and go to Algiers. It was, however, difficult to find transportation. I inquired at all the garages and taxi companies. No one was going north the next day. So stuck in Tamanrasset one more day, which was after all fine. Rick and I got a car that took us up into the Ahaggar mountains where we took a long climbing walk. Beautiful, quiet and deserted. A mixture of mysterious and majestic rock formations and sand dunes. It was also cool even though the sun was burning relentlessly. Rick was so taken by the mountains that he decided to stay in Tamanrasset and do a proper hike over several days in the mountains. I was a bit tempted to join him, but didn't.

When we got back to the car, the taxi driver was soundly asleep and it felt a bit cruel to wake him up, but of course we did and he didn't mind at all. He was probably happy to get back to town. So were we. All we had brought with us for our little excursion was each a bottle of water. It was of course to the same restaurant we went again and Jean-Claude joined us. He grew excited when we told him about our hike and decided to join Rick and the two of them started to plan.

Instead, I found transportation; at eight in the evening I was promised to accompany an Algerian towards In Salah. When he told me that I didn't have to pay for the lift, I became a bit wary and perhaps should have declined. But it was difficult to get a ride here so I did not.

At nine pm we left. There were only the two of us in a Land Rover, which was also a bit strange. So far, all the lifts had been packed with people. But Amid, as his name was, was nice, we conversed and he drove quite fast in the dark. How he found his way I did not understand but he told me that he often drives here.

"I have a small hotel in both Tamanrasset and In Salah, but I live in Ghardaia. So I drive quite often this way."

After two hours we stop to sleep. He spreads a blanket next to the car and says that we should sleep there together. But I don't want that, so I walk around the car to the other side and spread out my rain poncho and get into my sleeping bag. After a while he comes over and sits next to me.

"Why don't you want to sleep with me?"

I get up on my knees in my sleeping bag and explain that I just want to sleep, that I'm tired. Then he puts his hand in my sleeping bag and grabs my balls and smiles foolishly. I react instinctively and punch him in the face so that he falls backwards into the sand. I immediately regret what I'd done, but quickly get up on my feet, terrified of what's going to happen next. I look around anxiously but of course know that we are the only people between the horizons. Will he pull out a knife, will he jump on me, will he leave me alone here in the middle of the Sahara?

"I'm sorry; I didn't mean to hit you. But I was so surprised and I told you I didn't want to." He says nothing. He stands up slowly and stares angrily into my eyes. I'm a bit bigger than he is, so if we're going to have a fist fight, I think I have a chance. But after a while, he gets into the car, throws out my backpack, jump-starts the jeep, takes off and leaves me alone. I watch his red taillight disappear into the dark desert.

What do I do now? I look around but of course no other car lights are visible. It's pitch black; I hardly see the hand in front of me. Only the starry sky illuminates the sands of the Sahara. And lonely Erik. In a bit of a panic, I tell myself that other cars must surely be passing by here, if not sooner than later, tomorrow. The tire tracks in the sand we've followed indicates that it is not only Amid who drives here. I have some water in my bottle but decide not to touch it, not knowing how long I will have to wait tomorrow in the scorching sun. It's getting close to midnight and I can't do anything but sleep, I reason anxiously, hoping I'll wake up if a car comes by. I get ready to crawl into my sleeping bag alone in the Sahara. With the help of my torch I find some soft sand to bed down into.

Then I see two bright headlights approaching from the north. Has Amid changed his mind and turned around? Yes, it's his car. When he pulls up next to me, he hisses: "Get in! Let's go."

It was a quiet journey. In Arak we stayed and slept until six in the morning. This time without advances or a fight. We also had a puncture in the morning but quickly put on the spare tire, which we did together without a word. We also picked up three Senegalese who followed us to In Salah. And of course they had to pay and now I also had to. But I reminded Amid that he had promised I wouldn't have to. He swore angrily and when we arrived in In Salah at noon, I gave him 20 dinars. This infuriated him as he wanted 100 and threatened to go to the police. "Sure, do that," I said, foolishly cocky. The police would no doubt have sided with him, but he angrily jumped into the car and started up again, leaving me alone in the town square.

In Salah

I came to appreciate In Salah. It was a smaller town than Tamanrasset and with less tourism. Tamanrasset attracted with the mountains and the beautiful surroundings, but In Salah, which is said to mean the salty spring, was just a small oasis town on the road between Algiers and Tamanrasset. It rained perhaps every five years and is apparently the hottest in the Sahara; 55 degrees has been recorded in the shade. The size of the town made it easy to get around and out of. I slept on the sand dunes outside in a small grove of date and doum palms. I still remember those nights as magical. "Paradise – isn't that the desert at sunset? Blue shadows, violet days, crystal clear skies, the glowing red disk of the sun sliding down behind the horizon, sharp as the edge of a knife. And then the solemn feeling of eternity." Eva Dickson described it better than I can. But I did realize that a desert can have a variety of colours: yellow, grey, black, brown and pink; a cruel and fascinating landscape.

Here I fell in love with this desert geography. It's a love that I admit contains some desert romance, but I can at least claim to have crossed the Sahara, slept out in its cold, starry, desert nights. So when, later in life, I have spent time reading pre-Islamic poetry, qasida and ghazal, Bedouin poetry about love and camels, and Western desert narratives, I have done so without hesitation. Rather, I have enjoyed Isabelle Ebehardt, Saint-Exupéry, Pierre Loti, Gertrude Bell, Wilfred Thesiger, Charles Doughty, Paul Bowles and, of course, T. E. Lawrence - not claiming that all of their writings are romance.

It is interesting to compare Francophone writers such as Gide, Flaubert and Loti with Anglophone writers in such a literary context. While Gide and Loti experience the desert aesthetically and seek adventure and give full expression to their feelings and desires, often homosexually, in the tropics and the desert, in other words, are not afraid to 'go native', British writers rarely do. Not even Lawrence or Bell really leave the British, but serve it in their Arabic masks. More often English writers, like Conrad in several novels, depict the danger of being seduced by the exotic.

I stayed a few days in In Salah and let myself be a bit seduced. At daytime

I left my backpack leaning against a wall along the long main street, really the only one in town. I sat in cafés in the shade and drank endless cups of mint tea with too much sugar. Even if not as tourist crowded as Tamanrasset, I wasn't the only Westerner here. I had company if I wanted to, including a Finnish girl who had studied in Uppsala. Nice to speak some Swedish again. I also finished reading *Doctor Zhivago*, which was ultimately disappointing. How come he was awarded the Nobel Prize? Probably more of a political decision (which one can read about in Duncan White's fascinating book *Cold Warriors*). After reading *Anna Karenina* recently, I couldn't help but be disappointed with Pasternak. Now I started *Moby Dick* instead. I had also managed to swap *Zhivago* for *Tess of*, by Thomas Hardy. A good trade.

I wrote in my diary how carefree I felt in In Salah, how comfortable I was in the desert; as I wandered out of the city and into the dunes, in the intense light and the unyielding sun, I saw the mirage trembling on the horizon, a horizon that also seemed to be obliterated when land and sky met. I knew then that this, too, was what I had longed for and had now arrived at. I felt at peace in the Arabian desert world. Now, this was not Arabia per se, and the people were not Arabs, but I am not the only one to call this an Arab environment. There was something about the generous hospitality and being left alone when I wanted to be, and the complete trust I felt from everyone, that made me feel well. I never hesitated to leave my backpack at a café or leaning against a wall in the city. I can't recall ever leaving my rucksack like that for entire days anywhere else. I also kept a lot to myself. Took long walks alone in the oases around the city. Sat and read Melville in the shade without worrying about anything and was content, satisfied with the solitude. When evening came, I found company in a restaurant.

I was surprised to later read that Sven Lindqvist was afraid when he travelled in the Sahara. Albeit it was probably an almost existential fear of traveling: "I am afraid, therefore I exist," he writes in *Exterminate All the Brutes*. He is equally afraid when traveling between In Salah and Tamanrasset 80 pages later. When I read my journals from my trip, it is rather the absence of fear (except in southern Ethiopia) that is tangible. Today I find it a bit baffling. I was a 19 year old Swede traveling alone in Africa, I probably should have been frightened more often, or at least more cautious! But people everywhere in Africa were incredibly friendly,

254

so there was no need to worry, or room for fear. What should I be afraid of? And what was Lindqvist afraid of?

One evening, a large group of us had gathered, both hitchhikers and Algerians, in a dark restaurant. One of the latter said that if he were king of the world, he would shoot all Westerners except Swedes. I'm sitting outside the group so I don't hear him, but I see that several people turn to me and laugh. Then he understands that I am Swedish and comes over and hugs me. Once again, I experienced how good it was to be Swedish in Africa. And this also came to pass at a time when Sweden had a fine reputation among the world's developing countries. Back then, our politicians could spell to the word solidarity. I, however, do remember that I back then was very critical of the politics of the Socialdemocrats in power. And yet here I found myself a bit proud being Swedish: peculiar! But when you travel, you do become strangely and noticeably nationalistic, even though it is an 'imagined community.' And one has to be on guard against it. Nationalism is appalling and dangerous; the line between it and fascism has proven to be a thin one. Also nowadays in our Swedish parliament, and not only there, but almost all over the Western hemisphere, water-combed young racists in too small confirmation suits spread hatred and fear of the 'other,' marinated in nationalism. The remarkable thing is that while I was flattered here on behalf of Sweden, traveling humbled me; "one realizes what a tiny place one occupies in the world," as Flaubert wrote in a letter home from Constantinople in 1850: Traveling does inoculate one against nationalism!

Later that night I was joined in the dunes. More people dared to sleep outside after I told them how wonderful it was. But you had to be dressed and have a sleeping bag. The desert wind was warm, hot during day but cold at night. When you woke up to the first rays of the sun, it was still cold and damp from the dew. That it could be so dewy in this rather sterile environment surprised me. Now, the sun quickly wiped away all the moisture and soon it would burn mercilessly and then it was crucial to be up.

As I started to approach Europe again, I reflected on my traveling in my diary entries. How incomparably good it was to have no more luggage than could fit into a backpack, what freedom it gave, and "to be alone, needless, unknown, stranger and yet at home everywhere," as Isabelle Eberhardt wrote, is a joy to experience. And here in In Salah, I certainly did.

But soon it was time to move on.

Tuesday, March 28, Konrad, a German I teamed up with, and I arrived with a big truck to El Golea. He was in a real hurry as he had to be in Frankfurt by Monday and was aiming for a ferry between Algiers and Marseille over the weekend. The truck was supposed to leave at six in the evening but we had to wait a few more hours. When it was time to depart, we were told to walk out of town and wait for the lorry outside of town. Apparently it didn't want us as passengers when it passed the police patrol at the In Salah exit. We were also joined by eight Senegalese. And about 30 goats. The Senegalese knew what they were doing as they quickly occupied the front in the truck empty bed closest to the cab, then came Konrad and I, then all the goats. Konrad and I were in close contact with them all night. Every time the car slowed down they came falling over us.

This was before the great influx of refugees across the Sahara that Fabrizio Gatti describes so poignantly in his book *Bilal*. Here I travelled much the same route, but it was only in this truck that I became aware that I was sharing the voyage with migrants. They were all young men going to Europe to seek their fortune and were naturally curious about us if we could help them with addresses or in any other way, which we could not. I don't think we even wanted to.

Instead, we braced ourselves for a long night. Weren't we pushing and shoving with the Senegalese for space, it was with the goats we fought. The road surface was quite like a corrugated plateau and the flatbed seemed to have no shock absorbers. In other words, it was difficult to sleep. We now travelled over the Tademait plateau, the hottest and deadliest stone desert in the Sahara, "a terrible, sterile plateau," as Thorsten Orre writes. Now it was night and freezing cold. Both Konrad and I crawled into our sleeping bags and rolled into each other to try to find some warmth. Not very successfully. We mostly gritted our teeth. My jaw was really sore by the time we got to El Golea, I had been so tense all night. If we managed to fall asleep, the goats would stumble over us and wake us up and we had to push them away. A difficult and unforgettable night. The Senegalese seemed to feel better as they laughed and sang for long periods during the night. When we arrived, we discovered that the goats had both pissed and shit all over our luggage and sleeping bags, probably in reaction to the rough treatment the truck gave them.

At five am we could finally get off in El Golea and Konrad and I found a park where we fell asleep and managed to get a few hours before the sun ruthlessly woke us up. These temperature contrasts were hard to get used to. Also El Golea was nice. Quiet and slow. Thorsten Orre claimed in 1922 that it is the most beautiful oasis in the Sahara, with gardens, a small lake, migratory birds: a "complete paradise." He marvels when coming from a completely empty landscape to this oasis, where

> hedges of pines and cypresses line the oasis, immense eucalyptus, which otherwise do not go south of the Atlas, stretch their leafy crowns high above the palms. The rose bushes grow into gigantic thickets and fill the air with a numbing fragrance, mimosas scatter their fragrant, yellow little balls over the vine trees' luxuriant tendrils, the peaches shine bright and rosy among the darker gold of the Seville orange. [There] splendid butterflies hover among fragrant, wonderful flowers. Shining birds of paradise fly whistling through the air, ducks and wild geese dive in the reeds, snipes run among the tussocks. In the water, shiny fish strike, and the sacred marabou stork steps gravely onto the shore. There is singing and chirping and cheering, the scent of flowers and beauty and life - and just a few steps away is death and emptiness. (my translation)

Perhaps Konrad and I were not so overwhelmed, although we were certainly grateful to have arrived in El Golea. Konrad disappeared north the same day and the Senegalese I never saw after we parted in the early morning, but I stayed another day. And did nothing. In a hotel by the park I could borrow a bathroom and wash my pack and sleeping bag, which smelled terrible after the goats' cruel treatment. There were a lot of European travellers in El Golea that I came to befriend. In Thorsten Orre's time, early 1900-hundreds, El Golea was only a small military station, but he writes that he believes it will soon become "a real tourist resort." It wasn't in 1972, at least not compared to Tamanrasset. Nevertheless, I met several hitchhikers, most of whom were heading south and were curious about what the great African traveller from Stockholm had to say.

Mostly though I sat in the shade of the park's trees and read. I was soon joined by others and we even shared a couple of bottles of wine and ate dates. I had become fond of dates. The variety of dates seemed to be endless, both in the special date shops and in the street stalls; the tastiest were the light and dry ones. They went well with Algerian red wine in a park in El Golea, I also discovered. In the evening we found a good restaurant. Camel steak with fries. It was a nice evening with Santana and Hendrix on a small tape recorder that an Englishman was dragging around. I never understood how you could do that, while I on the other hand was happy to hear the music. Now we were a group of about ten from different corners of Europe, no other nations here, as was the case in East Africa. And many were girls, which was also nice and a bit surprising. However, the local girls were invisible. The women you saw were completely veiled in niqabs and sometimes only one eye was visible. I now and then tried to make contact with such an eye, but in vain.

We all slept in the park that night without anyone bothering us. Nice and kind of them.

The next morning I hitchhiked further north to Ghardaia together with French Alain, whom I first met in In Salah. It took a while, but eventually we arrived in a Land Rover with a British couple we had met earlier. It was stunning to arrive in Ghardaia; the journey there was through a dry and flat and seemingly dead stone desert, although we saw both gazelles and a jackal. Then suddenly a valley opened up and we saw a white, pink and light brown city down in the M'zab valley. Actually, there are five cities stretching along the valley and all are now on the UNESCO World Heritage List. The oldest architecture dates back to the 11th century, but it is the ingenious system of wells and canals that makes it possible to live well here. It was the Mozabites, a Berber people who first settled here and began collecting rainwater, digging wells and canals. Now the water runs underground throughout the valley and is accessed by wells, sometimes more than 100 meters deep.

Ghardaia was yet another town in the desert I grew fond of. (Only the second community along with Kano in Nigeria where my path crossed Eva Dickson's journey from Nairobi to Sweden.) I spent the first day with the couple in the Land Rover. We found a Hamam out in an oasis, where we spent some wonderful time and cleaned up. In the evening we bumped into a rather crazy Dutchman in a nearby restaurant. He told us that he worked as an oil prospector; he travelled alone in the desert for weeks looking for oil. Now, after two months alone in his Dodge jeep, he had a couple of days in Ghardaia and would first get drunk, but not too drunk as he was going to a brothel later. After that he planned to get really pissed. A strange fellow who was very entertaining to listen to.

And the evening became wild. After the Dutchman slipped away to the waiting girls, we became a group that continued to eat and drink. Larry, a colossally funny Irishman started singing Irish ballads and the rest of us joined in as best we could with the choruses. We almost raised the roof and when the Dutchman reappeared it got even wilder. I was laughing so hard my stomach hurt. I could never figure out who paid the bill, but at least it wasn't me - for which I was grateful. A memorable evening in the Sahara.

I ended up sleeping on the sand in another oasis that night with Alain and the Brits in the Land Rover. Another magical night in the desert. But the sun woke us up too early and cruelly and we realized that we might have had a few too many pilsners last night; "and hadn't the Dutchman offered something stronger?" Alain wondered.

The next day I said goodbye to both him and the British as they hurried north together. I wanted to stay a while in Ghardaia. In the town I found a cafeteria by a small sloping square that became my base for two days. There I had breakfast and drank several cups of coffee in exchange for leaving my backpack during the day. I was set on sleeping outside and not having to pay for a bed for as long as I could. It had been a long time since I had slept inside; I was not looking forward to it and wanted to wait until it was necessary.

It was now Holy Saturday (whatever that had to do with anything?) and I met a French couple at the next table who had met an Algerian who was going to guide them to one of the small walled villages outside Ghardaia: would I like to tag along? Yes, please, I replied.

We set off in his car and entered a small village which, according to Hassan, as he was called in my diary, was from the 13th century. In the square we stopped at a large well. We could hear women's voices but saw none at all in the square. Apparently there were passages under the square so the women could fetch water at the well without showing themselves in the square for lustful male gaze. Ingenious, but of course also sad. Poor women, and men, who had to live in such a ridiculous gender-segregated society. The city closed the gates when the sun set so it was important not to remain after sunset, there were no hotel in the village.

Back in Ghardaia, Hassan offered the French to spend the night with him if he could sleep with her. They did not take up on the offer. Later in the evening, almost the same thing happened. At my café I met some people I had run into before, including in Tamanrasset, and there was also a girl among them. They had all been offered to sleep at an Algerian's house, but had declined when he demanded to sleep with her for his generosity.

I walked out of the city and found my way back to the oasis where I had slept the first night. It was again fantastic to sleep outside, but I always woke up early when the sun rose, especially in the desert. Sometimes it would have been nice to be able to have a lie in. Instead, I found my way to my café, where I was one of the first customers. I sat with my back to the café wall with a view of the sloping square that was beginning to wake up. The café was not large but outside it had spread out, offering eight tables in the shade under trees and umbrellas, but only two inside; who wanted to sit inside? I had a simple breakfast, read Melville, and watched the city wake up. Then I walked around Ghardaia and saw some of what it had to offer, including several beautiful mosques and the amazing palace.

In the afternoon I sit again in the café, reading or writing or just listening to and watching the people in the square. A relatively loud group of Algerian students, as it turns out, is sitting at a few tables nearby. The girls are not veiled but dressed just as they are in Stockholm and Paris. So they are hardly local youngsters, I understand. One of them is a very beautiful girl with dark brown eyes that I can't take my eyes off. Since I'm the only European there, they notice me, also she. We make eye contact and we smile. Suddenly she gets up and comes over to me and asks if I would like to join them. Of course I would and do, and they shower me with questions about where I come from and what I am doing in Ghardaia. They seem to like the fact that I am Swedish and I ask them what they are doing here. They are on school vacation and are going to the festival that is now taking place in Ghardaia and the five cities. Otherwise, they are all studying at the University of Oran.

At five o'clock, they all have to catch a bus and take their leave. But the beautiful girl stays behind for a while.

"My name is Fatima; what is yours?"

"Erik, and you have the most beautiful eyes in the world."

I sense a blush on her chocolatey skin.

"Do you realize that we will probably never see each other again?" she asks.

"Yes, and it's sad: the curse of travelling. And right now terrible. I would love to get to know you."

"Why don't we exchange addresses, so we can at least become pen pals," asks Fatima. It was not often that I offered my address, but this time I am happy to do so. Then she disappears with the others. We exchanged letters for several years. A few years later, when she was studying in Paris, we even met one afternoon in the French capital. She was just as beautiful then.

The night was difficult. I had planned to sleep in the same little oasis as before, but it started to rain so I ended up crawling under a truck in a large parking lot and slept there. Not the best sleep I've had, but I didn't get wet. And it was free.

After breaking the night's fast at my usual café, I headed out of town and once there, I was the only one hitchhiking and soon got a ride with an Algerian who was going to Berriane, a small oasis 40 kilometres north of Ghardaia. He asked me if I wanted to sleep with him, and when I declined, he was okay with that. Me too, although I was getting a bit tired of having to constantly be on my guard for this: men hitting on me - a completely new experience for me during this trip. This must be how girls and women feel all the time when they are exposed to the lustful male gaze, I thought in my diary later. A useful experience, then, I guess.

As I was hiking out of Berriane, I met a couple of feisty French girls hitchhiking on their own around North Africa. Considering what I had just met, I wondered how they fared.

"No problem, but sometimes you have to give in," said one of them, laughing.

"Really?" I asked, telling them about what had happened in Ghardaia. They did not think it was strange at all but what you have to expect in North Africa. That's as far as we got, as they of course got a ride in the first car that appeared.

And soon it was my turn. A middle-aged Algerian couple stopped to photograph the small lake next to where I was sitting. They looked at me curiously and after a while they waved me over and I could join them to Laghouat. He spoke some English and wanted to practice it. His wife was more fun. She sang and laughed all the time. When I said I was a bit cold, she rolled down the window even more and laughed. At a small oasis we stopped and they offered me to share their lunch. Afterwards, when I and the man peed, she jumped into the car and took off so we had to walk a couple of hundred meters before she waited for us. Laughing. A rascal of a woman it was impossible not to like. They also played beautiful music on the cassette player in the car. I asked what it was and they told me it was Vivaldi's *Concerto for Two Mandolins*, and showed me the cassette; a record I bought as soon as I came home. When we got to Laghouat, they decided that I could go with them all the way to Algiers if I wanted to. I did.

It was again one of the most beautiful rides I have ever experienced. It had started in a flat stone desert where, despite a shining sun, it was cold. Then we approached the Atlas Mountains and sand and stone were replaced by flowers and flowers and more flowers. They told me that it was mainly yew bushes that were blooming. It was also hilly, rolling green and flowering moors, mountains and valleys with dramatic waterfalls as the road wound its way up the Atlas Mountains. We passed scores of nomads with long-haired camels - or dromedaries, as it were - and equally long-haired goats and donkeys. Their unkempt furs probably had something to do with the colder climate.

I decided not to continue into Algiers that late evening, but asked to be dropped off in Blida, 49 kilometres south of Algiers. I disliked coming to big cities in the dark and not knowing where to go. In Blida, I ate the leftover lunch they had given me along with a Pepsi. Then I met a student who spoke good English and he showed me to a hammam where I understood that men could sleep cheaply. It cost 2 dinars in the large shared bedroom in the bath, and 5 for a private room. I got my own room for 2 and thanked the attendant for it. "You will be raped if you sleep with the other men," he claimed. Then I went out to eat with the student in a small restaurant nearby. He also wanted my address and he got it. But I never heard from him. Anyway, he was nice and paid for the dinner. After that I took a nice bath for 2.50 dinar before turning in. I slept well even though it was humid and a bit chilly. My experience of the hammam was different from Flaubert's, when he visited similar establishments in Egypt and met young beautiful boys, but also older the men who washed him and offered to jerk him off. I was glad I to avoid that.

I was quickly on the road again the following day, and already at nine in Algiers. A beautiful white Mediterranean city that slopes down towards, or climbs up from, the Mediterranean, depending on the perspective. From what I saw then, the city seemed completely French, but I have seen *The Battle of Algiers* by Gillo Pontecorvo several times, so I know that there are Arab neighbourhoods here. Doubtful if I would have seen the film at the time, but probably, since it is from 1966 and of course was shown in the circles of the miscellaneous leftwingers I was part of. A fantastic movie, I still think.

But then, just after Easter in 1972, I was dazzled by the beauty of the city and the light of the Mediterranean. I found a coffee shop where I had some breakfast and could leave my backpack for the day. Then off to the Poste Restante where a letter from Tina was awaiting me with some bad news. She was short of both time and money, but maybe we could meet up in Spain, she wondered. I quickly scribbled a few lines that we could, and promised to get in touch and asked her to write to Marrakech. Then I was soon back in the café and on a bus to Blida again. I only spent three hours in Algiers - I regret that today.

Outside Blida it was again slow and tiring to hitchhike. I could not relax as there was lots of traffic. But no one seemed to want to pick me up. Eventually I got a ride with an Algerian family. He was a doctor in Oran and they both spoke some English. I shared the back seat with their mischievous five-year-old daughter. And my French was now good enough so I could play with her. It was a fun trip through a flowering, rolling landscape. When I told them my name was Erik, the driving doctor launched into Viking history, which I was assumed to know because of my name and heritage. When I started stammering out what little I remembered from school, his wife stopped me before I made a complete fool of myself. She said that Viking history was her husband's great passion. Among other things, he told me about a Viking chief who conquered Sicily and ruled with great generosity and tolerance towards

Christians and Muslims. I had no idea about that.

They dropped me off at one in the afternoon in the centre of Oran and I drank a café au lait at a café where I again left my backpack for a few hours to stroll around the city, which was as beautiful as Algiers. I found a record store where I could browse through a lot of new music I had not seen before. In a bookstore, I noticed that much of the literature on display was revolutionary: Che, Régis Debray, things I could sympathize with at the time. It confirmed the feeling I had in Algeria of a general anti-imperialist attitude. Maybe I imagined it, but I mention it in my diary several times and how it made me feel even more comfortable in the country. Probably a legacy of the liberation war against the French. But now I was going to leave it and I took a bus out of the city to start wagging my thumb towards Morocco.

I ended up in Ain-Témouchent where I found a hammam. There I again got my own small room; they didn't want me to sleep in the large communal dormitory here either. Next door was a small restaurant where I had a French menu dinner for 5 dinars.

The strange thing was that now that I had started eating European food again, properly and consistently, my stomach had started to protest. Several times over the past few days, I had come close to shitting myself. Had to rush into a café or behind bushes to save my reputation and pants. In the last hammam I had had to go to the toilet four times during the night. They even had a sitting toilet, but now I preferred the squatting toilet that I was used to. It was now Friday, April 7, and I took three stomach pills of some kind I had left over from Sudan. It apparently did the trick because soon I was in Oujda, and Morocco. The border crossing went smoothly. I had been warned that they didn't want any more hippies in Morocco and could therefore refuse a long-haired rascal like me from entering the country. But they didn't say a word against me. I was welcome.

Marrakech

Out of Oujda it was impossible to get a ride so I ended up in a decent hotel. A clean and tidy room for 5 dinars. I was not the only tourist in the hotel and the evening was spent in a room on the floor above mine with an American couple. Of course, marijuana was smoked. First time since Kenya I encountered it, but I declined. Wanted as long as I could be a little more moderate here than I was on Lamu. The American couple (no idea what their names were) had travelled around Morocco a few months but stopped hitchhiking as "you never get picked up in this country."

The next morning nevertheless found me outside the city with my thumb in the atmosphere; I didn't want to give up that easy. After half an hour, two Algerian guys who were going to Fez stopped. They kept playing Algerian (Rai?) music on their car radio, which made the trip pleasant. In Taza we stopped and they bought some food at a market which they shared with me at a rest stop outside the city. From where we sat we had a beautiful view of the snow-capped Atlas Mountains. I knew they were high but that they were covered in snow was a surprise. When we left Oujda, the country had been dry and desolate with steppe grass, occasional bushes, and a few lonely goats, but then it became greener and outside Taza really lush. And cooler. Oujda had been terribly hot.

In Fez, I found the youth hostel in the modern part of the city. But by the time I got there it was four hours before they opened, so I left my backpack in a nearby café and went for a walk. Bought an *International Herald Tribune* and read about what was happening in the world in another café by a square where everyone seemed to want to shine my shoes. I noticed that women and girls were less veiled here. And beautiful. I also saw a Gothenburg registered VW van.

At the hostel, I met a couple of nice Americans, Rob and Bob (they actually called themselves that). They knew no French, so I became their cicerone. The next day we went to the medina of Fez, the oldest of the four ancient royal cities: founded in 789, according to Wikipedia. The medina originated on the banks of the Fes River and has been a UNESCO World Heritage Site since 1981. Beautiful with narrow alleys, full of shops and people and donkeys and carriages and a hustle and bustle I hadn't seen since Cairo. A little boy decided to become our guide without us having any say in the matter. If we wanted to turn left, he meant right; if we went left anyway to get rid of him, he led us unconcernedly to the left. He, Tazim, even invited us home; without us having a clue where we were, we suddenly stood outside his home. The house looked run-down but when we entered it was beautiful and clean with tiled walls and floor. His un-veiled mother offered us lovely mint tea and showed us around parts of the surprisingly large house.

When we left his home after grateful word to his mother, Tazim took off with us. We had no idea where we were so followed him, even if a little hesitantly. He guided us into numerous carpet-, leather-, jewellery- and lamp shops. We thought it was a bit strange that shops offering the same goods always seemed to be next to each other; whole blocks of spice shops, other blocks of leather shops, others with gold or silver, etcetera. But there has to be a reason, we assumed. None of us wanted to buy anything, so it was always a bit strained in every shop, although the owners always were nice and far from unpleasant.

When Rob or Bob suddenly wanted to buy a leather belt each, I had to help them to haggle. I didn't mind. I always thought it was fun and managed to create a cheerful atmosphere in the bargaining, always important in order to get a good price, which I imagined I quite often succeeded in doing. (But of course I realized even then that they always won!) I did best if I did not want anything, but said that one dinar was all I wanted to pay, no matter what it was. They told me to get lost, only to often come running after me and give me whatever it was for one dinar. The Italian writer Elias Canetti discusses the logic of haggling, or lack thereof, in his fine little book from Marrakech. The initial price is a mystery, mainly because there are so many different prices, depending on the situation and the customer. The important thing for the customer is not to lose concentration, regardless of the salesman's arrogance or charm. A customer, Canetti recommends, ought to be dignified and articulate. I was more of a joker, I think; laughter always goes a long way, even in a medina.

After some time we got tired of all the people and hullabaloo, and asked Tazim to show us out of the medina. Then he suddenly wanted 15 dinars. We refused and kindly (rather cheaply, I think today) gave him

266

5. Then he got mad and quickly disappeared. There we were, having to rely on our own sense of locality. Rob and Bob were useless while I amazed myself and found the way out relatively easy. They were grateful as they had become worried and a little scared when it started to darken.

The evening at the hostel was pleasant as a German had a silver flute that I could borrow. I perhaps sat and blew for an hour or so. It probably did not sound too bad, as no one told me to shut up.

I stayed two days in Fez. I liked the old city and it was cool, even cold at night: consequently, I slept well. During the days I found myself mostly in the medina. I spent many hours there and found a small café where I could sit and chat with Moroccans to endless cups black coffee and mint tea. I actually bought a few things too: a cotton shirt for a dinar and a couple of wooden flutes. I had finally thrown away my blue-grey, long-sleeved T-shirt that had followed me since Högdalen and now looked more like a sieve with all its holes. Here I could replace it cheaply. But it was with some sadness that I parted with it; it had been through as much as I had and done me well!

When I left Fez for Marrakech, I first got a ride with some American hippies in a couple of VW buses, one of which broke down after half an hour. The other bus went back to Fez to try to find spare parts for the broken one. I wanted to move on but there were few cars so I sat with them and listened to John Lennon's *Imagine* album that had been released the previous year. Great music. If a vehicle suddenly appeared, I jumped up and waved my thumb.

A yellow US-registered VW Beetle drove by and stopped some distance away. An older white-haired woman got out and looked me over. After a while she waved and I was welcomed. Heather was 57 years old. A remarkable woman who had been traveling for three years. She had started in Australia, visiting her daughter, where she stayed for just over a year. Then up to Nepal and Burma, and by bus through India, Afghanistan and Turkey to Europe. In Germany she had worked at an American army base for six months and then bought the car I hitched a ride in. Now she had been on the road for four months in Europe and North Africa. She often slept in the car, but had a tent and camped whenever possible. Sometimes she stayed in a hotel if the weather was bad. Always alone. But now she had Swedish company. And it was clear that she craved company. She talked all the time and soon I knew most about her, her family and her friends in Virginia.

In Marrakech we found the campsite. I could sleep outside in my sleeping bag next to Heather's tent, without paying, no one noticed so it was a free night. I was also able to use their showers and other facilities.

In the evening I found a silver flute again. A group of campers were sitting around a small fire between the tents playing guitar and flute. After a while I asked if I could borrow the flute and they let me. I accompanied a couple of guitars and some singing. Almost the entire campsite joined us and it was insanely fun to play. We went on for a couple of hours before an older German gentleman from Das Rollende Hotel came over and told us in firm and understandable German to shut up. Some Brits objected: "We won the bloody war! Didn't we?" But it was getting late and everyone realized that it was probably time for silence.

When I went to bed, I sent the Municipal Music School in Stockholm a thought of gratitude. For three semesters I had learned to read music and roughly play the transverse flute at Hagsätra School - inspired by Ian Anderson in Jethro Tull. I had even intentionally misplaced the flute I had borrowed for my studies and paid a very reasonable sum for that negligence: the flute is still in my possession, even if it is many years since I played it.

Heather in the Atlas Mountains on our little excursion.

The next day, I joined Heather on an excursion up into the Atlas Mountains. She wanted to see the mountains and its Berber villages. We left at 6:30 am and brought some breakfast with us which we ate in a beautiful river valley after a couple of hours on the road. It was full of flowers and birds; Heather was an amateur birder and recognized several of them. There I took a photograph of her. One of about 50 black and white photos I took during this trip with my Kodak Instamatic. In light of today's hysterical photographing, it is crazy how few photos I have from almost a year in Africa. The 50 or so pictures I have from 1971/72 are of course extremely valuable, at least as I sit here trying to remember.

After breakfast, it was off again and we soon passed a ski resort in the snow, after which it went relatively steeply downhill on small dirt roads that zigzagged ominously along the mountain sides. A little scary, but she drove carefully. In a village with seven houses, we found a café where we each had an omelette and coffee. I wanted to contribute some for the gasoline but was absolutely not allowed to.

"I'm just so happy to have company. It wouldn't have been half as much fun on my own."

"And I am very happy that I was able to come along. I would never have seen the mountains on my own. But at least let me pay for this lunch." She did and I paid.

When we returned to Marrakech it was raining, so we both stayed that night in a hostel. The next day we went together to Essaouira. There we parted ways, but we had Christmas-card-contact for a few years before it dwindled; I never sought her out when I hitchhiked across America the next year: silly, perhaps.

In Essaouira I of course found Hotel du Pacha, or the Hippie Hotel, as it was also called. Everyone stayed there, including me - but that Jimi Hendrix had stayed there in 1969 when he was in town is probably only a fable the hotel entertains. It was nevertheless a nice hotel that played good music all the time, and you met all the other hippie-hobos. The rooms were simple and I came on my second day to share with Walter from Toronto. This meant that it was only two dinars a night.

Every night there was a party on the roof terrace or in the beautiful courtyard. The entire hotel was white, with blue furniture and various fabrics hanging in beautiful colours against the walls, along with lots of plants. It was impossible not to smoke here, as it seemed to be the major occupation of all the guests. And they always played great music. I remember Cat Stevens' *Teaser and the Firecat* was the most played album during my stay, and everyone agreed that it was as good as his previous album.

Next to the hotel there was a small yogurt shop that I still remember. They made their own yogurt which was heavenly together with running honey on top. It became a must for breakfast every day, a craving; so when they were closed on Fridays, we all suffered deeply. After breakfast we often set out of town to the beach for some swimming and body surfing. The water was a bit chilly but it was nice when the sun was shining hot. Of course, we all went skinny-dipping; we were all free-spirited hippies!

In Essaouira I finished reading *Moby Dick*. A fantastically rich and funny novel, vast in a way that invites re-reading. And I have done so once later in life. Then it was even better with a bit of scholarly guidance. Now I started reading Thomas Hardy.

There were a lot of Swedes in Essaouira, which was both annoying and nice. Even worse were the sad figures who had gotten stuck in the hashish cloud and were unable to get any further but walked around the city, high as kites all the time, begging food from us other slightly cleaner travellers. A few years later, I came across them again in Goa and Kathmandu, where they were more numerous and even more miserable: tragic individuals that even their own embassies had taken their hands off.

After a few days, Walter and I, along with two girls from Minnesota and some others, moved out to Diabat, four kilometres south of Essaouira. Back then it was a sleepy little village while today it is full of beautiful and adventurous hotels. We had found a small house, which really only consisted of a large room, a simple latrine and a small kitchen with a gas stove. And it cost almost nothing. But it was not for the money we moved lodging, but rather for the adventure. We were eight of us, so it was a bit crowded on simple mattresses that filled the whole room at night. There was a lot of cooking, grass-smoking and music playing, as there were a couple of guitars in the group.

After a few days Judith, one of the Minnesota girls, became ill and we took her to a hospital. There the three of us, me, Walter and Julie, as the other girl was called, sat waiting well into the dark evening for words on whether Judith would stay overnight or not. She did and the three of us walked the half mile to Diabet wrapped in blankets and Walter's sleeping bag. It was freezing cold in the wind and darkness but we sang and joked so before we knew it, we had arrived. A walk I remember.

The next day we picked Judith up from the hospital and moved back to the hippie hotel. The house in Diabet was no place for a sick girl from Minnesota, full of flies and cockroaches and other unidentifiable bugs, as well as goat droppings that were everywhere.

Walter and me outside Essaouiora.

After more than a week in Essaouira, where the days were almost identical, I hitchhiked back to Marrakech where I was expecting a letter from Tina. Would we meet up in Spain, or in Morocco, as I had suggested. A letter from her was indeed waiting at Poste Restante; we would meet in Barcelona.

Now I had rashes again! This time in the crotch of the thigh next to my balls. Big red blisters that itched and did not look healthy at all. In a clinic in Marrakech they decided that it was fungus. They gave me a lotion to apply daily. If that didn't help, I was told to come back or go to another clinic after a few weeks. I did so in Heidelberg, and later in

Stockholm, and a year and a half later in Los Angeles, where I finally got an ointment that killed the fungus once and for all.

The next day I ran into Julie, Judith and Walter. They were all staying in a hotel next to the Djemaa el Fna square. We had a few fun days together, even though I was staying in the youth hostel. We spent one day wandering around the Mellah, the old Jewish quarters. Not many Jews left though, barely over 100 from what we understood. At the beginning of the 20th century, they are said to have numbered over 36,000. At first it was not unlike other parts of the city, but soon it became crowded and poorer, we thought. Almost a bit threateningly scary, so we quickly moved back to the square. In the evenings we ate in the square and wandered around enchanted by all the activity that flourished: snake charmers, acrobats, jugglers, monkey trainers, storytellers and of course beggars and sellers of everything we were not interested in at the time. But the square was - and is - a magical place that still invites exoticism for a northern tourist.

We also got into a brawl with a Moroccan in a jewellery store, who took a ring from Judith. He wanted to look at it and then refused to return it. "You are so beautiful and I want to marry you and now I am keeping this ring and you can choose a new one in my shop." Judith wasn't interested in him nor a new ring, but wanted her ring back, which was a gift from her grandmother. But he refused and there was a hell of a ruckus and we screamed and shouted at each other until he simply disappeared into the back of his shop and we stood there with long faces and without Judith's ring. She was crying and Walter and I were so enraged that we had almost jumped on the guy. So it was a sad evening with a lost ring. But we probably smoked some grass, listened to some fine music after some fine food, and survived.

Early the next morning, after a quick breakfast together, the three of them took a bus to Fez and it was a very sad farewell. But short: long goodbyes only hurt more. With a sad lump in my stomach, I walked through an awakening Marrakech. Rarely had I felt so miserable by a farewell during this trip. And I realized why I felt so low,; I had a crush on Julie. However, I hoped to see her again in Germany (and did). But the four of us had also had lots of fun together and I had gotten used to company, in particular theirs, and become unaccustomed to being alone, which it now had been a while since I was.

It was, however, a lovely morning in "one of the most beautiful cities in the world, spacious and spread over a large area and surrounded by vast cultivations [with] magnificent mosques," as Ibn Battuta wrote in the mid-14th century. After a night of rain, the wet grass and flowers smelled wonderful, and the snow of the Atlas Mountains shone in the high air of the morning sun. Despite the tears in my belly, I was able to enjoy the morning, which so far was fairly still and quiet as I walked under the palm trees. I heard the Adhan, the call to prayer, probably the second of the day, from the minarets, or "lighthouses with voices instead of light," as Elias Canetti called them.

At the hostel I met Robert and Sheila, whom I had last seen in In Salah. So I ended up hanging with them for the rest of my stay in Marrakech. In the evening, we went to the movies and saw *Gimme Shelter*, it had great music, but was depressing in its depiction of what happened in Altamont during the concert. We ate hash brownies beforehand, which everyone said was a must. It didn't make any difference and just felt a bit stale and unnecessary. But it was cheap so no harm done.

The next day I aimed for Casablanca and quickly got a ride with a Moroccan couple all the way there. Once there, I settled into the youth hostel. It was a large, comfortable and clean hostel in Ahmed El Bidaoui Square with a friendly café across the street. I was told by a Frenchwoman that there were daily buses from Casablanca, both a morning and an evening one, to Ceuta, where you took the ferry to Spain. And my backpack was now so heavy with books that I decided to take the night bus, even though it cost an expensive 22 dinars.

I also found a Swedish consulate where I could read that Hammarby, my favourite football team, won their first match of the season. That cheered me up.

After the consulate visit I am sitting in the café opposite the hostel, starting to read *U.S.A.* by Dos Passos, when a polite gentleman in his 40s approaches me and offers me hashish. He is sitting at the table next to me, smoking openly with a couple of other middle-aged men in suits. I wonder if it is wise to sit and smoke so openly. "It's illegal, isn't it, after all?"

"Don't worry. You see those two sitting over there?" he asks, pointing to two other men in suits. I do.

"They are plainclothes police officers and they smoke too, as you can see. So we don't have to worry. In Morocco everyone smokes. We must have something to get high on, when our religion forbids alcohol."

"But I have seen drunken Moroccan youths."

"Sure, the young, who don't care about Islam drink, but you can bet they smoke pot too. Just like you hippies, right?"

Which, of course, I have to admit to. Then I take a few puffs on his hookah with hashish. But he has mixed it with sweet Arabic tobacco so it tastes bad and I cough violently. Which gives them all a good laugh.

My last evening on the Africa continent I spent in the café by the square and especially in the room upstairs. Everyone sat there and smoked kief. That's what the purpose of the room. During the day it was mainly Moroccan men, never women, who sat there smoking, while the hostel guests invaded it in the evening. On this, my last night on the continent, two Americans brought guitars, which they played admirably. We sat all evening smoking, singing and chanting together until they closed the place at midnight. I especially remember how we all joined in on the chorus of "Up on Cripple Creek, she sends me / If I spring a leak, she mends me / I don't have to speak, she defends me / A drunkard's dream if I ever did see one."

The next day, Sunday, April 30, was thus my last in Africa, so I felt a bit sad. And the strange thing is that I do so also now as I write this. I have read through my diaries, tried to turn them into a narrative, describing my journey 50 years ago, which was sometimes quite adventurous. And now my story is finished. I have nothing more to tell. It feels strangely sad even today, 50 years later.

The evening before taking the bus was almost as wild as the previous one. David and Keenan played their guitar also this evening, and at the hostel it was decided that there definitely had to be a farewell party for Swedish Erik. I could not escape that. So we sat a bunch on the square and smoked one last time for me. Nice. They knew that I would be leaving Africa after almost nine months on the continent. Then David accompanied me to the bus stop. 21.30 the bus left and I slept as well as I could on a night bus and at 08.30, I took the boat to Gilbraltar. On it I met a Mexican/American couple from Marrakech campsite and my first lift in Europe, to Malaga, was secured.

Högdalen

After seeing my first bullfight in Malaga, spending a week with Tina in Ibiza, a few days with my sister in Zûrich, where my last 1000 SEK were waiting for me and I finished reading *U.S.A.* (1200 dense Penguin pages of captivating reading) and visiting my high school friend Kicki, who was working at a hotel in Titisee in the Bavarian mountains for the summer, and then meeting Walter and Julie in Munich where I finally had a romance with her, as well as in Heidelberg, at Walter's grandfathers, whom we visited, and staying a few days in London, where I managed to see two great Stanley Kubrick movies, after which I ended up a few days in Amsterdam, where in the Kabul hotel I met Sean from Los Angeles, who was on his way up to a girl in Stockholm, and we hung out in Vondelpark, visited the Heineken brewery and the Van Gogh Museum, and hitchhiked together up to Stockholm - it grew into a lifelong and deep friendship, I on July 12, 1972, one year to the day after I left mom and dad crying on the balcony, walked down Harpsundsvägen and rang the bell at home. They knew I was coming, I had called from Zûrich, but not exactly when I would arrive. During my time in Europe, I had decided to come home for the anniversary and I managed, and mom and dad were as happy as I was. The first dinner was a wonderfully good meatloaf, brown cream sauce, lingonberries with firm, good, boiled potatoes.

I was mostly happy to see my parents and my brother, but of course also all my friends. Today, as I write these lines, I am thinking more about the trip. What kind of backpacker was I? "A traveller with a closed mind can tell us little except about himself," wrote Chinua Achebe in his essay on *Heart of Darkness*. Is it only about myself that I have told here? That would certainly be bad. At the same time, as the Swedish writer Kristoffer Leandoer writes in his latest book, "a certain degree of self-imposed narrow-mindedness for socio-economic contexts" is perhaps a prerequisite for the experience.

And is it possible to make the same journey today? Of course, but it would certainly be different. It would be more expensive but at the same time easier. Plastic cards and cell phones mean that many of the problems I faced would not bother me today. Would I now have a podcast or webpage to write my diary in for all to read while traveling? Make a fool of myself on that most anti-social of places: social media?

No, not me!

It is now 50 years since I came walking down Harpsundvägen to surprise my parents. I no longer wonder if I can remember myself in Africa; but it is not because I think I have found him, or me. Though I think I know why I travelled and what I found in Africa: the journey was itself enough: the road is enough in itself, as Kapuscinski claims! But is this really what happened to me? Have I remembered correctly? Reminiscence is treacherously full of insidious pitfalls. It is however all true according to my diary, humble knowledge and memory. On the other hand, maybe it doesn't matter; it has become a story, maybe even a good one: fine so!

What has struck me most as I have worked on my diaries, and hopefully also the reader who managed to get this far, is the friendliness of all the people, the almost boundless generosity I met everywhere. It began with Gun in Skillingaryd, whom I really should have stopped and visited when I passed by north on July 12. Would I encounter the same kindness in Skillingaryd and Africa today? I would like to think so.

It would probably be a bit more dangerous today to travel in some parts of Africa, though. Today I should avoid some regions and not wander alone through a baboon herd or nocturnally in 'Nairobbery.' But I would like to think that I would meet the same kindness in most Africa also today. The continent has a relatively bad reputation; it is mostly about poverty, war and famine we read. Rarely is everyday Africa depicted. An everyday life where most people have a decent life; they eat enough, even if not as hysterically much and varied as we do in Europe, perhaps the same food most days. They have a radio, maybe also a TV, a mobile phone and live in extended families and go to church on Sunday or the mosque on Friday. They live with friends and family in a way that we in the West can only dream of and enviously sense when we visit and then return to our more or less isolated existence. Western culture is individualistic which is why we find the generosity of Africa so surprisingly beautiful, or at least I did. Here I learned that all people have obligations to each other. "Everyone matters," as Kwame Anthony Appiah writes in his fine little book *Cosmopolitanism*.

What is remarkable is that there always seems to be hope in Africa.

Though people may struggle to make ends meet, in Africa they are rarely without hope for a better tomorrow. In most African languages, there is apparently no word for depression. Whining about doom and hopelessness is not often heard. Instead, joy when you expect that there should be no room for it. Something that makes traveling in Africa delightful. As a visitor you are always welcome, you are taken care of. And it is easy to fall in love with the continent, to become, as the French say, "Les fous d'Afrique," or as Eva Dickson put it: "Once captured by the enchantment of Africa, you will never be a free human again."

I nevertheless almost immediately started planning my next trip, and this time to America.